INTERVIEWING CHILDREN AND YOUNG PEOPLE FOR RESEARCH

CW00953052

SAGE was founded in 1965 by Sara Miller McCune to support the dissemination of usable knowledge by publishing innovative and high-quality research and teaching content. Today, we publish over 900 journals, including those of more than 400 learned societies, more than 800 new books per year, and a growing range of library products including archives, data, case studies, reports, and video. SAGE remains majority-owned by our founder, and after Sara's lifetime will become owned by a charitable trust that secures our continued independence.

Los Angeles | London | New Delhi | Singapore | Washington DC | Melbourne

INTERVIEWING CHILDREN AND YOUNG PEOPLE FOR RESEARCH

Michelle O'Reilly

Nisha Dogra

⑤SAGE

Los Angeles | London | New Delhi
Singapore | Washington DC | Melbourne

Los Angeles | London | New Delhi
Singapore | Washington DC | Melbourne

SAGE Publications Ltd
1 Oliver's Yard
55 City Road
London EC1Y 1SP

SAGE Publications Inc.
2455 Teller Road
Thousand Oaks, California 91320

SAGE Publications India Pvt Ltd
B 1/I 1 Mohan Cooperative Industrial Area
Mathura Road
New Delhi 110 044

SAGE Publications Asia-Pacific Pte Ltd
3 Church Street
#10-04 Samsung Hub
Singapore 049483

Editor: Jai Seaman
Editorial assistant: Alysha Owen
Production editor: Ian Antcliff
Copyeditor: Christine Bitten
Proofreader: Thea Watson
Indexer: Martin Hargreaves
Marketing manager: Sally Ransom
Cover design: Shaun Mercier
Typeset by: C&M Digitals (P) Ltd, Chennai, India
Printed and bound by CPI Group (UK) Ltd,
Croydon, CR0 4YY

Library of Congress Control Number: 2016940066

British Library Cataloguing in Publication data

A catalogue record for this book is available from
the British Library

ISBN 978-1-4739-1452-0
ISBN 978-1-4739-1453-7 (pbk)

At SAGE we take sustainability seriously. Most of our products are printed in the UK using FSC papers and boards.
When we print overseas we ensure sustainable papers are used as measured by the PREPS grading system.
We undertake an annual audit to monitor our sustainability.

CONTENTS

ABOUT THE AUTHORS

Dr Michelle O'Reilly is a Senior Lecturer for the Greenwood Institute of Child Health, at the University of Leicester, working for the School of Media, Communication and Sociology, and the School of Psychology. Michelle also provides research support to practising clinical professionals working for Leicestershire Partnership NHS Trust. Michelle's research interests are broadly in the areas of child mental health, psychiatric research, family therapy and qualitative methods, and she has a particular research interest in Autism Spectrum Disorder, having recently edited a special section in the *Journal of Autism and Developmental Disorders*. Michelle has recently edited two handbooks (with Jessica Lester) – *The Palgrave Handbook of Child Mental Health* and *The Palgrave Handbook of Adult Mental Health*. For more details please consult: https://www2.le.ac.uk/departments/npb/people/michelleOReilly.

Professor Nisha Dogra is Professor of Psychiatry Education and Honorary Consultant in Child and Adolescent Psychiatry, at the Greenwood Institute of Child Health, University of Leicester. She is also Course Director for the Masters in Child and Adolescent Mental Health. She undertook some training in hospital and community paediatrics before training in psychiatry and then as an academic child psychiatrist. She currently works as a generic child and adolescent psychiatrist within a multi-disciplinary team (MDT). She has been involved in the development and delivery of a wide variety of teaching and training events in undergraduate and postgraduate education, locally, nationally and internationally. Professor Dogra worked on diversity in healthcare as part of her Commonwealth Fund Policy for Health Care Harkness Fellowship 2005–2006. She was a runner up for the Times Higher Education Innovative Teacher of the Year 2011. For more details please consult: https://www2.le.ac.uk/departments/npb/people/nishaDogra.

ACKNOWLEDGEMENTS

We would like to offer our appreciation to several people who have helped to make this book happen. We thank the anonymous reviewers for their suggestions to develop areas within the book and all of their ideas. Of course we thank our families for their personal support during the process of writing, for their patience and understanding. Finally, we thank SAGE, for facilitating this book from inception to publication, particularly Jai Seaman and Alysha Owen.

ABBREVIATIONS

AMA = American Medical Association

BSc = Bachelor of Science

CA = Conversation Analysis

CAMHS = Child and Adolescent Mental Health Services

DA = Discourse Analysis

DP = Discursive Psychology

DVD = Digital Versatile Disc

IPA = Interpretive Phenomenological Analysis

IQ = Intelligence Quotient

IRA = Irish Republican Army

NSPCC = National Society for the Prevention of Cruelty to Children

SRA = Social Research Association

UK = United Kingdom

UN = United Nations

UNCRC = United Nations Convention of the Rights of the Child

USA = United States of America

PREFACE

Interviewing is considered to be the most popular form of qualitative data collection and many researchers choose to use this to learn about people's lives. Many, if not most, of the qualitative approaches argue that there is value in the interview for gaining an understanding of people's opinions, experiences and feelings about particular phenomenon. Furthermore, some quantitative researchers use the interviewing method to gain structured information from participants. While not without criticism, the use of interviews in research is growing and is commonly taught on research methods programmes on undergraduate and postgraduate training courses, as well as on vocational training courses for practitioners in various areas of practice, including education, social care, health and medicine.

This book is designed to take the reader through the whole process of undertaking a research project with children and/or young people using interviewing. The book is an accessible and practical guide for the reader and is designed to help students, practitioners, researchers and academic scholars in designing, planning, undertaking and analysing their interview study with children and young people. This is a timely text as there is a vast literature on interviewing as a technique for collecting data, and the literature on using this method of data collection with children and young people is expanding. However, while there are general textbooks to guide research with children and there are general textbooks on interviews, the focus on interviewing children and young people in one resource is up to now limited.

DEFINITIONS

In this book there are a range of terms used. Generally, we use the pronoun 'we' throughout the chapters to identify us as the authors of the book, and use 'you' to refer to the person reading the book. This book is about interviewing children and young people and we use a range of terms where appropriate to refer to this group. Generally, we use the term children to refer to populations who are under the age of 18 years old. We use the term young people to refer to those in their teenage years, and we use the term adolescents when being more technical. Throughout the book we refer to the parents and guardians of the children and generally use the term 'parents' throughout to encompass all adults who have legal responsibility for children including biological parents, foster parents, adoptive parents, step-parents, local authorities, carers and other legal guardians.

THE BEST WAY TO USE THIS BOOK

While some readers may have experience of interviewing adults, we note that working with children requires different kinds of skills and this book is designed to help. Other readers may have practice-based experience of working with children but may be less confident in conducting research. Again this book is designed to help develop those skills and to consider the important issues in the decision making process. Throughout the text we use our combined clinical and academic experiences and knowledge to develop the book.

We begin the book with chapters that provide context for interviewing children and young people. Early chapters focus on the value of the method of data collection and providing guidance for designing the study, while outlining different options that interviewers have to make in the process. This includes choices about the format of the interview and some of the practical decisions that need to be made in terms of the practical considerations. The book continues with some specific considerations such as the use of participatory methods, their value and their limitations, as well as considering the structure and form the interview might take. In doing interviews with children it is essential that the interviewer works within an ethical framework and the book provides useful and important information about how to do this. Additionally, there are particular factors related to the child and to the researcher that need some attention in the process and we devote attention to these in detail. The final sections of the book focus on the analysis methods and the process of reflexivity and reflection. Throughout the book we provide activities and vignette exercises to help you reflect and consolidate your learning. The answers are provided within chapters or at the end of the book.

We recommend that you read through this book to develop a broad perspective on interviewing children and to engage with the suggested materials and recommended reading. This book may help you to identify areas for further training and we encourage you to develop your skills base using this book as a benchmark for doing so. It is common to have questions after reading a book, and this is a good thing as it promotes better quality research. Engage with your colleagues, supervisors and other scholarly materials to help you develop this further.

1

THE IMPORTANCE OF INTERVIEWING CHILDREN FOR RESEARCH

━━ **LEARNING OUTCOMES** ━━━━━━━━━━━━━━━━━━━━━━━━

By the end of the chapter the reader should be able to:

- Define what constitutes an interview.
- Assess the difference between interviewing adults and interviewing children.
- Describe the rights of children to participate in research.
- Evaluate the necessity for child-centred approaches.
- Recognise why research with children was historically avoided.
- Critically assess the benefits of using interviews with children and young people as a research method.

INTRODUCTION

Involving children in research is a fairly modern endeavour and more recently children's rights to participate in research have been increasingly recognised. This has led to a greater encouragement to include children's voices through research. However, researchers who are new to doing research with children may find it quite daunting, especially if undertaking qualitative research interviews without much experience of either conducting interviews or of doing research with children. Undertaking research interviews with children and young people can be challenging for several reasons, including varying chronological ages, developmental abilities and expectations of the research. This introductory chapter outlines various issues, many of which are explored in greater depth later in the book. This chapter introduces you to the reasons why interviewing children is so important and we benchmark this against the issues of the child's position in society, child-centred practices and children's rights. We introduce you to the notion of child-centred research and the significance of this for interview research. We contextualise this against a discussion of the position of children in society and the UN Convention on the Rights of the Child. We conclude the chapter by providing the benefits and limitations of interviewing children and young people to demonstrate the usefulness of the method.

DEFINING AN INTERVIEW

Intuitively most people have some sense of what an interview is like and some of you may have been interviewed in some context, such as for a job or market research. An interview is considered to be a conversation between two or more people, where one party (the interviewer) asks particular questions to elicit responses from the other (the interviewee). There are many different types of interview – consider some examples listed below:

- Job or careers interview
- News interview
- Market research interview
- Health interview
- Psychiatric or clinical diagnostic interview
- Police interrogation interview
- Chat show interview
- Qualitative or quantitative research interview.

Clearly the type of interview we are focusing on in this book is the research interview, with a key focus on interviewing children. However, reflecting on your general knowledge about how interviews work is a useful starting point for any research project. In the research context an interview will be more personal than a questionnaire as the interviewer always works directly with the interviewee and has the opportunity to ask further questions based on the responses given. The common framework for interviewing of any kind is that the interviewer sets an agenda and asks questions, and consenting interviewees provide responses, although the balance of this may be dependent on context and purpose. We provide an example below from our own interview study with children to illustrate what this looks like (see Box 1.1).

━━ Box 1.1 ━━━━━━━━━━━━━━━━━━━━━━━━━━━━━

Example of research interview

This example is taken from a study with children aged 8–10 years old who had both mental health and educational needs.

Interviewer: Okay. And how were you feeling when you were at school?
Child: Um, okay but upset.
Interviewer: Mmm. Okay, and did you speak to anybody until the day, before the day when you got really upset?
Child: I tried telling mum but mum but I – Mum said something before that she thought it was, um, oh what's it called? Umm [Pause] trying to be noticed.

It is clear from this example that the interview follows a traditional format whereby the interviewer asks the child a question, and the child provides an answer. Notice that the interviewer then follows up the child's answer by latching the next question to the response previously given by the child.

INTERVIEWING ADULTS AND INTERVIEWING CHILDREN

Historically, interviewing children and their families was mostly avoided as there was a general belief that children and young people did not have the social competence to recall credible accounts of their experiences (Fraser et al., 2014). Furthermore, because of the potential complexity of interviewing younger participants some researchers felt uncomfortable as they lacked the necessary skills to engage children and young people in an interview. Over the last few decades however, there has been a growing interest in treating children as a distinctive population that warrants some inquiry in their own right. Initially, child research focused on children's development and their abilities, but this gradually received criticisms for treating children as objects to study.

Contemporary research has an emphasis on doing research *with* children, treating them as agentive subjects in the process and this perspective has led to interviews with children and young people becoming more commonplace (O'Reilly et al., 2013a). This is in part due to changing attitudes regarding children and childhood, and a greater emphasis being placed on child-centred attitudes and children's rights. The objective of this type of research is to include children's voices in decisions that impact on them and their environment.

CHILDREN'S RIGHTS

Respecting children's rights is a fundamental attitude in most modern societies. There is now a greater emphasis on recognising children as active participants in their own decision making and this is reflected in a recent report by National Voices (2015). Notably, this new discourse of children's rights is juxtaposed against a pre-existing culture of paternalism towards children that still infiltrates all levels of society and causes tensions between realising children's rights in practice and protecting them from harm. Consequently, the debates around children's rights and voices in practice is nuanced, and also contested in typically subtle ways.

The conceptualisation of children's rights was first recognised internationally by the Geneva Declaration of the Rights of the Child (1924) when it was adopted by the League of Nations. In 1989, the United Nations Convention on the Rights of the Child was adopted and has since been ratified by 195 countries (UN, 1989). The Convention has 54 articles that cover all aspects of a child's life and set out the civil, political, economic, social and cultural rights that all children everywhere are entitled to. It also explains how adults and governments must work together to make sure all children can enjoy all their rights. In 1989, all governments across the world but two promised all children the same rights by adopting the UN Convention on the Rights of the Child (aka the CRC or UNCRC). The Convention changed the way children are viewed and treated – in other words, as human beings with a distinct set of rights instead of as passive objects of care and charity.

Four of the 54 articles are known as overarching general principles. These are:

- **Non-discrimination (Article 2):** The Convention applies to all children whatever their ethnicity, gender, religion, language, abilities, whatever they think or say, no matter what type of family they come from, whatever their circumstances.

> For example… A child in care has the same right to an education as a child who lives with his/her parents.

- **Best interest of the child (Article 3):** A child's best interests must be a top priority in all decisions and actions that affect children. All adults should do what is best for children and should think about how their decisions will affect children. Determining what is in children's best interests should take into account children's own views and feelings.

> For example… Children in hospital may need lifesaving treatment, and they should be consulted about the process of the treatment.

- **Right to life, survival and development (Article 6):** Children have the right to life and governments must do all they can to ensure children survive and develop to their fullest potential. The right to life and survival guarantees the most basic needs such as nutrition, shelter or access to healthcare. Development – physical, emotional, educational, social and spiritual – is the goal of many of the rights in the Convention.

> For example… The right to education, access to information, freedom of thought or right to play.

- **Right to be heard (Article 12):** Every child has the right to express their views, feelings and wishes in all matters affecting them, and to have their views considered and taken seriously. This principle recognises children as actors in their own lives and applies at all times, throughout childhood.

> For example… In the research context all children have a right to participate in research and express their views of a subject matter if they choose to. This is regardless of their abilities, age, social circumstances, race, gender, etc.

> Important point: It is important that you respect the rights of the children to participate in your research project and allow them to participate on their terms.

An important article in this convention for researchers was Article 12, which proposed that children and young people have the right to be engaged in decision making and should have their views respected, and Article 13 which stated that children have the right to freedom of expression.

Before you go any further with the chapter we suggest that you try the activity in Box 1.2 so that you can reflect on the nature of children's rights.

■ **Box 1.2** ■

Activity on children's rights

Aside from the four overarching rights we have discussed, what civil, political, cultural, social and economic rights do you think children should have in research? What might the challenges be of ensuring those rights are realised in practice in an interview-based study with children? You may find looking at the UNCRC on the UNICEF website helpful in developing your answers: http://www.unicef.org.uk/Documents/Publicationpdfs/UNCRC_PRESS200910web.pdf.

It is challenging to consider the exact nature of the rights children hold in research as the researcher has to balance including them in the interview and allowing them some agency in directing the trajectory of the interview, against protecting them from possible psychological or physical harm and promoting their best interests. Historically some groups of more vulnerable children have been excluded from research as it was deemed necessary to protect them, but by taking such a position this has excluded their voices and removed participation rights from them. Some examples of groups considered most vulnerable and thus the most likely to be excluded historically (although note that some of these groups have been researched more than others) include:

- Children with physical disabilities or with chronic illness.
- Children with mental health problems or severe mental illness (and in inpatient care).
- Children with speech, language and communication problems and with learning disabilities.
- Children suffering from a terminal illness or young carers caring for parents with chronic or terminal illness.
- Children from ethnic minority groups, including refugees or asylum seekers.
- Children living in poverty or who are homeless.
- Children looked after by the State (in foster care, children's homes or adopted).
- Young offenders and those in young offending institutions.
- Children excluded from school, or at risk of exclusion.
- Gypsy, Roma and Traveller children.
- Teenage parents.
- Children who have been victims of crime or abuse or from families where there was domestic violence.

In contemporary research it is recognised that it is important to sensitively undertake research with these groups and it is, therefore, important not to discriminate against any group of children and to respect their decisions to participate or decline participation in the research. It is through your interview research that different children's voices can be heard. It is arguable that children should at least have the right to consider participating in your interview, even if they require the assistance of a parent or guardian in making that decision.

CHILD-CENTRED APPROACHES

Doing research interviews with children and including young populations in research is part of a broader framework of child-centredness. In most areas of practice in the modern world, those who work with children are guided to practice in a child-centred way and this is also true for researchers. There is no universal definition currently of child-centred practice as this is culturally contextual, but it should be understood as part of the broader discourse of the rights of the child. In other words, in order for society to ensure that children's rights are being recognised and implemented there needs to be directives to ensure that institutions and individuals are adopting a child-centred way of working (UNICEF, n.d.).

> **Important point**: Working and researching in a child-centred way is a truly global initiative, as 195 countries have promised to adopt the UNCRC. This means that research nationally and internationally should respect the child's perspectives.

Making sure that you consider child-centred practice as central to your interviewing of children can be challenging as this is influenced by many factors. The essential tenet of a child-centred interview is to make sure that the children are involved in any decisions that affect them, both in terms of promoting their participation in the interview if they desire it, and in terms of allowing them to lead and develop the research and interview agenda. It is essential that children's viewpoints are represented (Söderback et al., 2011) and respected (Flewitt, 2014), as typically children's best interests have been reflected from an adult perspective (Lansdown, 2000). Despite the enthusiasm in the research community to research in a child-centred way it is easy to slip into more adult-centric ways of interviewing and care needs to be taken. To be child-centred you need to actively consider the role of the child and we provide you with some tips in Table 1.1.

Table 1.1　Tips to be child-centred

Tip	Description
Reflect	Reflect on perspectives about the place of children as this may influence how hard you need to work to ensure that your approaches and behaviours are child-centred.
Certainty	Be certain that the child is willing to participate.
Give information	Inform the child of what is expected and find out what they expect from you.
Focus	Focus your interview on the child.
Control	Offer the child some control over the interview and also offer the child some control over the recording device.
Questions	Provide an opportunity for the child to ask you questions.
Language	Use child-friendly language.

YOUR OWN POSITION ON CHILDREN AND CHILDHOOD

Before we start considering the ways in which children have been positioned within society we recommend you start with the activity in Box 1.3. This is useful as it encourages you to think about what you think about children and how this might influence the way you conduct your interviews.

━━ **Box 1.3** ━━━━━━━━━━━━━━━━━━━━━━━━━━━━

Activity on positioning children

Before you read any further we suggest that you make some attempt to write down what you think about children's position in society.

- Do you think they have rights?
- Do you think those rights have limits?
- Do you think they need to be protected?
- Do you feel they are born innocent and are shaped by their environment?

Just a short general list of points will be sufficient.

───

The very notions of children and childhood are non-specific and developmentally relate to a range of chronological years typically referring to the period between infancy and adulthood. Arguably childhood is a sociological construct as opposed to being a natural one and over time, our understanding of it has changed considerably. This is because any understanding we have of children and childhood is culturally, politically and historically influenced, and therefore it is useful to consider childhood as a dynamic process. In other words, the ways in which children are viewed and understood will change as the perspectives of society change. Nonetheless, the way in which we view children is important as this has an influence on how they are treated and prioritised by organisations, politicians, policy developers and society. Furthermore, this will also influence how children are viewed and treated in research by us as researchers and by other stakeholders.

In research terms therefore, when beginning your interview project, it is important that you plan carefully, choose a relevant topic, develop a research question, and consider the relevance of theory. Qualitative research specifically requires careful consideration of the research question as this drives the project (see Chapter 2). This is important as the research question reflects the theoretical stance of the researcher and helps to inform choice of methodology and method. This will determine whether interviews are an appropriate data collection tool to address your question. In other words, you need to address your epistemological position, and most specifically your theoretical understanding of children.

Epistemology is a concept that is widely discussed in methods books and we do not want to go into much detail here as you can read about this in many other places (O'Reilly and Kiyimba, 2015; Silverman, 2013). However, what we are referring to in this section is how your world view influences the way you see children and the way you work with them. This relates to your epistemological position, that is, how you can know what you know; it refers to the relationship between you as the researcher and the nature of the knowledge produced by the research. So in other words, the way in which you view children will influence the way in which you go about seeking knowledge about their lives. Thus, your epistemological position will shape the project and therefore it is helpful to be reflexive about your views of children and childhood from early on in your interview research.

The concept of children and childhood in relation to chronological age and developmental age are not universal, and defining childhood and its relative components is dependent upon the changing values, definitions and expectations of any given society. In the contemporary western world children are now considered in terms of social equality and social order, and have been categorised according to their age. As mentioned earlier in the chapter this notion of social equality has led to the idea that children are entitled to socio-cultural and moral rights. Thus, children belong to a group in society with rights and are worthy of moral consideration (Paul, 2007). However, conversely, children are still viewed as in need of protection from a range of social, psychological and physical harms and despite the rights-based framework are still restricted in terms of practising their citizenship. For example, children in most western cultures cannot:

- Vote
- Drive
- Engage in sexual intercourse
- Smoke
- Drink alcohol
- Get married

These activities are restricted until a particular age and vary according to country.

The tension in views of children and childhood, and arguments regarding children's rights inevitably will have an effect on the way in which you carry out your research. As mentioned earlier in the chapter, research involving children tended to be avoided in the past, and when new ideas emerged it was the case that researchers conducted their research *on* children. However, as we have already noted, modern research now considers this a collaborative endeavour, and as we noted earlier, research *with* children is more standard. Notably, this transition from doing research on children, to doing research with children, began toward the latter end of the twentieth century, which marked a period of including children in research design, consulting children on issues that matter to their lives and engaging children more directly in research planning. However, importantly this was also a period that marked a greater concern with protecting children in research. This period saw a tightening of ethical protocols and stricter guidelines in how children should be treated in research (we return to this issue later in Chapter 8).

When you engage children in your interview research therefore, it is important that you are reflexively aware of how you view children and childhood. This is because your views have potential to shape and direct your interviews. It will be important that you engage in the children's cultures so as to represent their views as accurately as possible and do some work to manage the inherent power relationship that exists (Holt, 2004). There are many different ways in which you might view children and the common ways of conceptualising them was offered by Alderson (2005) which we outline in Table 1.2.

Table 1.2 Views of children and childhood (Alderson, 2005)

Views of children

1. The child as innocent and needing protection.

2. The child as criminal and needing control.

3. The child as ignorant and requiring education.

4. The child as disabled and a victim of a rejecting society.

5. The child as deprived or disadvantaged and needing resources.

6. The child as resourceful.

7. The child as excluded and needing special opportunities.

These different positions on children and childhood have complicated the research picture in terms of how researchers should approach and engage children in interviews. From these positions three key ideas to researching children have emerged and these were described by Punch (2002):

- when researchers interview children they should use the same methods and approaches as interviewing adults.
- children are different from adults and therefore require a different style and method to engage them.
- children are similar to adults but have different competences and therefore the typical adult strategies require some modification and adaptation to be effective.

To help you think about this further we provide a vignette exercise in Box 1.4. We suggest you look at this now.

▬ Box 1.4 ▬

Vignette – Adam

Adam is training to be a teacher and is specialising in arts and crafts. He plans to teach young children aged between 4 and 11 years old. As part of his training course he is required to undertake a small scale research project with children and he has decided to interview six children aged 5 years old about their opinions of art in school. He thinks that children should help shape the curriculum and that their views are

(Continued)

(Continued)

important to the methods used to teach them arts and crafts. He therefore thinks their opinions are very important to teaching delivery.

- What position on children and childhood does Adam seem to have?

Take a few moments to write down what you think Adam's perspective is on children. Does he take a paternalistic view of protecting children or a rights-based view?

For a response to this question please refer to the answer pages at the end of the book. There we provide some suggestions about Adam's perspective on children.

BENEFITS OF INTERVIEWING CHILDREN AND YOUNG PEOPLE

Arguably interviewing children and young people can yield a great deal of rich and interesting information. There are many benefits to using interviews as a data collection technique with children and young people. Indeed, this form of data collection has been very popular with researchers and the number of research studies that report on interview data with children of all ages has increased. This literature has proven important in a range of areas including health, education, social care, social policy and so forth and has had some impact in terms of how we view children and childhood.

Thus in terms of using interviews with children and young people for your own project you might want to consider how and why they are a useful form of data collection.

- Interviews are a flexible method of data collection and there are various different types of interview you can undertake. They are flexible in the sense that you are able to decide which questions you ask, what order you ask those questions in, which lines of inquiry you pursue in more detail, and you can change the wording of the questions to suit the individual child or young person.

> **For example…** You may be interviewing children across a wide age range. While your research agenda and topic may remain the same, the nature of the questions may need to change to reflect the developmental and chronological age of each child interviewed.

- Interviews provide data that is rich and interesting. The data obtained has depth and allows you to explore things in more detail than quantitative methods (such as questionnaires) might allow. The use of interviews allows you to probe further into areas of interest and you can prompt children to expand on their answers.

> For example… A questionnaire might ask children about their weight and exercise. It might ask the child how many times per week they engage in sporting activities, to which a child may reply '0'. However, if interviewing the child, you may find out that the child had experienced significant bullying during sporting activities in school and thus steps had been taken to ameliorate this by allowing the child to abstain from sports. Alternatively, you might find out that the child has a particular disability which prevents him/her from participating. Alternatively, you may find that the child takes dancing classes on a weekend but does not see that as exercise and therefore misinterpreted the question. By interviewing the child, you can establish that the child does not play sport, the reasons for that and also find out how the child feels about it. The data is likely to be richer than if obtained through a written questionnaire.

- Interviewing as a technique provides you with a means to engage the child directly and gives you some opportunities to check that the child has understood the question. Interviews give you the flexibility to build a rapport with the child and follow-up interesting or important issues that the child raises during the interview. This will also be relevant if the topic is sensitive or difficult.

> For example… If you are interviewing children and young people about their feelings and experiences of being in a family where there is domestic violence, then you can be sensitive to their body language and any distress. This means you can phrase your questions carefully, ensure that they have the opportunity not to answer any questions they find too difficult, and provide them with a safe space to express their views.

- The use of interviews with children provides an opportunity (if needed) to explore more sensitive issues and topics with the child as they provide a context whereby these issues can be carefully managed. The interaction between researcher and child means that the interviewer can be sensitive to verbal and non-verbal cues from the child for any distress or anger.

> For example… You may be interviewing children about their relationships with their friends and a child may talk about the fact that he thinks he has not got any friends and is lonely. This might be something you had not considered in your interview schedule, but because of the rapport you have built with the child the topic may be appropriate to pursue if the child is comfortable with doing so.

CRITIQUES OF THE INTERVIEW METHOD

Although you may have chosen to conduct interviews with children and young people for your project, it is important to be aware of the limitations of this method of data collection. If you are writing up your research for a proposal, thesis, dissertation or even a journal article, you will need a rationale for your choices and an awareness of the limitations of your research. Often the use of interviewing as a technique, particularly in qualitative approaches, is taken-for-granted and interviews are especially popular. Problematically, the idea that an interviewee can 'tell it like it is', that he or she is the incontrovertible expert on his or her own experiences, that respondents are transparent to themselves, still remains the unchallenged starting point for most of this qualitative, interview-based research. (Hollway and Jefferson, 2008: 298)

There are several limitations to interviewing and some of these can be overcome with some effort from you and others are inherent to the method. We begin with those that you have some control over.

- The interview context can be quite a formal situation for some children and younger children particularly may be anxious about participating.

You can play an important role in helping to overcome this limitation. You will need to be sure that the children are well aware of what the interview will entail and what to expect. You will also need to spend some time getting to know your participants and building rapport. In practice this means that some of the time you have with the child will need to be spent on the two of you getting to know one another. You can tell the child about yourself, who you are, where you are from and so on but ensuring you share only age and context appropriate information. You can ask the child simple questions about their favourite colour, what school subjects they like, about their pets and so on. This will help the child to feel more relaxed. We return to this issue again later in the book.

- Interviews may not be the most suitable mode of inquiry for children or young people who find verbal communication difficult.

This will partly depend on the topic you are exploring and which children you include to be interviewed. If it is just one child with communication difficulties, then you may want to adapt the interview to suit. If all children have communication difficulties, then you may want to think of ways to do text-based interviews or use a different method. Alternatively, you may need an interpreter or someone who speaks sign language for example.

- It may be the case that you have little experience conversing with children or little training in this respect. Additionally, even if you have experience with children you may have little experience of research interviewing and this particular modality of communication.

The planning stage of your research will be essential in overcoming this limitation if this is the case. You will want your interview to be as relaxed and natural as possible so practice talking with children in other contexts where possible. One option is to do some volunteer work with children or meet up with friends who have children of their own. Remember it is easy to slip into using adult-centred language and you need to make the interview child-friendly.

- Some children will be reluctant to share their experiences with you or may be too shy to open up.

You need to ascertain whether the child truly wants to participate or not, and provide them with the opportunity to withdraw in case this is their preference. There are different ways of ensuring this, for example, if possible you can check with the parents/guardian and make sure that they have consulted with the child (they know them best), you can ask them directly, you can look for signs that they are uncomfortable, distressed, or reluctant to answer questions, or offer them the opportunity to stop at fairly regular intervals.

However, if you are certain that the child is happy to participate then there are things you can do to encourage them to feel more relaxed. While these will be discussed later in the book (see Chapter 6), you may want to use arts and crafts or toys to help them to feel more relaxed. You can also spend time getting to know the child and reschedule the interview for another day, giving the child an opportunity to get to know you a bit better first (if time permits).

Of course there are some limitations that are inherent to the method itself and difficult to counter through active strategies. This relates mostly to the theoretical assumptions of the research. Thus there have been challenges to the taken-for-granted assumption that qualitative interviews should be the first choice of method (Potter and Hepburn, 2005). The data collection method of interviewing should be congruent with your own theoretical assumptions (as we mentioned earlier in the chapter). However, quite often researchers fail to make clear the relationship between their method of data collection and their underpinning framework and this can result in their interview being treated as a generic research tool (Wimpenny and Gass, 2000).

Potentially problematically, it is the researcher that sets the agenda and directs the conversation (Brinkman and Kvale, 2005) and it is therefore necessary to consider the role of the researcher in the production of the data (Potter, 2002). In other words, it is you as the interviewer who will shape and direct the interview and it is you that will determine what gets asked and

> Important point: It is important to remember that interviews are not neutral tools for gathering data; rather they are active interactions (Fontana and Frey, 2003).

what does not. It is necessary to remember this as you develop your project and to consider the ways in which the questions you ask shape the responses you get. Thus the methodological perspective that is guiding the interview will have an impact on the questions that are addressed, the nature of the relationship between interviewer and interviewee, and the ways in which the questions are delivered (O'Reilly and Kiyimba, 2015).

SUMMARY

From reading this chapter you should now be able to appreciate that there is value in conducting interviews with children and young people. We have illustrated that the interview method allows the researcher to explore in depth the interests, opinions, views, experiences and feelings of children and young people which can have an impact in many different disciplines. We have demonstrated that there are some important issues to account for when thinking about engaging children in interviews. We have shown that contemporary views on children and childhood, discussions of children's rights, and the concept of child-centredness play an important role in how research is shaped and how your interview is conducted. We have encouraged you to reflect on your own views and positions, and given you some useful information to consider. We concluded the chapter with a more critical discussion of the general benefits and limitations of the method as a benchmark to consider as you progress through the book.

RECOMMENDED READING

Qualitative research generally

Ritchie, J., Lewis, J., McNaughton-Nicholls, C. and Ormston, R. (eds) (2014) *Qualitative Research Practice: A Guide for Social Science Students and Researchers.* London: Sage.

Silverman, D. (2013) *Doing Qualitative Research* (4th edn). London: Sage.

Research with children generally

Clark, A., Flewitt, R., Hammersley, M. and Robb, M. (eds) (2014) *Understanding Research with Children and Young People.* London: Sage.

Greenstein, T. (2006) *Methods of Family Research.* London: Sage.

O'Reilly, M., Ronzoni, P. and Dogra, N. (2013) *Research with Children: Theory and Practice.* London: Sage.

Interviewing

Flewitt, R. (2014) 'Interviews', in A. Clark, R. Flewitt, M. Hammersley and M. Robb (eds), *Understanding Research with Children and Young People.* London: Sage. pp. 136–153.

Potter, J. and Hepburn, A. (2005) 'Qualitative interviews in psychology: Problems and possibilities', *Qualitative Research in Psychology, 2*: 1–27.

Understanding theory

O'Reilly, M. and Kiyimba, N. (2015) *Advanced Qualitative Research: A Guide to Contemporary Theoretical Debates.* London: Sage.

Ravitch, S. and Riggan, M. (2012) *Reason and Rigour: How Conceptual Frameworks Guide Research.* California: Sage.

2

DESIGNING YOUR INTERVIEW STUDY

━━ LEARNING OUTCOMES ━━

By the end of the chapter the reader should be able to:

- Appreciate the benefits of maintaining a research diary.
- Recognise the relationship between the research question and the interview design.
- Critically assess the design of interview schedules.
- Evaluate the usefulness of piloting the interviews.
- Evaluate the influence of the child's age on the interview.
- Plan the process of transcription and recognise the associated challenges.
- Describe the precautions needed to stay safe in the field.

INTRODUCTION

The purpose of this chapter is to help you with the key design issues in your interview study. There are several important facets to designing your research interviews and we provide you with practical advice in approaching each of these. Keeping a research diary can be a useful way to monitor your research and we provide some advice on the appropriate ways to maintain this. To successfully meet the aims and objectives of your interview project it will be necessary to have a clear research question. In addition to the overarching research question which guides the project, to maximise the likelihood of success it will be necessary to develop a clear schedule of interview questions. Most research guides will advise you to pilot this schedule and we provide you with some useful steps for doing this, along with a rationale for why it is important. In this chapter we consider how the age of the children and young people you recruit might shape and direct the style, content and trajectory of the interview, and draw your attention to some of the age-appropriate issues you may need to cover. We also consider practical challenges for transcribing it once you have collected your data and how to plan for this in advance. We conclude the chapter with some discussion regarding the location of the interviews, and provide tips on the benefits and challenges of interviewing children in their own homes. This is considered against a critical discussion of researcher safety and we provide you with some advice for staying safe in the field.

KEEPING A RESEARCH DIARY

Keeping a research diary is considered essential in qualitative projects, but is also useful for mixed methods and quantitative research. The function of keeping a diary up-to-date is that it provides you with a chronological account of events, decisions and questions that have occurred throughout your research (Burgess, 1981). Although this can be time-consuming it is beneficial as it helps you to track your thought processes, decisions and reflections, rather than relying on your memory. There are many different ways of keeping a research diary depending on your preference: you may prefer to use your computer/tablet to keep an electronic folder of documents with your diary entries; or you may prefer to buy a note book with divider pages built into it and colour code the different types of entry; or you may prefer to use a calendar style diary, either in hard copy or on the computer whereby the actual dates are printed and you can record events and decisions on a particular date.

There are three main reasons why you should keep a research diary for your research project and these were outlined by O'Reilly and Parker (2014a). We outline these in Table 2.1 below.

Table 2.1　Purpose of a research diary (O'Reilly and Parker, 2014a)

Purpose	Description
Factual information	Facts can be recorded in the diary, such as references that have been recommended to you, dates of events or meetings, forthcoming appointments, and information about your participants.
Reflexivity	This is particularly important in qualitative research as you are required to be reflexive through the process of your research which means you will need to reflect on your personal reactions to events and during the data collection process. So this is an opportunity to write down your thoughts and feelings as they were experienced at the time.
Decisions made	You will make many decisions throughout your project. Some of these will be minor and others will be much more significant. It is useful to write these decision processes in the diary to show how and why those decisions were made.

THE ROLE OF THE RESEARCH QUESTION

Your research question is a central component of your research as it informs many of your methodological choices. In other words, your choice to conduct interviews with children and/or young people will have been guided by the research question. Although your first iteration of a question is likely to be tentative and exploratory, it will be an essential tool for articulating the primary focus of your study (Agee, 2009).

It can be quite challenging to come up with a good research question and we suggest you consult with as many people throughout the process as you can. One of the best ways you can develop your question is to brainstorm your ideas and consider all the aspects of the topic that are of interest. See Figure 2.1 for an example where we brainstorm topics of interest related to children's views of crime.

Important point: A badly designed research question is likely to result in a loss of focus and direction (Agee, 2009) and therefore it is important to ensure that you have a clear, focused question from the design stage of your project.

Once you have a general brainstorm map it is necessary to start writing down questions in relation to your identified brainstormed areas; write down all questions no matter how silly or unfocused they might initially seem. See some examples below (in reality we would probably come up with twice if not three or four times as many as this):

- What do children think crime is?
- How do children perceive criminals?
- What are children's fears about crime?
- What are children's attitudes towards the police?
- Why might children fear criminal behaviour?
- How do young offenders perceive themselves to be treated by the justice system?
- Where do child victims of crime go for help?
- What characteristics do young offenders have?

It should be clear that some broad area of interest such as 'children's views of crime', while an interesting topic, is not a focused question and needs refinement to become a proper research question. Once you have come up with a long list of general questions it will be

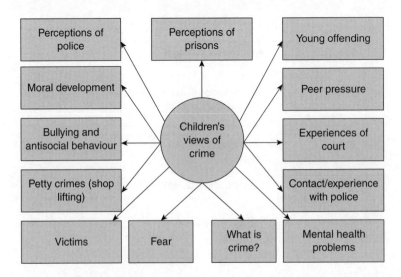

Figure 2.1 Brainstorming topics

important to organise your thinking and a useful way of doing this is to use the 'STEPS' model (O'Reilly and Parker, 2014a); see Figure 2.2.

This model provides a useful way to think about how to write your research question as it refers to both the 'what' aspects of a good question, i.e., enquiry, participants and subject, as well as the 'how' aspects, that your research question should be specific and timely (that is, contemporary and filling a gap in knowledge). The 'how' parts are general overarching aspects of the question, but the 'what' aspects are quite specific.

Before applying the specifics of the model at this stage of your thinking you need to narrow down your focus to help you develop a proper question. If you look back at Figure 2.1 and the short list of questions generated you can see that there is little focus. 'Children's views of crime' is a very general area and to simply interview children about what they think of crime is arguably too broad a project. You need a focused question which is answerable so before applying steps it is useful to consider what you are really interested in and it can be helpful to look at the literature on the topic (in this case children and crime) to help you narrow it down. For example:

- 'Children' is a broad category encompassing birth to 18. This might be ambitious so you need to be more specific. Are you interested in a particular age group (teenagers, young children)? Are you interested in those who have committed a crime or have been a victim of crime? Are you interested in those who have witnessed crime? Being specific in your category of 'children' can help you think about what it is that you are trying to address.
- Crime itself is also a broad category. This includes minor misdemeanours through to very serious assault and murder. Depending on your reading you might want to focus on particular types of crime, such as antisocial behaviour, shoplifting/theft, bullying, or more serious dangerous crimes such as assault, domestic violence, armed robbery and so on.

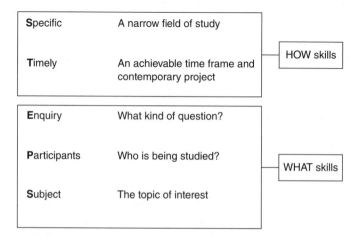

Figure 2.2 The STEPS model (taken from O'Reilly and Parker, 2014a: 61)

From this you can select relevant questions from your list and refine them. So for the sake of an example, we will focus on young offender's perspectives on the justice system. From our original list of questions these ones were still relevant:

- What are children's attitudes towards the police?
- How do young offenders perceive themselves to be treated by the justice system?
- What characteristics do young offenders have?

We can now apply the STEPS model to these questions (of course you should have more than three from your own longer list). So the core three ingredients outlined by O'Reilly and Parker (2014a) are:

- Enquiry.
- Participants.
- Subject.

They argued that the enquiry aspect of the research question relates to the nature of the question and in qualitative research this is typically represented with question words such as 'what', 'why' or 'how'. These prefaces to the question will determine the direction of your research question. So in the examples we have given you, the words 'what' and 'how' are used to indicate the direction of the question and shows what kind of a question it is. Thus all three questions have an enquiry element.

The second ingredient is participants, and refers to the sample or population you intend to research. O'Reilly and Parker argued that it is useful to give some indication of the demographic characteristics of the sample within the question. So in our first question the participants are described as 'children' and in our second and third questions they are 'young offenders'.

The third important ingredient according to the STEPS model is the subject, the topic area of the research. It is useful here to be relatively specific. In our first question the overall topic is the police, but more specifically it relates to children's attitudes towards this group. In our second example, the topic is the justice system and more specifically how young offenders feel they are treated in the justice system. Finally, our third question has the topic of young offender's characteristics.

Once you are satisfied that you have included these three key ingredients you then need to take a broader conceptualisation of your research question to satisfy the first two ingredients of the STEPS model. In other words, you need to be sure that your research question is specific enough to be answered through your research and that it is timely, in the sense that it addresses a contemporary issue and fills a gap in knowledge. We can now look at each of our questions in turn and examine them more closely for these two aspects.

- What are children's attitudes towards the police?

While this question has all three of the main ingredients, it lacks both specificity and possibly timeliness. As we noted earlier the general category of 'children' is a little vague and there does not seem to be a sound rationale for needing to explore children aged 0–18 years and their attitudes of the police force. Again you would need to consult the literature to help you with this decision, but you need to think about the gap in knowledge. By consulting the literature, you can see what we already know about children's attitudes toward the police to determine if there is a gap in our understanding and thus whether it is timely. However, even if it is the question would need refining to be more specific.

• How do young offenders perceive themselves to be treated by the justice system?

Again this question has the three core ingredients needed and in this case is more specific than the first example. We have a more defined sample: 'young offenders', and the topic under scrutiny is also fairly specific: 'the justice system'. This helps to narrow down the focus of your interview study, although you may need to be more specific about the age range of your young offenders. Ostensibly it seems timely, as young offenders historically have not been given full attention due to the assumed vulnerability of the group and the difficulty in accessing these populations. Again you would need to consult the literature to ensure that this focus would address a gap in knowledge and thus be timely.

• What characteristics do young offenders have?

While this question also has the core three ingredients it is a rather closed down and vague question. It is not clear what is meant by 'characteristics' and there seems little rationale for providing a list of the demographics of this population. While it would be necessary to again consult the literature to see what we already understand about the general demographics of the population, there is little specificity or timeliness to this question.

> **Important point**: Do not underestimate how long it will take you to develop a good research question (White, 2009). A good question will take you a long time, and should be revisited over several days or even weeks.

Remember that your research question is a work in progress and should be refined over time. Do not expect to write it in five minutes and not have to return to it. It should be informed by your interests and the gap in the literature and you will need to revisit it on many occasions. A clear research question will help you to construct a directed and purposeful literature review, which in turn will help to inform any changes to the research question (Andrews, 2003). Ultimately your research question and topic should be guided by the literature to ensure its originality (Kinmond, 2012). Remember also that you may need to develop sub-questions that relate to your overall question for your research project. While your overarching question will provide your direction for the study design and data collection, it does provide the potential for developing more specific questions during the research process and these sub-questions allow for a greater level of discovery and give direction to the kinds of data that are needed (Agee, 2009). So, for qualitative research you will have one broad research question that guides your project, but you may need two or three related sub-questions that fall under that broad question.

We now suggest you turn to Box 2.1 and try the activity.

━━ Box 2.1 ━━━━━━━━━━━━━━━━━━━━━━━━━━━━━━━━━━

Activity on STEPS

If you have not done so already, try to write down your research question and see if it conforms to the requirements of STEPS. If you are not ready to develop a research question yet try to make one up and see if that conforms to STEPS. Use this as an opportunity to practise writing research questions.

───

DEVELOPING AN INTERVIEW SCHEDULE

An essential part of the success of your interviews will rest on the development of a good interview schedule. Typically for most types of interview flexibility in the schedule is useful and important. Do not develop too many questions on your agenda as they are to some extent guided by the participants and the interviewer will follow the natural trajectory of the conversation. It will be important that you understand the purpose of your interview as this will help you to make decisions regarding the types of questions you will be asking.

> Important point: Remember that the interview questions reflect the aims and objectives of the project and should enable you to address your research question. The research question and the interview schedule questions are different things with a different purpose, so do not mix them up.

You will no doubt be aware of the fact that questions can be phrased as open or closed questions (which we will discuss further), but it is important to remember that questions do not exist in an abstract way. You may ask an open question, but you may do so in a way in which the child hears that you have not indicated an interest in their response. In other words, your body language and tone set the context of the question for the child and the way the child hears the question is as important as the way you ask it.

Using closed questions

While of course a quantitative interview schedule is likely to have many of these, qualitative interviewers tend to avoid closed questioning. However, as you are interviewing children and young people some closed questions may actually be useful. In interviews with children, closed questions can help you to elicit essential information that informs

For example… In a study on social media usage in teenagers you might ask 'Do you have a Facebook account?' as a platform for your open questions such as 'in what ways do you use Facebook?' or 'please give me an example of the comments you make on Facebook?'

For example… In a study on teenagers' perceptions of mental illness, you might ask 'do you know anyone who has experienced depression?' At this point in the interview you might want to explore additional areas but later you might come back to this answer to elaborate with something like 'you said your cousin had depression last year, tell me about the treatments they had for that'.

Important point: Do not be tempted to have too many closed questions and remember that you will probably have to modify them or change the order they are asked during the interview itself and may need to rephrase some of them for different children.

the broader objectives of the project. Closed questions are those which lend themselves to yes or no answers, or a statement of fact, for example:

Do you enjoy swimming?

What is your favourite colour?

Typically, researchers see closed questions as generating short or one word answers and therefore these kinds of questions can restrict the responses of your participants. However, just because the question is phrased in a closed way does not mean that your participant will not elaborate on their 'yes' or 'no' reply (Roulston, 2010). Some children, particularly younger children, can be difficult to engage in an interview and time needs to be taken to help them relax. By asking them several short closed questions about simple things such as their favourite colour, how many pets they have, whether they enjoy particular activities and so forth, it can help the child to feel that they have something to offer. Furthermore, it is possible to use closed questions to clarify your understanding of details given in response to previous open questions. Possibly more importantly, closed questions can be used to open up a topic of inquiry which can be elaborated on in the next question or later in the interview.

Using open questions

While closed questions may have their place on your schedule, it is more likely that you will need several open questions to really explore the relevant issues for your research question. Open questions or statements are those questions that invite the respondent to open up and provide a narrative about the issue. They encourage the respondent to widen the scope.

Open questions allow participants to formulate their responses to you in their own words and talk around the subject. These questions will be crucial for you in meeting the aims of your study and in addressing your research question. Open questions encourage participants to provide longer responses and help you ask questions based on what they have said. For example:

- Why did you do that?
- How did that make you feel?
- What happened the last time you visited the swimming pool?
- Which friends help you with your homework?

When conducting interviews with children, open-ended questions can provide an opportunity for the participant to bring in topics and modes of discourse that are more familiar to them (Eder and Fingerson, 2001). Remember also that open style 'questions' or phrases can be used successfully with children in a more narrative style or unstructured style of interviewing. You can encourage the child to tell their versions, stories, and express their feelings through open style statements to reduce the traditional question–answer sequence style interview, for example:

- Tell me about what school is like for you.
- Please give me an example of when you felt sad.

Using prompts and phrases, nodding and encouraging the child to talk can mean that you do not need to ask many questions in your interview. You can simply encourage the child to tell you about life for them, their experiences of particular instances, and slowly build a rapport with the child as they narrate their stories.

It is often suggested that interviewers should start with open questions or statements that invite the respondent to talk freely. Then as the interview progresses, the interviewer can use closed questions for clarification or further details (for example, DiCicco-Bloom and Crabtree, 2006). This should be a gradual shift but it will depend on the topic under discussion and whether the interview is structured or not and if specific information is required.

Morse and Field (1995) suggested that after rapport is established, for an unstructured interview a simple statement such as 'Tell me about …' should enable the participant to tell their story with relatively little interruption. However, this might be more difficult for some participants, particularly children. Therefore, researchers working with children might need to consider that some closed and direct questions may be needed to engage the child with the topic (Irwin and Johnson, 2005). Irwin and Johnson suggested the need to be prepared and have an alternate structure to the interview to meet the needs of individual children and also to be prepared to go off the research topic to facilitate the conversation.

Practical choices

When you are developing your interview schedule it is important that you think in a practical way about the best way to develop it. Do not be afraid to ask for help from more experienced researchers if you need it. There are several factors you need to consider when you develop your interview schedule:

1. Use the literature to help you. Remember that there is a great deal of methodological literature out there, as well as people who have done research with children and published their project findings. Both of these types of literature are important. It is helpful to have a sense of the themes that have been investigated in the area of study as well as the conceptual and theoretical knowledge in this area (Kvale and Brinkman, 2009). This will help you think about the general areas that need to be covered in your schedule of questions.

2. Before you design your interview schedule it can be helpful to think about the core issues at stake for your research and map these out. Think broadly to start with and conceptualise the key areas of interest in relation to your research question. You can then design your interview schedule questions around these core areas of your research agenda.

3. Discuss your questions with the rest of your research team or your supervisor and peers if possible. Having critical discussions about the questions you have included on the schedule will help you to foster a more creative style of thinking as you develop your questions (Gaskell, 2000).

4. Ask some children you know. If you have access to any groups of children who are a similar age or sample type to those you intend to study, then ask them to help you develop some of your questions. They will bring a unique and important insight to your schedule (be mindful of the possible breaches of ethics in doing this).

5. Keep the schedule concise. Remember that on the day of the interview you will need to be flexible and adapt to the participants' reports. You may need to change questions, ask them in a different order, ask new questions, or omit questions depending on their responses. The schedule should be approximately one page and focused around broad headings that reflect the research agenda (Gaskell, 2000).

> Important point: Remember that the schedule is there to guide you and it is not a script that you follow meticulously (Gaskell, 2000).

There is no key template for an interview schedule but it should not be too long, should reflect your research question, should reflect the literature and should be organised around the core issues that you have identified. You must remember that the questions are merely a guide and you will need to ask questions on the basis of the answers you are given by the children and be prepared to move between questions on the schedule and ask new questions to pursue an area raised by the child that you may not have thought about. For some guidance we present an example interview schedule in Figure 2.3 below. This is an example of what a schedule might look like and is based broadly around the issue of children's perceptions of being bullied.

PILOTING THE INTERVIEW QUESTIONS

It will be necessary to pilot your interview schedule before you start collecting your data so that you can get some feedback and refine your questions. By not conducting a pilot study you risk missing out on the opportunity of refining your study that could impact on the quality of your research and this is likely to impact on your dissemination (Sampson, 2004).

It may be useful to mention the pilot phase in your ethics application (considered later in the book).

There are several benefits to conducting some pilot interviews:

> For example… By testing the recording equipment you might find that you need an external microphone because the sound quality is poor or that you placed the recording device too far away from the interviewee.

- Allows you to test out any materials you have developed. Not only can you test the purpose of the questions, but also

Interview schedule example

Area 1: Peer relationships

1. Tell me about your friends

    Prompt: Tell me about your best friend

    Prompt: What do you like to do during school break times?

2. What happens when you fall out with your friends?

    What do you do when your friends (name best friend if possible) fall out with you?

Area 2: Defining bullying and peer conflict

3. In your opinion what do you think bullying is?

    Prompt: Give me an example from the television of some bullying

    Prompt: What is the difference between friends fighting and bullying?

(Note: Could ask the children to draw bullying)

Area 3: Types of bullying behaviour

4. Tell me about your use of social media

    Prompt: Do you use Facebook/Twitter/YouTube?

    Prompt: Have you ever received nasty messages on Facebook/Twitter?

5. Tell me what you think cyberbullying is

    Prompt: Tell me about any experiences you or your friends have of nasty messages by text message/Facebook.

Area 4: Experiences of bullying

6. When was the last time you were bullied?

    Prompt: Please give me an example of that

7. How did you deal with the bullying?

8. Who did you tell about the bullying?

Figure 2.3   Example interview schedule

check that they are worded in a way which your potential participants can understand on your interview schedule. You can also test out the recording equipment.

- Allows you to check ethical procedures. This will give you an opportunity to test your informed consent procedures and check whether the ways in which you explain key ethical principles are understood by children who fit your sampling criteria.

- Examination of interviewing skills and feasibility of data collection. By piloting your interview schedule you will be able to examine your interviewing style

> For example... You may find that the terminology you are using to explain what the project is about is too sophisticated and that the children in your pilot struggle to understand what it means. This means that with their help you can revise the wording you use.

> For example... You might find that you are not relaxed enough when asking questions or that you rush onto the next question without taking the opportunity to explore the child's initial answers. By reflecting back on the recording and asking your pilot participant questions at the end you can improve your techniques.

and skills, check the questions and their child-appropriateness, and obtain useful feedback on improving your interviews. You will also be able to check that children are willing to engage with you and why, as well as identifying any barriers or issues that might arise (van Teijlingen et al., 2001).

> **Important point**: Remember that pilot studies will vary in length, depth and intensity and the choices you make will depend on the purpose of your pilot study. If major complications arise from the first pilot study you may need to undertake a second one.

CONSIDERING THE AGE OF THE INTERVIEWEES

It may seem fairly obvious that the age of your interviewees will have some impact on the shape, trajectory and style of the interview you conduct. While it is important not to make assumptions about the competence of the children and to be aware of any other factors that may influence the interview (learning difficulties, mental disorders, speech problems and so on), it is useful to have a broad awareness of the influence of age (this is something that we return to again later in the book in Chapter 9).

Very young children – under 4 years

It is unusual for interviews to be undertaken with very young children; however, it is not impossible to do so as most of them do have some vocabulary and some experience of communicating with adults. Very young children are likely to have a limited competence to engage, and it is likely to be difficult to create reliable meaning from their talk due to issues of grammar, semantics and syntax (Cameron, 2005). They may also not have any concept of the topic under research. You will usually need to be experienced to talk to this age group and sensitive of difficult issues. These very young children are a particularly vulnerable group, and may benefit from having their parent present to facilitate the interview.

If you are going to interview children of such a young age, then you will need a very carefully developed interview schedule with simple short questions. It is a good idea to bear in mind a range of interviewing tips, which we present in Table 2.2.

Table 2.2 Practical tips for conducting interviews with very young children

Tip	Description
Familiarity	Make reference to things that they are likely to be familiar with (check with the parent before you ask these questions), for example, children's television characters, story books, toys or activities can all provide a platform for a question.
Use pictures	You can use pictures to help facilitate discussion. You can take photographs of particular objects or find colourful pictures from the internet and use them to stimulate discussion.
Keep it short	Keep your interview short. Just get the key information you need as the child may become tired or bored. Equally choose an appropriate time to do the interview. Try not to choose a time when the child would normally be napping or eating for example. If necessary, you may need to conduct more than one interview to yield the data you require.

Tip	Description
Parent facilitation	Allow the parent to join in the interview and help you. Parents are probably best placed to get more detailed answers out of their child and will know the best ways of asking your questions. We return to this issue later in the book.

Young children – 5 to 11 years

Conducting interviews with this age group is more common, but presents its own set of challenges. If you plan to conduct your interviews with children in this age category, then you will need to consider a wide range of issues. You will need to use methods that reflect the children's interests, values, experiences and routines and you will need to pay attention to the issue of power. Remember that children of this age group are used to being given directions from adults. They are less used to having a degree of control or saying no. However, in your interview it will be beneficial to give the child some control, to be flexible in how and when you ask questions, and it will be helpful to encourage them to lead the interview and tell you their stories (O'Reilly et al., 2013a).

Important point: Remember that children in this age group have a tendency to give the answers they think the adults want to hear so phrase your questions carefully and in a non-leading and non-judgemental way.

There are several practical tips to consider when interviewing children in this age group and we outline these in Table 2.3.

Table 2.3 Practical tips for interviewing young children

Factor	Description
Child's vocabulary	It will be helpful if you familiarise yourself with the child's vocabulary and to do this you could spend some time with children this age to get used to the way they communicate with each other and how they communicate with adults. However, remember some vocabulary will be related to the context.
Encouragement	Encourage the children to ask you lots of questions about a range of topics including those less relevant to your research.
Get advice	Seek advice from teachers, parents, youth leaders and anyone else to pitch your questions at the right level.
Rapport building	Allow the child some time to get to know you (this is even better if it can be done in advance of the interview rather than on the day).
Communication style	Remember that the older children (aged 11 years) may communicate in different ways, have different interests and have different competencies to the younger children (aged 5 years). You will need to adapt your interview style accordingly if you are interviewing children across the age range.
Individuality	Remember that children are individuals and some may find the process easier than others and their personalities will vary. Be flexible and have a range of topics to make conversation with them. Find out what the current 'craze' in the age group is – even if they do not like it they are likely to have a view.
Participatory methods	Consider the use of participatory methods (discussed in Chapter 6).

Older children (young people) – 12 to 18 years

If you are undertaking interviews with young people, then clearly the techniques you employ will differ from interviewing younger children. Young people have a greater capacity to understand the questions you are asking and the purpose of your interview. However, this age group has greater pressure on them in terms of their physical development, changing social relationships and academic stress. It can be difficult to engage young people in interview research as they may be less motivated for the interview, may be more resistant to opening up, or may fear reprisals or judgements. While some forms of participatory methods such as video-vignettes, social media, or photography may help facilitate the interview, it is important to remember that young people may find their inclusion patronising.

For an example of research using participatory methods refer to Box 2.2.

▬ Box 2.2 ▬

Research case example of participatory methods

A research study exploring young people and their welfare by Samantha Punch (2002) included the use of a range of participatory methods. The study investigated young people's perceptions of their problems, coping strategies and help-seeking behaviour using both group and individual interviews. Accordingly, the author used a range of task-based activities including spider diagrams and charts and stimulus materials such as video-clips and common phrases, as well as a new innovative technique, 'the secret box'. Punch found that the participatory methods facilitated the engagement of the young people, maintained their interests and stimulated discussions about sensitive topics. Additionally, these methods helped to reduce the unequal power relationship between researcher and participant.

Most young people (in the western world at least) live in an age of social networking, computer technology, the internet, computer gaming and so on and this can be used to your advantage when you design your interview study. You might even think about using the internet to conduct your interview as outlined in Chapter 4.

There are important issues you need to think about when conducting interviews with this group and we provide some practical tips in Table 2.4.

Table 2.4 Practical tips for interviewing older children

Tip	Description
Consider power	The issue of power is still pertinent when interviewing young people and you will need to spend some time getting to know your interviewees before the data collection phase. There is a risk you may influence their responses and you need to adopt an open style of questioning and encourage them to direct the interview agenda as much as possible. You could also give them some control over the recording device to show a level of trust and control. You need to be clear about your role in the research, who you are, why you are there and what you want from them before you proceed with the interview.

Tip	Description
Atmosphere	Try to nurture an atmosphere where the young person is positioned as the expert and you are there to learn from them.
Manage anxiety	Like with younger children, young people may be anxious about responding to your questions for fear of retribution or embarrassment. You will need to spend some time assuring them that the data will remain confidential.
Talk on their level	It may be tempting to try to treat them like adults or for you to act like a teenager to be on their level, but this is not advisable. Try to talk to them on their level but treat them with respect and acknowledge who you really are. Young people will pretty easily pick up if they think you are being disingenuous.
Presence of others	Young people are more likely to disclose information and open up to you if parents and/or teachers are not present and therefore you may have to negotiate some privacy. Of course if they do request the presence of someone else (maybe a friend or social worker rather than parent) during the interview you should try to accommodate it.
Rapport building	Remember that some shy young people will take time to warm to you so you need to put them at their ease and reassure them and give them more time. Go at their pace through the questions and allow them space to reflect on their answers before leaping in with your next question.
Respect confidentiality	Some parents find it difficult when they are told they do not have access to what their teenager said during the interview. You will have to respect the confidentiality of the young person while reassuring the parent. Remind the parent that you have a duty to disclose safeguarding issues but the rest is confidential.
Culture	Be aware that older children tend to have their own discourse styles and peer cultures (Eder and Fingerson, 2001) and it is useful to have some familiarity with these.

TRANSCRIPTION

Although transcribing your interviews is something that actually happens after the data has been collected, we are dealing with it here in this chapter as transcribing your data is not as straightforward as it may seem and it is something you need to plan for. Traditionally transcription was viewed as a technical task but transcripts actually reflect the goals of a study (Ochs, 1979). It is now agreed that transcription is an active process and one that is understood as theoretical, selective, interpretive and representational (Davidson, 2009).

The first decision to be made is whether to transcribe your interviews yourself or to pay a professional transcriptionist.

There are benefits of undertaking the transcription yourself:

- You can familiarise yourself with the data as you transcribe.
- You can spot any errors or problems during the process.

- Some methodological approaches advocate undertaking your own transcribing and thus you remain congruent with your approach.
- You heard the interviews so will more easily pick up quietly spoken or muffled words that a transcriptionist may miss.
- Transcribing can facilitate the learning process, which will be important if you are undertaking an educational qualification.

There are some benefits to paying for a professional service:

- It will save you time which can be important if you are working to tight deadlines.
- It provides you with a verbatim transcript which you can tidy up according to your needs.
- You can focus on more important aspects of the project such as the analysis.

However, it is important that you provide your transcriptionist with some clear guidelines regarding what you need from them. They should have a good understanding of what you want in the transcript, how you want the turns of talk laid out, and what level of detail you need included. Furthermore, if you have sensitive or potentially upsetting data then you will need to brief and debrief your transcriptionist and offer them a means of support. Transcribing this kind of material can be potentially upsetting for the person listening repeatedly to the recordings (Wilkes et al., 2014; Kiyimba and O'Reilly, in press a and b). Remember that transcription requires repeated listening to the data and hearing the voices of the participants can trigger an emotional reaction (Shopes, 2013).

You will need to think about how much detail you include in your transcript. You will need to decide how you are going to indicate who is speaking (numbers, names, roles), whether you include sneezing, coughing, laughing and so on, whether you time the pauses and how you include non-verbal gestures. Some of these decisions will relate to the methodological approach you are using for your interviews.

Children's talk and transcription

You need to remember that children tend to speak differently to adults as their language is developing and this will need to be considered in your transcription. Of course the age of your sample will make a difference to how sophisticated their vocabulary is and their ability to articulate themselves. You will need to decide whether you transcribe slang terms, swear words, accents, and whether you transcribe exactly how a word was pronounced (e.g., 'brover', as opposed to the tidied 'brother') or not. See the two examples in Box 2.3 from our own research taken from an interview with an adopted child.

■ Box 2.3 ■

Examples of transcription

Verbatim but tidied up

Interviewer: Really?

Child: Yes and Dad was like oh we should have come earlier then we could have put you on that train, but it was okay because all that they were doing is just sending these children down the next line and then back again which was really weird because we missed it.

Transcribed exactly

Interviewer: Really?

Child: Yeah an' Dad wuz like oh we <u>shoulda</u> come earlier then we coulda put ya on that train but it wuz okay cuz all that they wuz doin' is jus' sendin' these children down the next line ((coughs)) an' then back again which wuz <u>really</u> weird cuz we missed it

Transcribing children's speech can be challenging as children's language typically involves sudden shifts in voice and key (Davidson, 2009; Hamo et al., 2004). There may be occasions during the interview where children use noises instead of words and these can be difficult to transcribe as there are no orthodox transcription notations, although they have been referred to as 'active noising' (O'Reilly, 2005). Furthermore, some children may have communication and speech problems or stutter which can be difficult to represent.

Again the issue of power can become problematic in transcribing. The ways in which researchers represent children's talk can emphasise adult speaker's turns and can inadvertently privilege the adult's voice (Ochs, 1979). It will be important that you find ways of representing the children's voices in your transcripts. The inclusion of non-verbal turns can help to show that the children provided responses to questions or expressed their views through looking away, shrugging, covering their face or initiating topic shifts. These can be important at the analysis stage to convey to the audience that the child did take a turn.

CHOOSING A LOCATION AND STAYING SAFE IN THE FIELD

When planning your interviews, it will be important for you to consider where you are going to conduct the interview. You may choose to conduct your interview within the institutional setting you have recruited from, such as the school or health setting (clinic, hospital, hospice) or you may choose to conduct the interview in the community, in a village hall, scout hut or leisure centre. Alternatively, you might choose to conduct your interview in the child's own home.

If you choose to conduct your interview in an institutional setting, then you will need to plan carefully and check that the setting is mutually acceptable. You will need to ensure that you have a quiet room available to carry out the interview and one that is going to be free of interruptions. There is little point using a school staff-room near break times when teachers will be using it.

Important point: Schools are busy places so even if it is supposed to be a quiet period this may be hard to guarantee, so if the topic is sensitive the venue might be less suitable than if the topic is somewhat safer.

It will be important to put a sign up on the door so that people are aware of the need for privacy. You will also need to think about where the child will be comfortable. Will a child be able to relax and talk to you in the staff-room at school, a room they are not typically allowed to enter?

If you choose to conduct your interview in the community, then you can face similar challenges. You will need to secure access to a building that is public enough for safety, but private enough for confidentiality. If you are conducting an interview on something potentially embarrassing such as sexually transmitted diseases, then the teenager may not feel comfortable entering a building set up for interviews knowing that if they are seen people will know why they are going in. Again you will need a room that is quiet and low risk for interruptions.

If you decide that it is sensible to conduct your interviews in the child's own home, then you need to think about the challenges that this can raise. The family home can be chaotic and you will need to negotiate a private and quiet space in the house. It can be difficult to negotiate this as family members have access to all rooms and you are not in a strong position to remove the family pet, turn off the television, or rearrange the furniture (Bushin, 2007; MacDonald, 2008). The child's bedroom may be allocated to you, but do not assume that the child has autonomy over this space (Punch, 2007). It may also feel uncomfortable to invade the child's space. Furthermore, the bedroom might be the child's safe haven to return to after the interview, particularly if the interview had emotional or distressing content. It is preferable to communicate with parents prior to the interview and raise the issue of a private space in advance.

Your physical safety

For example… Getting the train back late at night can be risky, going to a stranger's home alone can be risky, and researching issues such as substance abuse or domestic violence may lead to risk. So the very location of your interview or the nature of the topic might pose some risks to your physical safety.

It is easy to forget your own safety when out collecting data and it is easy to dismiss the potential risks you might take especially when working with children. However, it is imperative you undertake a risk assessment and think about any potential risks to you. Although infrequent there have been cases of physical violence (Bloor et al., 2007) or threats (Parker and O'Reilly, 2013) in the field. Although physical risk is less common than emotional risk, preventing it is important. There may be obvious physical risks, such as the risk of infection if you are carrying out your interviews in a hospital, but there are other potential problems that may occur.

In Table 2.5 we provide some advice for staying physically safe.

Table 2.5   Staying physically safe

Tip	Recommendation
Do a pilot study	By undertaking a pilot study, you will be able to reflect on some of the possible dangers more carefully (Sampson, 2004).
Undertake some safety training	It is important that you have some training on what to do in a threatening or compromising situation (Social Research Association (SRA), 2005).
Be prepared to change the venue	If you feel uncomfortable to think there may be some risk that cannot be managed then arrange to meet your interviewee somewhere more public (Faulkner, 2004).
Follow your safety protocols	Your institution should have some safety protocols in place which you should familiarise yourself with and do follow them (Parker and O'Reilly, 2013).
Visit the neighbourhood in advance	Some neighbourhoods are known for their criminal activity so do your research but do not assume safer places will be safe without assessing potential risk (Paterson et al., 1999).
Plan for the inherent risks in the setting	Some settings are more dangerous than others. For example, prisons/young offender's institutions can be hostile (Liebling, 1999).
If possible, take another researcher with you	The participants can be told that they are there to observe or sort the equipment (SRA, 2005).
Check in with someone	Make sure someone knows the address of where you are going and have an agreed time to call them post interview.

Your emotional safety

It can be easy to get distracted preparing for any physical risks that you forget the potential emotional impact that interviewing children or young people might have. Some areas of research are more emotionally sensitive than others and it can be quite difficult to stay detached during the interview and after. Some of these emotions may just be mildly uncomfortable whereas others can feel more traumatic and long-lasting (Hubbard et al., 2001) and impact on future interviews.

You also need to be aware of the risk of burnout due to a cumulative response to traumatic material (Coles and Mudlay, 2010). In Table 2.6 we provide you with some practical advice for staying emotionally safe.

Overall therefore there are many important areas to think about and O'Reilly and Parker (2013) made core recommendations to those undertaking qualitative fieldwork:

> For example... If you interviewed young children about a topic that did not seem too sensitive, such as children's attitudes towards healthy eating, and found that one of the children got upset because they had an older sister who had died from an eating disorder, this could be very unexpected (and unlikely). This may make you risk averse in interviewing children again and you may become anxious when interviewing other children about other topics in case something unanticipated and distressing occurs.

- *Raise awareness of researcher safety:* It was recommended that researchers share their experiences and become more aware of any potential danger in the field.

Table 2.6   Staying emotionally safe

Tip	Recommendation
Be prepared	Some topics are obviously sensitive and risk an emotional response in you. Be ready for this and plan for it. Build in support for post interview debriefing.
Acknowledge your emotions	Do not fight your emotions – they are natural. It might be useful to get some training on how to manage stress and distress (Johnson and Macleod-Clark, 2003). However, do not unload your emotions on to the child.
Enlist the help of a second researcher	If possible it can be useful to have a second interviewer that remains mostly silent to ease the intensity of the one-to-one relationship (Brannen, 1998). It can also be useful to discuss your emotional responses with a colleague.
Write it down	Use your research diary to write down your thoughts and feelings as the act of writing and getting them out can be cathartic.
Take breaks	If you or your participant feel emotional during the interview then it can be useful to take a break from it (Hubbard et al., 2001).

- *Need for training:* It was recommended that research institutions, such as universities, are active in developing and providing training for researchers and their managers about risk.
- *Perform a transparent risk assessment:* It was argued that the researchers, in consultation with their supervisor/manager undertake a formal risk assessment prior to data collection and that the SRA guidelines are useful in doing so.
- *Ensure space for debriefing:* It was recommended that research teams should create space for debriefing so that the interviewer can talk about any emotional or other experiences that have affected them. Thus a team approach was advocated by O'Reilly and Parker.

What we have dealt with here is your safety and the importance of keeping safe in the field and through the process of analysis. We have not really mentioned the safety of children in this section, as this is an area which is multidimensional and relates more specifically to ethics and safeguarding, and thus we deal with this later in the book in the chapter on ethics and in Chapter 7.

SUMMARY

This chapter has dealt with a range of important issues that you need to consider when you are designing your interview study, including the benefits of keeping a research diary. You should now have a clearer idea of how to develop your research question, as well as design-ing and testing out your interview schedule, and be able to evaluate the usefulness of piloting the interviews. From reading this chapter you should have thought about the chronological and developmental age of the children you plan to interview and how this might shape the direction and style of your data collection. In this chapter we have also considered the practical issues of transcribing your interviews and have drawn your attention to some of the related practical challenges. It is important to plan this carefully. We concluded the chapter with some advice for staying safe and recommend you read about this further.

RECOMMENDED READING

Transcription

Davidson, C. (2009) 'Transcription: Imperatives for research', *International Journal of Qualitative Research,* 8(2): 35–52.

Location and safety

Bloor, M., Fincham, B. and Sampson, H. (2010) 'Unprepared for the worst: Risks of harm for qualitative researchers', *Methodological Innovations,* 5(1): 45–55.

MacDonald, K. (2008) 'Dealing with chaos and complexity: The reality of interviewing children and families in their own homes', *Journal of Clinical Nursing,* 17(23): 3123–3130.

Parker, N. and O'Reilly, M. (2013) '"We are alone in the house": A case study addressing researcher safety and risk', *Qualitative Research in Psychology,* DOI:10.1080/14780887.2011.64726.

Social Research Association (2005) *Staying Safe: A Code of Practice for the Safety of Social Researchers.* Available at: www.the-sra.org.uk (accessed 18 October 2014).

Planning a project

Fraser, S., Flewitt, R. and Hammersley, M. (2014) 'What is research with children and young people', in A. Clark, R. Flewitt, M. Hammersley and M. Robb (eds), *Understanding Research with Children and Young People.* London: Sage. pp. 34–50.

O'Reilly, M., Ronzoni, P. and Dogra, N. (2013) *Research with Children: Theory and Practice.* London: Sage.

Developing research questions

O'Reilly, M. and Parker, N. (2014) *Doing Mental Health Research with Children and Adolescents: A Guide to Qualitative Methods.* London: Sage.

White, P. (2009) *Developing Research Questions: A Guide for Social Scientists.* Basingstoke, Hampshire: Palgrave MacMillan.

3

DIFFERENT TYPES OF INTERVIEW

■ LEARNING OUTCOMES ■

By the end of the chapter the reader should be able to:

- Compare and contrast the different types of interview: structured, semi-structured and unstructured.
- Recognise the challenges of conducting interviews with children and young people.
- Critically assess the different approaches to conducting an interview with children and young people.
- Evaluate the different ways of doing interviewing, founded in approaches such as ethnography, feminism, phenomenology, narrative, and the use of naturally occurring data.

INTRODUCTION

Interviewing is the most popular data collection method in qualitative research. Interviewing participants effectively requires particular skills and can be challenging for those who are less experienced. In this chapter we consider why interviewing children is a popular method of inquiry. The main focus of this chapter is to introduce you to the different interview methods that are available for use with younger populations. We begin by outlining the three common forms of interviewing, i.e. structured, semi-structured and unstructured. We consider the benefits and limitations of using these with children and young people. We also introduce some of the alternative types of interviewing that go beyond traditional interviewing techniques, for example the ethnographic interview, feminist interview, phenomenological interview, narrative interview and the naturally occurring interview. We propose ways in which these can be useful for research with children.

TYPES OF INTERVIEW

You will need to decide which form of interviewing is most appropriate for your project. We introduce you to the four main types of interviews in Table 3.1. We acknowledge however

Table 3.1   Different types of interview

Interview type	Description
Structured interview	This type tends to be used for quantitative research and requires rigidly going through a series of predetermined questions.
Semi-structured interview	This is a qualitative technique that requires the researcher to have a schedule of questions, but implements them flexibly allowing the participant to guide the direction of the interview.
Unstructured interview	This is a qualitative technique whereby the researcher has a few questions to guide the interview, but this type resembles a conversation developed around a theme.
Naturally occurring interview	These are interviews that take place in the natural social world that are not performed for research purposes but may be later used to fulfil a research agenda.

Important point: Remember that your choice of interview type should reflect your research question, the aims and objectives of your project, and will be determined by what you hope to achieve from the interview.

that the distinction between these different types is more complex than is often considered, and that the terminology used may be understood differently by researchers representing different qualitative perspectives. However, they remain a useful heuristic in guiding interview-based research.

The structured interview

If you are conducting a qualitative project, it is unlikely that you will use structured interviews as they are quantitative in nature and they are often used as an alternative to written questionnaires. This means that quantitative criteria, such as reliability and validity are pertinent to the interview design and the questions must be asked in the same way, in the same order to every participant. For example, consider the three questions below:

1. What is your favourite food?
2. Do you like fruit?
3. How much fruit do you eat in a day?

You would have to ask all of the children these three questions in the same order. So if the child said that they did not like fruit in response to question 2, you would still have to ask them question 3, despite it being a silly question knowing the answer to question 2.

The structured interview is considered to have an advantage over questionnaire design as it seeks to engage the young participant in the research which means that the researcher can explain more challenging questions directly. The use of the structured interview is also favoured over the questionnaire as a way of improving response rates. It is well known that response rates to questionnaires vary, but are typically poor; especially for those that are longer (see Roszkowski and Bean, 1990). This is compounded further with younger populations as gatekeepers, such as parents, may be too busy to help them fill out their answers (particularly for younger children). In conducting a structured interview, it will be important to agree a time slot with the parents and this may increase the likelihood of the interview taking place (although there is no guarantee and you may need to send them reminders) (O'Reilly et al., 2013a).

The semi-structured interview

Semi-structured interviews are perhaps the most common type of interviewing technique and are generally favoured by qualitative researchers. The semi-structured interview allows the researcher some flexibility in how they ask their questions and in what order they present them to the participant. This means that the researcher can actively listen to what the children say during the interview and use these responses to modify or change questions, or even ask new ones that are relevant to the individual experience of the participant.

For an example of the semi-structured style of interviewing see Box 3.1.

■■ Box 3.1 ■■■■■■■■■■■■■■■■■■■■■■■■■■■■■■

A research case example of semi-structured interviewing

In a recent research study of ours we interviewed young children (aged 8–10 years old) about their experiences of having both educational and mental health difficulties. As part of those interviews we were interested in their views and experiences of attending a child and adolescent mental health service (CAMHS). By giving the children some freedom to open up, but directing them through questions, we were able to ascertain that these children were quite fearful prior to their appointments, but after they had settled in they were able to appreciate the value of the service. We provide two examples of questions below:

Example 1

Interviewer: You were a bit scared?
Child: [child nods]
Interviewer: Can you remember what you felt a bit scared about?
Child: I didn't know what we were going to do.

One useful technique is to mirror the child's words. Here the interviewer checked that the child did say that they were scared prior to the appointment and this was confirmed by a nod. In pursuing the reasons, the interviewer could have said 'why were you scared?', but why questions can feel interrogative or account-seeking and therefore by asking the child to recall it a gentler way of finding out was used and thus was successful in eliciting a reason.

Example 2

Interviewer: One of the reasons I come round talking to children is to try and find out if we can make any changes to make things better?
Child: Yeah, um, if there's just some more stuff to do while you are waiting.

(Continued)

(Continued)

Interviewer: Okay, what kind of stuff would you like?
Child: Um, I could read a book

In this example the interviewer provided some context for the child for the basis of the questions and allowed the child the opportunity to provide a suggested improvement to the service. This open style was successful as the child offered a suggestion. It is important to remember that young children (and these children also had educational and mental health problems) are likely to provide fairly short responses and so you can encourage them to elaborate as this interviewer did in asking what kind of things she would like in the waiting room.

For a published example of this work see Bone et al., 2015.

Bone, C., O'Reilly, M., Karim, K., and Vostanis, P. (2015). 'They're not witches…': Young children and their parents' perceptions and experiences of Child and Adolescent Mental Health Services. *Child: Care, Health and Development*, 41(3): 450–458.

> **Important point**: Remember that it is through the interview that the researcher can attempt to appreciate the world from the point of view of the participant (Kvale, 2008).

Semi-structured interviews are a useful technique to use with children and young people as they allow you to explore issues and ideas that you might not have thought about yourself when designing your interview schedule. You may find that children introduce new ideas or issues that are relevant to your research question, which provides you with the opportunity to add new questions for subsequent interviews. Furthermore, the semi-structured nature of the schedule means that you can adapt existing questions to suit the participant in front of you and tailor the interview to suit the individual's needs (Flewitt, 2014).

The unstructured interview

The unstructured interview resembles the semi-structured interview in many ways. For example, the questions used in an unstructured interview are open questions and are designed to encourage the participant to open up regarding a particular topic or issue. However, in the unstructured interview the participant is afforded significant control over the direction and content of the interview, although the researcher plays an active role in guiding it (Corbin and Morse, 2003). This can be particularly useful with children and young people as research indicates that they want to be consulted about the issues they feel are important to them and that they want the researcher to listen to all their views and not just the ones dictated by the research agenda (Stafford et al., 2003), and thus the unstructured interview offers this opportunity.

It is important that you consider the value of using an unstructured interview with younger participants. While potentially empowering to give children control over the trajectory of the interview, very young children may struggle with the task. Again it is important for you to consider your aims and objectives and think about what you are hoping to achieve by handing over control to the participants (this is something we consider in more depth in later chapters). Remember that while the unstructured interview resembles a conversation

For example… Alström Syndrome is a rare genetic disorder that occurs in children. There is some literature on this syndrome, but qualitative work is limited. It may be the case therefore that you choose to interview children suffering from this and use an unstructured interview so as to fully gain the perspectives of these children (of course recruitment and other issues may make this difficult). Remember that although the interview is unstructured in style it still needs a research focus and still needs to address your research question and so the limited questions and your encouragement of the child to narrate should be around particular areas, such as treatment experiences, feelings about school or family support for example.

in some ways, it is different as conversations reflect mutual interests and this is not the case with an interview (Kvale, 2008; Flewitt, 2014). Unstructured interviews can be particularly useful when there is very little known about a topic, event, or condition as the schedule of questions does not constrain the process by the researcher's agenda.

We now suggest you try the activity in Box 3.2.

■ Box 3.2

Activity on types of interviewing

We have now introduced you to the three most common types of interview. Before we discuss the alternative types, we recommend you take a few moments to reflect on the differences and consider which one is suitable for your own research and why. Remember that the type of interviewing strategy you adopt needs to be relevant to the research question you have developed. If you are a qualitative researcher you should be keeping a research diary and you could note down your initial thoughts in there.

CHOOSING AN INTERVIEW TYPE

While the categories of structured, semi-structured and unstructured interviewing still provide a useful and important heuristic, it is important that you recognise that there are many other ways of interviewing. Over time there have been several ways of interviewing developed, often intrinsically tied to philosophy, theory and underpinning assumptions of a particular perspective. While some of these draw upon semi-structured or unstructured types others transcend them completely. It is important that you have a clear rationale for the type of interview you plan to conduct, which should be connected to the research question and the aims of your project. It is important that you remember that there needs to be congruence between your research design, research question, methodological approach, data collection method and analysis (O'Reilly and Kiyimba, 2015).

We now move on to introduce you to some of the more common ways of interviewing, including:

- Ethnographic interviews.
- Feminist interviews.

- Phenomenological interviews.
- Narrative interviews.
- Naturally occurring interviews.

Each of these types present an alternative way of conducting an interview with a child or young person that goes beyond the traditional heuristic of the three categories discussed so far and are tied to a particular perspective.

The ethnographic interview

It is important to remember that children and young people are a heterogeneous group, reflecting diverse cultures, ethnicities, social backgrounds and so forth. Ethnography specifically seeks to describe these cultures and in order to do so researchers engage in extensive fieldwork. Thus those researchers seeking to understand children's worlds from an ethnographic perspective will typically engage in a range of data collection methods. Interviewing is a common method utilised, but these researchers engage with ethnographic interviews as this is congruent with their aims and objectives. Ethnographic interviews are qualitative interviews and are grounded in cultural anthropology where typically interviewing took place on site (Heyl, 2001). Ethnographic interviewers place an emphasis on culture and symbolic meaning, and by immersing themselves in the worlds of their participants, they design their interviews to explore the meanings that individuals ascribe to events in their cultural worlds (Roulston, 2010).

In some ways the ethnographic interview is similar to a friendly conversation, although of course the interviewer is promoting a particular research agenda (Spradley, 1980). The key task for the ethnographic interview is to generate data that includes the participants' own language to describe their culture, as well as seeking out explanations and definitions of the terms used to explore how they are routinely used by members of that culture (Roulston, 2010). Thus, ethnographic interviews are distinguished from other types of interviewing as they seek to empower their informants to shape the questions asked and in some cases the focus of the research (Heyl, 2001). Importantly therefore, ethnographic interviewing can have important practical applications.

For an example of ethnographic interviewing see Box 3.3.

▬ Box 3.3 ▬▬▬▬▬▬▬▬▬▬▬▬▬▬▬▬▬▬▬▬▬▬▬▬▬▬

Research case example of a study using ethnographic interviewing

A study by Westby (1990) illustrated that ethnographic interview findings can provide important information to develop culturally appropriate interventions for families and children. Westby argued that the findings from ethnographic interviews can help professionals in their practice to ask the right questions in the right way in order to help families in meeting the needs of their children. This is because the ethnographic interviewer has considered the cultural aspects of these families' lives although the interpretation may be subject to the researcher's own perspective.

The feminist interview

At first thought it might be difficult to see the relevance of feminist interviewing to children and young people. However, you might be choosing to interview teenage girls, and thus the feminist perspective might become very pertinent to these young women. Second, children and young people are sometimes classed as one of the minority groups, and thus the principles of feminist interviewing might be translatable to your research. For these two reasons we give you a brief introduction to this form of interviewing here.

Feminist interviewing as a distinguishable form of interviewing technique emerged in the 1970s/1980s as this was a time when researchers were starting to use open-ended interviews from a feminist perspective. Feminists have argued that the research methodology should focus on the need to empower their research participants so as to produce more ethical research outcomes and the purpose of the feminist interview specifically was to promote an egalitarian relationship amongst female researchers and female participants (Bhavani, 1988; Roulston, 2010). This is why feminist interviewers typically rely on open-ended questions and usually interview each participant more than once (Roulston, 2010).

Feminist interviewers pay a great deal of attention to the relationship they have with their participants. Specifically, they reflect on the power dynamic that operates between them and their participant and seek ways to empower the participants. It is easy to see how this is also important in research with children and young people, as interviewers seek to find ways to empower children in the process. It is argued that a reflexive style of interviewing can facilitate this empowerment as the interviewer scrutinises the implications of the power dynamics during their interactions with participants (Del Busso, 2007). Thus, when conducting a feminist interview, the interviewer should use terms and categories that are used by women in their daily lives, and they should listen carefully to how women construct their accounts and experiences (DeVault, 1990). However, assumptions may be made about the heterogeneity of 'women' as women have many facets to their overall makeup of which gender is one facet.

> For example… You might be interested in teenage girls' experiences of obesity and bullying. You could choose feminist interviewing as your data collection technique to allow the girls to shape the research agenda, influence the nature of the questions asked and tell their side of the experience.

The phenomenological interview

Researchers tend to adopt phenomenological interviewing when they seek to generate data regarding the lived experiences of their participants and aim to generate detailed and in-depth descriptions of human experiences (Adams and van Manen, 2008). Clearly this type of interviewing is grounded in the tradition of phenomenology, and this perspective will guide the nature of your research, how you interact with your participants and how you conduct your subsequent analysis. You may choose to use phenomenological interviewing

For example... 'Tell me about your cancer treatments' (as opposed to 'what treatments did you have?')

For example... 'Describe to me what it is like at school' (as opposed to 'what is school like?')

For example... 'What does your autism mean to you?' (as opposed to 'how do you feel about your diagnosis of autism?')

with children if you want to take a small sample and explore in depth how they have experienced some phenomena or event.

Importantly the phenomenological interview is an approach that is reflective and open in its style and thus the questions used tend to be designed to generate detailed information about the participants' experiences (Roulston, 2010). Probing questions ('give me an example'), acknowledgement tokens ('uhum' and 'right') and encouragement ('go on') can all facilitate a freer narrative from the child.

The traditional perspective of phenomenology advocates that the interviewer must 'bracket off' parts of the self during the interview as by bracketing these preconceptions and presuppositions about the world it is possible to see it as experienced by the participants (Bevan, 2014). This means that when interviewing children and young people, it is essential that you take a detached position and that any assumptions you have about children and childhood is suspended during the interview. This can be achieved more easily by beginning the interview with a very general open question allowing the participants to direct the level of detail, as well as trying to use the participants' words in subsequent questions (of which there are usually only one or two) (Roulston, 2010).

The narrative interview: beyond the question–answer method

An important example of an alternative style of interviewing is the narrative interview, as this seeks to transcend traditional question–answer styles that are associated with structured, semi-structured and unstructured interviews. Basically, the narrative interview is one that requires the 'informant' to tell a story about an event in their life, and for children this can encourage them to tell you about something that has happened to them. The narrative interview is in-depth, unstructured and goes beyond question–answer formats as this imposes a structure by selecting the theme and topics, by ordering the questions and by formulating questions in the language of the interviewer. In practice therefore to conduct a narrative interview, there are four key phases as outlined by Bauer (1996):

1. Initiation – the initial topic is formulated for narration and visual aids may be used.
2. Move through narration – the interviewer does not interrupt the informant and only uses non-verbal encouragement.
3. Questioning – some expansion questions may be asked – for example 'what happened then?' – but no opinion questions should be asked and no arguments made.
4. Small talk – general chat to close down the interview.

Evidently the traditional interview format can be adult-centred and impose an adult vocabulary on the child, even when attempts are made to be child-friendly. Problematically in traditional interviews the interviewer takes for granted that the words mean the same to both parties and that the question asked will be the one understood and that is not necessarily the case (Hollway and Jefferson, 2008).

> For example… The interviewer may ask what CDs the child likes to listen to, but the child may only listen to mp3 format music.

Alternatively, in the narrative interview there is no imposition of structure and everyday communication is used through storytelling which allows the inform-ant to use their own spontaneous language to narrate the events (Bauer, 1996). As Hollway and Jefferson (2008: 307) stated 'eliciting stories has the virtue of indexicality, of anchoring people's accounts to the events that have actually happened'. Notably this can

> For example… The interviewer may ask what it is like to act gaily, and the child might think that they are referring to sexual preferences rather than emotions.

be a useful way of interviewing children. Indeed, children develop and learn the skills of storytelling early on, typically in parent–child interaction (Irwin and Johnson, 2005).

The naturally occurring interview: beyond researcher generated questions

Another alternative interview type is the naturally occurring interview which is often not considered by researchers, and has sometimes been overlooked in general methods text-books. Nonetheless, this type of interviewing can be a useful way of yielding data from children and young people and is typically contrasted with researcher-generated inter-views. For an overview please see Table 3.2.

Naturally occurring data are considered to be those conversations and interactional events that would have taken place regardless of whether you researched them or not. It has been argued that these would have taken place even if you had never been born or if for some reason you were unable to go and record them (Potter, 1996, 1997). So for example, when social workers interview children about their abuse experiences or when children are interviewed in a documentary about some topic of interest, these are naturally occurring.

Table 3.2 Difference between naturally occurring and researcher-generated interviews

Researcher-generated interview	Naturally occurring interview
The researcher-generated interview can be structured, semi-structured or unstructured. It can occur as a one-to-one interview or be done with groups of children/young people. This type of interview is created specifically by the researcher for the purpose of addressing a research question, and the questions asked are generated by the researcher.	The naturally occurring interview takes the form dictated outside of the control of the researcher. Thus it may be fairly structured or unstructured and this will depend on the interviewer and the purpose of the interview. The naturally occurring interview is one that occurs naturally, without the intervention of the researcher and for a purpose other than research.

For example… Police interviews with child witnesses can be a useful source of naturally occurring interview data and these take place every day regardless of whether they are recorded for research purposes. A good example of this is a conversation analysis project by Johnson (2002) who recorded such interviews with both adults and children carried out by a range of police officers in the UK. Johnson explored the ways in which questions were asked in these interviews and looked at topic-marking and movement within the narrative agenda. Of course recording naturally occurring interviews raises important ethical considerations (discussed in Chapter 8) that are potentially very sensitive, due to the context, topic, age of the participants and so forth.

Naturally occurring interviews tend to be contrasted with those that are considered to be researcher-generated and these are deliberately 'set-up' as an interview by the researcher in order to address their research questions. So in terms of the project cited above, if Johnson had undertaken a researcher-generated version of the project, she would have conducted interviews with police offers or child witnesses to ask them about their experiences of interviewing child witnesses, or being one in a retrospective manner. This would likely yield different types of data to the naturally occurring interviews

Important point: Ultimately, your choice regarding whether to use researcher-generated or naturally occurring interviews for your own work will depend on the nature of your research question.

that were recorded. However, your choice will depend on how you intend to study the issue at stake and the nature of your research question.

You may find it useful to consider this more carefully now by turning to the vignette exercise in Box 3.4.

■ Box 3.4 ■

Vignette – Alicia

Alicia is undertaking her Master's degree in forensic science and is expected to undertake a research project as part of her education. She is interested in victim's views of the criminal justice system. She has decided that interviewing a sample of victims of crime is the most appropriate method of data collection to address her research question 'what do teenage victims of crime think of the criminal justice system?' She has decided to sample teenagers as she believes that this will increase her chances of recruitment.

• What type of interview method would suit Alicia best for her study?

Take a few moments to write down your rationale in your research diary.

For a suggested answer please see the answers page at the back of the book.

We also include an activity at this point to help you think more about the types of interview. Please look at Box 3.5 for this.

━━ Box 3.5 ━━━━━━━━━━━━━━━━━━━━━━━━━━━━━━━━━━

Activity on benefits and limitations of interviews

You have now been introduced to many of the different types of interview techniques. Before you go any further with the book try to create your own bullet point list of the benefits and limitations of using the different types of interviews based on the three chapters you have read so far. Remember to do this with respect to interviewing children and young people.

SUMMARY

From reading this chapter you should now be able to appreciate that there are different types of interviewing, including structured, semi-structured and unstructured, and we have shown that it is important to reflect on the aims and purpose of your research when selecting an interview approach. We have also introduced you to a range of alternative types of interviewing techniques including ethnographic, feminist, phenomenological, narrative and naturally occurring. From this you should be able to see that interviewing choices need to be linked to the research question, tied to the aims of the project and are linked to the overall theoretical framework of the interviewer.

RECOMMENDED READING

On different types of interviews

Bevan, M. (2014) 'A method of phenomenological interviewing', *Qualitative Health Research*, 24(1): 136–144.

Del Busso, L. (2007) 'Embodying feminist politics in the research interview: Material bodies and reflexivity', *Feminism and Psychology*, 17(3): 309–315.

On conducting interviews

Flewitt, R. (2014) 'Interviews', in A. Clark, R. Flewitt, M. Hammersley and M. Robb (eds), *Understanding Research with Children and Young People*. London: Sage. pp. 136–153.

Roulston, K. (2010) *Reflective Interviewing: A Guide to Theory and Practice*. London: Sage.

4

DIFFERENT WAYS OF CONDUCTING INTERVIEWS: FACE-TO-FACE, TELEPHONE AND ONLINE

■■ LEARNING OUTCOMES ■■■■■■■■■■■■■■■■■■■■■■■■■■■

By the end of the chapter the reader should be able to:

- Distinguish different ways of conducting interviews with children and young people, including face-to-face, telephone, computer-mediated, email, Instant Messenger and Skype.
- Appraise the challenges of undertaking these different types of interviews.
- Critically assess the benefits and limitations of these different ways of conducting interviews.
- Recognise the most appropriate ways of recording the interview.

INTRODUCTION

An important decision you will have to make for your data collection is regarding how you will conduct your interviews with your participant group. There are now many different ways in which you can carry out an interview with a child or young person. First we discuss the popular and traditional method of face-to-face interviews and we consider the potential value of this method. However, with shrinking resources and new emergent technologies, some researchers now use alternative ways to collect their data. In this chapter we explore some of the benefits and challenges of interviewing children and young people via the telephone and the issues that are faced by doing so. Additionally, children and young people are living in a digital age, with large numbers accessing the internet on a regular basis and/or using advances in mobile phone technology. In this chapter we introduce some of these new ways of conducting interviews and present an overview of the key benefits and challenges associated with them as well as some of the key decisions needed when choosing a modality of recording them.

Before going any further take a couple of minutes to do the activity in Box 4.1.

 Box 4.1

Activity on interview preferences

Before you read the chapter, take a few minutes to write down your preferred way of interviewing children. Try to come up with three reasons why this is the case.

FACE-TO-FACE INTERVIEWS

Important point: While it is traditional to sit in an interview situation in a small room, remember that face-to-face interviewing can take place in any space, and it is important for the child to feel comfortable.

Traditionally researchers have conducted their interviews with children face-to-face. Such face-to-face interviews are characterised by synchronous communication in time and space. In these interviews, the interviewer and the participant sit in a quiet and comfortable room to talk. In this format the researcher will make provision to find a private space to question the child about a particular topic or issue, and stay with them for the duration of the interview. In this way the interviewer is able to monitor the reaction of the child to each question and monitor non-verbal behaviour (and possibly capture it in the recording). They can also attend to any needs that might arise from the interview as they are able to directly observe the child. Researchers should be aware that a face-to-face interview may be carried out as they play or in outdoor spaces (Irwin and Johnson, 2005). The decision will depend on the topic being explored and may be jointly made by the child and researcher as the venue should support the child, but also needs to be appropriate for the purpose. You can ask them where the interview should occur. However, remember that you will need some privacy to protect the child, you need to think about what you will do if the child becomes distressed and you will need to consider the technical aspects of recording (for example, background noise). Also, think back to the advice we gave you earlier on assessing for risk and protecting your own safety.

Benefits of face-to-face interviews with children and young people

Interviewing your participants face-to-face has been the favoured approach over time and while this was partially due to limited viable alternatives, it was also due to the benefits that face-to-face interviewing can offer. There are some benefits of face-to-face participation that are particularly pertinent to children and we offer these below:

- There is an obligation of researchers to safeguard children's best interests and protect them from harm. Although we detail this further in Chapter 8 where we consider the ethics of interviewing children, conducting an interview face-to-face can facilitate such safeguarding.

For example… Building rapport is necessary for safeguarding and can be time consuming; by undertaking a face-to-face interview it provides an opportunity to chat with the participant prior to the start of the interview (Irwin and Johnson, 2005). This can build trust and help the child to feel more relaxed. For example, it can be useful to spend some time either before the day of the interview, or before the interview starts just chatting about the child's school, siblings, pets, hobbies and so on.

- It is easier to check for any signals of dissent or potentially forthcoming distress and through the constant monitoring and non-verbal cues the interviewer can be responsive to the needs of the child.

For example… Children and young people can find it especially difficult to let the interviewer know that they wish to stop the interview and despite their right to withdraw the interview may carry on. However, when face-to-face with the participant, the researcher can observe the non-verbal language which may show dissent such as the child checking their watch, yawning, looking distracted, pulling faces, looking at the door, or generally looking uncomfortable. They can then offer to end the interview or withdraw the child from the study.

- The presence of the child in front of the interviewer has the potential to ensure clarity in establishing the purpose of the interview. It has been argued in the literature that children may not fully understand the purpose of the research interview and by spending time (maybe even 2–3 previous meetings) with the participants it can facilitate a working relationship with the child which facilitates explanations regarding the research (Irwin and Johnson, 2005).

For example… If you spend time with a group of children in their class, helping them with their maths or art classes and get to know them a little before they participate in the interview, it will build rapport. Alternatively, you might spend time with those children/young people in a youth centre, sports club, book-club and so on. This will help you to get to know the communication style of those children, break down potential barriers, build trust and ultimately will help you to explain the purpose of the research and be more certain that they have understood it.

- By being face-to-face with the child there is an opportunity to reduce the power dynamic that probably exists. You can achieve this by sitting at the same level as the child, giving the child some control over the recording equipment, and positioning them as the expert.

Important point: It is essential to consider the power dynamic that exists between you and your participants. Some researchers fail to acknowledge that often in society children are treated as of lower status than adults and generally lack any power (Eder and Fingerson, 2001).

> **For example…** As power is an issue you could try to be quite flexible in your interview, allowing the children to have a greater say in setting the terms for the conversation and you could encourage them to take charge of their narratives through storytelling (Mauthner, 1997). However, you need to ensure that the choices you give them are age appropriate and not overwhelming. You also need to ensure that you do not give them responsibility they cannot manage. Overall it is important that you take practical steps to reduce the power of the researcher such as giving children some control over the recording, reminding them that they have rights, checking in that they are okay, sitting at their level, and allowing them to ask you questions.

- Using face-to-face interviews potentially provides greater scope to actively engage the child in participatory techniques such as drawing as you are present to help them to develop their artwork. Furthermore, an ongoing dialogue can be encouraged while the child engages in the activity (see Chapter 6 for more information on this).

> **For example…** If interviewing very young children whose vocabulary is less developed, you might sit with them and help them to produce artwork that is associated with the research topic. As they draw, you could ask questions about their choices of colour, shape and design and as such obtain some useful information for your interview.

Challenges of face-to-face interviewing with children and young people

Although face-to-face has been the favoured form of interviewing, particularly with younger populations, there are some limitations and challenges of using this modality. It is important that you are aware of these potential difficulties and that you take these into account when making your decision of how to interview the children in your sample, while recognising that not all of these are under your control. We outline some of the key challenges below:

> **For example…** If you wish to conduct interviews with children and young people with different parts of the country then you will have to spend a considerable amount of time and resources reaching those participants. If you do not have this budget, then you may be restricted to interviewing children who live locally.

- Conducting face-to-face interviews can get expensive. Most commonly you will have to travel to a location that suits your participants and this is going to incur a travel expense (and in some cases the cost of an overnight stay). Of course it may be that your participants travel to meet you, but ideally you ought to be refunding any out-of-pocket expenses they incur in doing so. If you do not have a budget this can be problematic as you should not expect your participants

> **For example…** The purpose of the project may be to explore teenager's attitudes towards alcohol. You are aware that there are cultural differences in alcohol consumption and therefore you may feel that it would be useful to have a sample that includes teenagers from different countries. If you do not have a budget to travel using face-to-face in person interviewing could be too expensive.

to be inconvenienced by such costs. Where possible if funds are low, try to recruit participants locally to reduce any expenses in travel.
- By choosing face-to-face interviews as your method of data collection, you restrict the opportunity to include children that cannot physically access your location. Of course,

this may not be necessary for your research but if a wider sample would be appropriate this method may be unnecessarily restrictive.

- Not all children and young people are comfortable talking to people that they do not know well and for others verbal communication is either not desirable or possible. Increasingly children may be more familiar with social media and digital communication than more traditional methods. Whilst it is possible to build up rapport and trust by spending time with these children before commencing the interviews, this is time consuming and will add to the project expense. There may also be considerable pressure on children as they may find the process too stressful.

- Children may find it more difficult to change their mind and withdraw from the study in your presence.

- Children with physical disabilities may find it difficult to sit and talk for any length of time. Furthermore, children with a mental health condition may by the nature of that condition find it more challenging to sit with you face-to-face.

> For example... Some children are more socially awkward and shy than others and may not want to engage with an interviewer. This does not mean that they do not want to have their views heard or be part of the study, but that a more suitable data collection method is required. This is even more likely to occur if you are talking about a potentially difficult to talk about topic such as teenage pregnancy, bullying or criminal behaviour.

> For example... Children have the right to withdraw from the interview, or terminate it prematurely should they wish to. However, social conventions, fear of reprisal and general respect for authority may prevent them from expressing their wishes. Being face-to-face, this potentially asserts additional pressure to complete the interview as it is more difficult to disengage from someone who is physically present (however, as aforementioned the interviewer can look for signs of dissent).

> For example... A child with obsessive–compulsive disorder might be preoccupied with the cleanliness of the room or may have anxiety about sitting with a stranger. Additionally, a child with autism spectrum disorder by virtue of the disorder may struggle with face-to-face communication and social cues although they may well be less bothered by social convention.

> Important point: It is important to be aware of any special needs that each of your participants may have so that you can have strategies in place and adapt your interviewing style or technique to match the needs and abilities of the child (Wilson and Powell, 2001).

TELEPHONE INTERVIEWS

The use of the telephone for interviewing adults has become more commonplace as this form of interview can be easily recorded and negates the costly need for travel. Furthermore, comparative studies of face-to-face versus telephone interviews have shown that there is little difference in the number or quality of responses (Sturges and Hanrahan, 2004). Telephone interviews are synchronous in terms of place and can be a useful way of reaching a wider participant sample (Opdenakker, 2006). When deciding whether to use the telephone or conduct your interviews face-to-face, you will need to consider the requirements of your task, the depth of the responses you require (Shuy, 2001) and what your research question is aiming to address.

Although there has been less work on interviewing children using the telephone, most children (particularly older children) are familiar with this modality, and many of them own their own mobile (cell) phone. However, it is important not to assume that your child participants are comfortable in telephone conversing and you should check this out prior to the interview.

Benefits of telephone interviews with children and young people

There are several benefits of using the telephone to interview your young participants and we outline these below.

- Using the telephone to interview can be advantageous for managing your own and the parents' busy schedules (Holt, 2010).

For example… Parents tend to be very busy, picking up their children from school, taking them to their extra curricula activities and hobbies, working, domestic duties, visiting extended family and so on. Your interview is unlikely to be a priority for them and they may even forget you have scheduled it. However, rather than have you turn up at their home when they have forgotten or are busy doing other things, a telephone call is less intrusive.

- Using the telephone negates the need for travel.

For example… As there is no need for travel you can reach children who live a long distance from your research institution at the cost of a phone call. However, international dialling can prove more expensive and you may have to consider this when planning (although it is still cheaper than getting on an aeroplane and visiting the country).

- Telephone interviews provide an opportunity to reach respondents who are reluctant to communicate face-to-face (Tausig and Freeman, 1988). Telephone interviewing offers some level of anonymity as it puts some distance between the interviewer and interviewee, which can reduce their anxiety about participating (Sturges and Hanrahan, 2004).

For example… Children particularly might be anxious about meeting you and by using the telephone this may reduce their anxiety. However, this can impede rapport building and trust, and they may still feel some anxiety about talking to a stranger.

- During a telephone interview the interviewer is able to make field notes without distracting the participants (Sturges and Hanrahan, 2004).

> For example... Children are easily distracted and if you are making field notes while talking to them face-to-face they may start asking you questions about what you are writing or may want to contribute to the notes, and this may disrupt the interview process. Nonetheless by allowing the child to do this it can help reduce the power differential. This is, however, negated by interviewing over the telephone as they cannot see the note pad and recording is less intrusive.

Challenges of telephone interviews with children and young people

While telephone interviews can overcome some of the challenges associated with face-to-face interviews, there are some challenges of using this modality, particularly with children and young people, and again some of these may be beyond your control.

- Non-verbal communication is typically lost over the telephone (Holt, 2010).

> For example... Children use a lot of non-verbal communication, such as nodding, smiling, shrugging their shoulders, and so forth. This will be lost in the telephone interview and yet may be important for the interaction or flow of the interview.

- Accessing your respondents by telephone relies on their ownership of a telephone (Sturges and Hanrahan, 2004) and the opportunity of accessing it privately without being overheard.

> For example... It can be easy to assume that the children or young people have access to either a landline or mobile (cell) phone, but not all families own a telephone. This is particularly true in areas where there is poverty and families have limited resources. Even if there is a phone the child may not be able to use it to have a private conversation.

- The telephone interview contains more limited opportunities to create a good interview ambience (Opdenakker, 2006).

> For example... A good quality interview relies heavily on the relationship between interviewer and interviewee, and the depth of responses from the child. The general atmosphere of the interview can be facilitated with face-to-face interviewing through such aspects as good lighting, warmth, comfortable seating, refreshments, laughter, and physical presence and it is more difficult to obtain this over the telephone.

COMPUTER-MEDIATED INTERVIEWS

Many young people (adolescent age particularly) have social networking accounts, use Instant Messenger, have email addresses, text regularly, and are familiar with Skype. While younger children may have reduced access to some of these modalities due to their age, there are still many who are comfortable with computers and computer-mediated

Important point: Despite the popularity of the internet, there is still some inequality and so it is important to think about the demographics of the children in your sample when making your decision about whether to use it as an interviewing tool.

communication. The rise of the internet has augmented the ability of individuals to interact regardless of geographical constraint (Hinduja and Patchin, 2008). Indeed, communicating through the internet has become an important part of many young people's lives and the majority of children (at least in the western world) have access to the internet at home or school, and often know more about it than their parents. Notably a report from the US showed that 82% of young people aged between 14 and 17 years old have a social networking page, and 55% of 12–13 year olds have one (Lenhart et al., 2005).

The growth in popularity and access to the internet provides new ways for researchers to interview children and young people. The rise of digital technology and the continuing familiarity of younger age groups with these technologies have provided unique potential for researchers to engage children in new and novel ways. Notably computer interviews with children or young people can be text-based or verbal; and they can be synchronous or asynchronous (Mann and Stewart, 2000). Synchronous interviews are those that require the interviewer and interviewee to be using the internet at the same time, through text or talk. Alternatively, asynchronous interviews are those that do not require the interviewer and interviewee to be on the computer at the same time. Thus computer-mediated interviews (whatever form they take) have some general benefits as well as posing some general challenges, which we provide below. Before you go on further with the chapter try to do the activity in Box 4.2.

■■■ Box 4.2 ■■■■■■■■■■■■■■■■■■■■■■■■■■■■■■■■■■■■

Activity on benefits and challenges of computer-mediated interviews

Before you read about the benefits and challenges of computer-mediated interviews, try to write down what you think the main advantages and limitations of interviewing children and young people in this way might be. Once you have done this compare it to our list below.

General benefits of computer-mediated interviews

Before we consider the specific different types of computer-mediated interviews with children and young people, we first draw your attention to some of the general broad benefits and challenges of using this mechanism to collect your data as these are pertinent to most of the different types. Thus, the key benefits of this way of interviewing are listed below:

- This type of data collection method provides certain groups of respondents the opportunities to be included in research from which they might otherwise be excluded (Ison, 2009).

> For example… Some groups of participants find it difficult to communicate through traditional face-to-face interviews and these groups are thus underrepresented in research, but using computers can encourage their participation and inclusion (Hinchcliffe and Gavin, 2009). Children, or even adults, with disabilities may find the internet a useful modality for social interaction (Ison, 2009).

- Computer-mediated interviewing may be a more efficient use of limited resources as it is an inexpensive and convenient way to allow participants to give their views and opinions (Gunter, 2002).

> For example… Imagine if you wanted to interview children and young people about their television viewing, but as a student undertaking a project as part of a Master's degree you have no funds. You have the opportunity to choose one of the computer-mediated ways of doing an interview and by doing so can include a greater number of children from different places, with very little financial cost to you or your participants.

- One of the more expensive costs associated with qualitative interviewing is that of transcription. Transcription is time intensive and can be costly, but all of the text-based computer-mediated interviewing techniques negate the need for transcription.

> For example… If you were to use emails as for your form of interviewing then the participant types out their responses for you to analyse, no need to transcribe or record.

For an example of computer mediated interviews in research see Box 4.3.

▬ Box 4.3 ▬

Research case example of a study using computer-mediated interviewing

In a recent research study Barratt (2012) conducted computer-mediated Instant Messenger interviews with young people aged 17–32 years. The purpose of the study was to evaluate the feasibility of interviewing vulnerable young people (drug users) online. Barratt selected the interviewees from a larger sample of 837 Australians who self-reported using drugs and 29 interviews were conducted in total. They found that interviews of this nature varied in length from 1 hour to 2.26 hours but despite this being a long time the participants were not deterred from participation. Barratt reported some challenges, including interruptions such as a cigarette break, or other friends coming online or physically to the participant's house. It was noted that only two of the participants became disconnected from the Instant Messenger. Barratt concluded that this form of interviewing can be a very useful mechanism for interviewing young people.

Barratt, M. (2012) 'The efficacy of interviewing young drug users through online chat', *Drug and Alcohol Review*, 31: 566–572.

General challenges of computer-mediated interviews

The very nature of computer-mediated communication creates some challenges for using this medium for interviewing children and young people, and while you may be able to help combat some of these others will be more difficult for you to control or mediate for. For example:

- Computers can crash, power cuts may interrupt the flow, and a loss of internet connection can terminate an interview (Jowett et al., 2011).

> For example… You might be interviewing a young participant about a particularly sensitive event in their life using Instant Messenger. This might be something that is rather difficult for them to talk about, such as a mental health condition, experience of abuse, being a victim of harassment or bullying and so on. Just at a crucial point as they begin to show signs of being emotional (through style of language and use of emoticons or emojis*) your computer (or theirs) crashes, or one of you loses the internet connection and you cannot get that young person back. This is very problematic as now you have left your young participant in a potentially distressed state with no support.

- Many of the computer-mediated interviewing forms lack the visual cues of communication, which can interfere with the meanings conveyed (Hinchcliffe and Gavin, 2009).

> For example… If you are using email, text messages, or Instant Messenger, it is possible that subtle forms of meaning such as sarcasm, humour and so on are lost in the text. There is a greater risk of misinterpretation in the communication too.

- Online communication tends to have its own form of paralanguage, which includes a range of internet abbreviations (e.g., lol = 'laugh out loud', but can also mean 'lots of love'!), the use of emoticons and/or emojis (smiley face – ☺ – to denote smiling) and the use of asterisks to denote bodily actions (e.g. *grin*) and these can convey emotion (Jowett et al., 2011).

> For example… You will need to be familiar with this use of language if you are to respond appropriately. However, it can be difficult to be certain whether your participants are actually uncomfortable or happy with a particular line of questioning just from this language (Jowett et al., 2011). They may use a sad face ☹ to indicate that they were unhappy at the time of the event they are narrating about, rather than at the current time during the interview.

- Some participants may have some concerns regarding how they are articulating themselves through text and be worried about their spelling and grammar (Hinchcliffe and Gavin, 2009).

> For example… Children and young people are regularly in environments whereby they are having their spelling and grammar appraised, in schools for example, and thus are potentially conscious of the way they express themselves to you in a text-based interview.

- There is a risk that the participant may feel detached from the interview and it may feel a little mechanistic.

> For example… The child may become distracted from the interview and drift away from the focus of the text-conversation or they may reveal more about themselves to you than they may otherwise feel comfortable doing so because it does not feel 'real' to them.

---

* emoticons are those visual representations through text to display an emotion, e.g., ☺ and an emoji is a visual representation of emotion through an image.

We recognise that there are many different ways of interviewing children through the use of a computer and these pose their own specific benefits and challenges and we discuss the more common types of computer-mediated interview here.

EMAIL INTERVIEWS

The email interview has some similarities to the face-to-face one, but tends to take place over the computer, and tends to be used with one participant in the exchange rather than a group, over a longer period of time. Many children and young people have access to email, either through having their own email address or through their parents.

> Important point: Privacy and anonymity of the interview may be a problem if the child or young person is using someone else's account to email you from.

The literature on email interviewing is developing, but tends to be quite limited in its discussion about effectiveness and value with younger populations. Nonetheless, there is some useful general advice predominantly in relation to email interviewing adults that translates for children and young people should you choose this mechanism and we provide this in Table 4.1.

Again, as with any of the computer-mediated interviewing techniques, it is important that you think about the benefits and challenges of using email with young participants and we consider some of these below.

Table 4.1 Practical advice for conducing email interviews

Tip	Description
Simultaneous interviewing	You can be conducting more than one email interview with more than one participant during any given time period (Hunt and McHale, 2007).
Include instructions	It is necessary to include some instructions and some sense of the time frame in the initial email communication (Meho, 2006).
Be flexible	Do not forget to make your email interview strategy flexible enough to capture the stories of your participants (Hamilton and Bowers, 2006).
Plan a time frame	Remember that your email exchange of questions and responses will last over several days or even weeks, unlike the traditional face-to-face one (Hunt and McHale, 2007).
Check understanding	It is necessary that you check that the questions you have asked have been understood by your participants (Berger and Paul, 2011).
Respond appropriately	You will need to regularly check for responses and respond appropriately and quickly (Meho, 2006).
Do not ask too many questions	Do not write too many questions in any single email as this can diminish the value of each question (Burns, 2010).

Benefits of using email interviews with children and young people

The use of email for conducting interviews with younger participants does have a number of advantages:

- The use of email offers your participants some flexibility in terms of fitting addressing your questions around their other commitments (Ison, 2009), such as their school schedule, hobbies, homework and so on.

> For example... By allowing your participants to respond to your questions by email, they can fit this activity around their lives, and/or put it to one side while they think about their answers. So, if they have an important exam coming up, they may choose to delay response until after they have finished their revision, or even the exam itself.

- Using email for interviewing means that you will be creating an audit trail and this will give you the opportunity to develop reflective questions throughout the process, and use the responses to help you pursue interesting or important areas (Hamilton and Bowers, 2006).

> For example... Because you can read through older emails sent to you, you can take time to reflect on the issues that are coming up and this means you can ask additional questions that you might not have thought about.

- Using email allows your participants to give more thoughtful and detailed responses, as well as allowing them to type at their own pace (Ison, 2009). This is particularly useful for topics with a more sensitive nature (Cook, 2011).

> For example... Some children may type very slowly and thus for other modalities such as Instant Messenger may feel under pressure to respond quickly. Using email means that they can take their time, draft and save an email, and build up their response to you before they respond. This means that they do not become fatigued (important if they have a disability), and can generally think about what they want to say.

- Because email is asynchronous, it will allow you to interview participants in different time zones (James and Bushner, 2006).

> For example... If you have practically and ethically secured access to children from other countries who are significantly behind or ahead of your time zone, then it is easier to use email to communicate than trying to find a time when you or your participant are not sleeping.

Challenges of using email to interview children and young people

While there are some clear benefits of using email, there are also several challenges and limitations and it is important that you are aware of these. Some of the challenges you can take steps to overcome, but others are more inherent to the method.

> For example... Building up a rapport and sense of trust is essential when interviewing children or young people, and much of this is achieved through body language, facial expression and time spent with the individual. Over email much of this is lost, and it will take you longer to build a relationship this way.

- Building a rapport with participants over email is more difficult, and through email the interviewer needs different ways to show they are 'listening' (Hamilton and Bowers, 2006).

- There are barriers to participation in an email interview, particularly if the participants have limited literacy skills, cannot read or type, or do not have computer skills (Fleitas, 1998).

> **For example…** Although some young children are exposed to computers, tablets, e-readers and the internet from a very early age, this should not be assumed. Children of different ages may have limited or no exposure to digital technology (although it is growing rapidly).

- As email interviews take place over a prolonged period of time, there is a risk that the enthusiasm or attention of the participant may wane (Hunt and McHale, 2007).

> **For example…** Children typically have short attention spans and will be easily distracted by other things. They may forget they are in an email exchange with you, they may forget to check their emails regularly, or may simply lose interest in the research.

- There is always a risk that the emails might not be authored by the intended participants (Ison, 2009).

> **For example…** Just because the email is from the email account of your young participant does not mean that they wrote it. One of their peers may have written it (with or without the knowledge of your participant), or parents may construct a response on the child's behalf.

INSTANT MESSENGER INTERVIEWS

Given the popularity amongst young people of instant messaging as a form of communication with their peers, this too has great potential as an interviewing method for researchers. Instant messaging software displays a conversation window for both parties to write and receive messages. There are various forms of Instant Messenger available.

> **For example…** Skype has a messenger function (see Figure 4.1) and so do many social networking sites such as Facebook.

In the case of any Instant Messenger software the interviewer and participant both need to be available at the same time as the chat is synchronous, and the conversation occurs online in text format. Usefully, most of these Instant Messenger formats illustrate to the other party when one writer is typing out a message so that it is possible to be aware that the other is still present. The use of instant messaging for interviewing any population is

> **Important point:** Remember that there are many different versions of Instant Messenger software so it could be useful to allow your child participants to choose which one they prefer for their interview.

fairly new and this is a developing field of literature. Nonetheless, there have been some arguments put forward that have considered how this might be beneficial or challenging as a method of interviewing, particularly for children or young people.

Benefits of using Instant Messenger for interviewing children and young people

There are many ways in which instant messaging software can be used to aid the interviewer in the data collection process:

- Like face-to-face interviewing, this form of interview occurs in real time and it more strongly resembles a conversation than other text-based methods such as email (Flynn, 2004).

> **For example…** This synchronous approach to text-based interviewing has the advantage of encouraging participation. However, the child may still get bored or distracted and stop sending you responses. The lack of visual cues will mean that you are less likely to know why they have stopped or whether they are coming back to the conversation.

Figure 4.1   Instant Messenger window (from Skype)

- Instant messaging is popular amongst the younger generations and they are familiar with its format.

> **For example…** As your target population is the younger generation it can be useful to use tools that they are familiar with as this has the benefit of making them feel more comfortable.

- Most Instant Messenger software has settings for automatic saving which can be useful if the computer crashes or the internet connection is lost (Fontes and O'Mahony, 2008).

> **For example…** Imagine you have nearly completed an interview with your child participant and you have been sending messages back and forth for 45 minutes when your computer loses power due to a power cut or simply crashes. The internet goes down and your window is lost. After 2 hours of trying everything you finally get the software back up and running. Your participant may at this point have given up and left the internet, but at least you can salvage the interview from the saved function.

- There is potentially less pressure on participants than in a face-to-face interview.

> For example… In a research study using Instant Messenger software to conduct qualitative interviews, respondents reported that they felt less pressured when using this medium than they had/would in a face-to-face context. This was because they were in the comfort of their own home and felt able to interrupt if they wanted to (Fontes and O'Mahony, 2008).

The challenges of using Instant Messenger for interviewing children and young people

As with other methods there are several limitations to using this modality to collect data from younger populations:

- Instant Messenger interviews are likely to take longer than face-to-face ones, and will be even longer if your participant is a particularly slow typist.

> For example… Children or young people may curtail their responses because of the physical need to type out their answers so you may actively need to encourage them to elaborate or expand further. It may also be necessary to conduct the interview in two or three parts, to avoid the participant getting bored or losing concentration (Opdenakker, 2006).

- Most approaches to interviewing require the interviewer to take some field notes while conducting the interview. This can be easily overlooked when having to keep typing questions and prompts into text boxes.

> For example… It can be quite challenging to keep your focus on two writing tasks at one time and your notes may suffer as a result.

- The use of instant messaging can curtail spontaneous responses to questions and the participants may censor their answers.

> For example… Children and young people may 'tone down' their responses, leave out important but more sensitive details, or generally not include responses that could be useful to the interview as they 'censor' their answers. In face-to-face interviews this censorship may still occur but is likely to be reduced because of the immediate time pressure to respond, as well as the visual and social cues that can encourage conversation.

- Terminating the interview on Instant Messenger can be more challenging and it has the potential to feel abrupt to both the interviewer and the interviewee (Opdenakker, 2006).

> For example… In ordinary face-to-face conversation, closing down an interaction takes some time, relies on politeness convention and much of it is achieved non-verbally. In text this is more difficult to manage as there are no non-verbal cues to gauge the other person's response.

SKYPE INTERVIEWS

Not all computer-mediated interviews need to be text-based as some technology allows the advantage of a face-to-face interview, while both parties are in separate locations, such as Skype. Skype is a useful forum for cutting the cost of national and international calls and allows for synchronous video-chat (Bertrand and Bourdeau, 2010). This allows for most of the benefits of face-to-face research, but has the additional benefits of cost-effectiveness. Furthermore, it is possible to record the calls made on Skype, which facilitates analysis. Thus, as with the other forms of computer-mediated interview there are specific benefits and challenges of using Skype to interview children and young people.

Benefits of using Skype interviews with children and young people

Using Skype to interview children has many of the benefits of face-to-face interviews, but does present some unique benefits in the context of computer-mediated interviewing and we list these below:

- There is software available that will allow you to record both the talk and the non-verbal aspects of your interview.

> For example... Given one of the main benefits of face-to-face interviewing is that you can monitor the body language of your child participants, for analysis and also for signals of distress or dissent, the visual aid and potential for recording the non-verbal (with consent) is very useful. This can be particularly helpful when you come to analyse the data as nodding and shaking the head can be important responses and thus recording these has benefits.

- Because the child is able to see your face and respond to you in real time, then it will be easier to build some level of rapport.

> For example... As already stated building a rapport is necessary for the safeguarding of the child and the quality of the interview, and therefore it is important you spend some time building a relationship with your participants over Skype. Because it is cost-effective, it is possible to have two or three general conversations with the child over Skype before setting up the interview, in the same way as you might with face-to-face interviewing.

Challenges of using Skype interviews with children and young people

We would remind you that while Skype interviewing has a lot of similarities with face-to-face interviews, they are still different, and there is still a vast physical space between you and your young participant. It is necessary therefore to think about some of the challenges that this can create.

- It is difficult to make eye contact over Skype as this means looking directly into the webcam and this can be uncomfortable (Bertrand and Bourdeau, 2010).

> For example... You need to think about where you locate your webcam so that it is not too high or too low, in order that the young person can see your face. Also, looking directly into the webcam may feel uncomfortable because of where it is positioned or it may have a small light on it.

- Not all children are comfortable talking to a computer screen, especially if they are more familiar with text-based communication (O'Reilly and Parker, 2014a).

> For example... Not all children and young people will have used Skype (or other similar programmes) prior to the interview and might find it strange to be interviewed in this way.

- There is potential to lose some of the visual and interpersonal aspects of the interaction (Evans et al., 2008), particularly if the signal breaks up or there is a second or two delay in the exchange.

> For example... Sometimes a poor internet connection can result in a delay of exchange and this will lead to a more fragmented conversation. This can make the interview particularly difficult. Furthermore, the physical distance between you and the child/young person can mean that some of the subtleties of face-to-face interaction become lost.

You might find it useful to look at the vignette in Box 4.4 at this point in the chapter.

■ Box 4.4 ■

Vignette – Manjit

Manjit is undertaking her PhD in sociology and is interested in the broad social issue of children living in poverty. She is at the beginning of her project and is designing her research. She is taking a broadly macro-social constructionist position[1] and has decided to interview young children aged between 6 and 11 years about their experiences of living in poverty. She does however need to decide whether to interview children in her country of origin (India) or in the country where she is doing the PhD (UK). Furthermore, she needs to decide how she is going to carry out those interviews.

- What are the challenges that Manjit faces by interviewing children in India?
- What might be an appropriate way of conducting those interviews using computer-mediated interviewing?

Possible answers can be found on the answers page at the end of the book.

---

[1] Macro social constructionism is the view that knowledge is produced through interaction and our constructions are linked with power relations (Burr, 2003). This is different to micro social constructionism which argues that knowledge is not static but co-constructed through everyday life, and is focused on situated interaction and local culture (Gubrium and Holstein, 2008). See O'Reilly and Kiyimba (2015) for a full overview.

CHOOSING A RECORDING DEVICE

An important decision to be made is whether to audio- or video-record your interviews. We live in a digital age and children and young people in the western world tend to be quite familiar with recording devices. This growth in digital technology means you have choices regarding the best way to capture your interview. If you are going to be carrying out qualitative interviews of any kind, then it will be necessary for you to record it and not simply rely on field notes. By recording the interviews, you will have a semi-permanent recording which will allow you to refer to your data long after it has been collected. Additionally, by using a digital recording device you will be able to edit, disguise and manipulate sounds and images which can be useful when you come to present your research.

> Important point: Remember that you will need good sound quality so think about the quality of the recording equipment, remember to check the microphone and think about where you place the recording device during the interview.

There are some clear benefits of using audio devices for recording your interviews with children/young people:

- Audio can be less intrusive to the participants as modern devices tend to be fairly small and discrete.
- Audio devices tend to be cost-effective.
- Audio recordings provide you with a semi-permanent record of everything that was said in the interview.

Of course there are limitations to using audio recordings:

- It is not possible to capture the non-verbal gestures which may be important for the interview. For example, children often nod or shake their head to indicate yes or no, without verbalising a response.
- It can be difficult to identify who is speaking in a multi-party interaction, and thus if you are doing a group interview this can cause problems, especially if two or more children speak at once.

You may choose to use video to record your interviews as this has the scope to capture the visual as well as the audio aspects of your interview. There are some advantages of recording in this way:

- By recording using video you will be able to capture the non-verbal responses of the child as well as the verbal ones.
- If you are conducting a group interview the video will enable you to see subtle interactions between the different members that took place outside of the main interaction.
- Children tend to be fairly familiar with being in front of a video camera (or smart phone version) and therefore will hopefully not be too unduly influenced by its presence.

There are of course some disadvantages of choosing video to record your interviews:

- Good quality video equipment tends to be more expensive than the audio alternative and can be more difficult to set up.
- The use of video will raise additional ethical sensitivities that you will need to think about when planning your project.
- You may need more than one device if you are conducting a group interview to fully capture all of the children on the screens.
- Despite the probable familiarity with video some children may feel uncomfortable in front of it and contribute less to the interview, or refuse consent because of this modality of recording.

It is useful to stop and think about your own research here. Look at Box 4.5 for an activity on this.

▬ Box 4.5 ▬

Activity on audio or video

At some point when you write up your interview research you will need to give a rationale for your choice. Make a decision now whether you are going to use audio or video for your interviews and try to write a sentence as to why.

___

Once you have decided how to record your interview, you will need to decide about whether to buy or borrow the recording device. There are many different digital devices and many of the newer ones have a large storage capacity and files can be transferred easily onto your computer (Paulus et al., 2013). Typically, most devices have a built in microphone but you will need to be sure that this is adequate for your needs. Some microphones have noise cancelling functions and will filter out background noise which can be very useful depending on where you carry out your interview. Some mobile 'smart' phones have recording devices on them and you may find this sufficient for your study, particularly as some of these have good quality video capability (Paulus et al., 2013). You will need to think about the storage capacity, the battery life and how you will protect the data. You will want to transfer the file from the phone to a computer as soon as possible and delete the original once you are certain that the file has transferred properly.

Practical issues when recording children and young people

Although many children will be familiar with modern technology, do not assume that all children have access to a computer or that all children are used to being in front of a camera or comfortable with the medium. Recording children for research may make them nervous and they may not necessarily tell you this (Grant and Luxford, 2009), but there are some ways you can help put them at ease. Bottorff (1994) outlined four useful ways to achieve this:

1. Be careful where you put your recording device, particularly video, to ensure that is not obtrusive.
2. Remind the participants that you will protect the recordings and maintain their confidentiality.
3. Provide a clear rationale for your use of recording equipment.
4. Give your participants details about the process of data collection and how you will be recording them.

There are several challenges that you could face in recording your interviews with children:

• Children may become embarrassed to talk to you in front of the device.

It will be important that you give the child some time to get used to the presence of the device. Let them hold it and press some buttons. Give them a chance to record you pulling funny faces or speaking into the microphone. Importantly you will need to reassure the child that they can stop the device at any point in the interview and ask for a break (Bottorff, 1994; O'Reilly et al., 2011).

• Children may have some concerns about what they look like (or sound like) on camera (Grant and Luxford, 2009).

Teenagers particularly may have concerns about their appearance or their ability to artic-ulate themselves. It is important that you give them plenty of notice about the presence of the recording device and give them time to think about their appearance. You could ask them to wear their school uniform so as to remove any pressure about choosing clothes. Consult their parents before the interview if you have any concerns if this is possible.

• The presence of a recording device may complicate existing power relations (Sparrman, 2005).

In the interview you will want to take as many steps as possible to reduce any asymme-try between you and your participant. It is important that you give the child some control over the recording equipment if possible and allow them to press the stop but-ton. If you have a remote control this can be helpfully placed on the table, in the middle between you, and you can make it clear that you both have the option to press the stop button.

SUMMARY

From reading this chapter you should now be able to appreciate that there are many different ways in which you can conduct your interviews with children and young people. We have shown that while face-to-face interviewing is still the most popular and traditional form of interviewing there are possible cost-saving alternatives such as using the telephone or computer-mediated communication. We have demonstrated that there are benefits and challenges to each of the different types of interviewing and that these need to be carefully considered with interviewing young populations, particularly due to the safeguarding and ethical issues that can arise, especially with sensitive topics. We have also discussed choosing a recording device.

RECOMMENDED READING

On internet and computer-mediated interviews

Hamilton, R. and Bowers, B. (2006) 'Internet recruitment and e-mail interviews in qualitative studies', *Qualitative Health Research,* 16(6): 821–835.

Jowett, A., Peel, E. and Shaw, R. (2011) 'Online interviewing in psychology: Reflections on the process', *Qualitative Research in Psychology,* 8; 354–369.

On telephone interviews

Holt, A. (2010) 'Using telephones for narrative interviewing: A research note', *Qualitative Research,* 10: 113–121.

On general digital tools and the internet

Mann, C. and Stewart, F. (2000) *Internet Communication and Qualitative Research: A Handbook for Researching Online.* London: Sage.

Paulus, T., Lester, J.N. and Dempster, P. (2013) *Digital Tools for Qualitative Research.* London: Sage.

5

PLANNING YOUR INTERVIEW: KEY DECISIONS AND PRACTICAL ISSUES

━━ LEARNING OUTCOMES ━━━━━━━━━━━━━━━━━━━━━━━━━━━━

By the end of the chapter the reader should be able to:

- Recognise when parents may need to be present during the interview.
- Review the possible benefits of a family interview.
- Differentiate group interviews from focus groups.
- Decide between single and multiple interviews.
- Evaluate different sampling issues for interview studies with children.
- Critically assess different recruitment methods and the role of the gatekeeper.
- Critically assess the usefulness of involving children as stakeholders during planning.
- Critically assess the potential of involving children as co-researchers.

INTRODUCTION

When you are planning your interview it is important that you consider the options available to you. By this stage in your reading we have introduced you to many different types of
interviewing. Interviewing children or young people however raises some additional issues
and in this chapter we introduce you to some of the key decisions you will need to make.
One such consideration is whether you interview the child while their parent/guardian is
present and the extent to which that adult might be active or passive in the interview.
Depending on the research topic and question you might choose to conduct a family interview with all members of the child's family. The group interview can also be a useful tool of
data collection whereby you can choose to interview several children together and in this
chapter we differentiate group interviews from focus groups. An important decision to be
made is how many interviews you will conduct with each child, which is linked to issues of
recruitment and communicating with gatekeepers. In this chapter we provide guidance on

how to make these decisions and offer practical tips for communication. During this planning stage it can be useful to consult with a stakeholder group, which can include children, as this can inform your decisions and plans for the project. The benefits of involving stakeholders or children as co-researchers are also critically considered in this chapter.

PARENT/GUARDIAN PRESENCE IN AN INTERVIEW

One of the key considerations you need to think about when planning your interviews with children or young people is whether you are going to have an adult present. Furthermore, you will also need to consider what part the parent plays and hence their placement in the room (for example, are they part of the interview or merely an observer?). Parental presence has the potential to compromise the integrity of the data as parents or guardians (henceforth – parents) may lead the child's response, but on the other hand they can scaffold their child's responses adding richness and depth to their stories (Irwin and Johnson, 2005). The decision regarding whether or not to have a parent present during the interview is likely to be influenced by several factors and we outline these in Table 5.1.

Table 5.1 Factors influencing decision of parental presence during the interview

Factor	Description
Child's age	Younger children are more likely than older ones to be comforted by a familiar face in the room.
Wishes of the child	The child may wish for their parent to be in the interview with them.
The nature of the topic	Having a parent present could curtail responses on particular issues if the child does not want to reveal that information in front of someone close or if it is embarrassing for them. For example, they might not want to reveal that they have had a sexual relationship in front of their mother.
Vulnerability of the child	Some children who may have physical or mental health problems, or traumatic past experiences may prefer to have someone familiar present.
Communication issues	Some children may be too young to have much of a vocabulary or may have communication difficulties which make it difficult for them to articulate themselves. For example, some children with autism have problems with spoken language and the social conventions of communication.
Role of the researcher	It may be that the researcher does not feel comfortable being left alone in a private room with a child for fear of accusations of inappropriate conduct (this may be more likely for male researchers or if the research topic relates to abuse).
Wishes of the parent	Some parents may only provide consent for you to interview their child if they are also in attendance – this can create a tension if the child expresses a wish for the parent to leave.

Remember that the quality of your interview data will be dependent upon your management of the interaction between you and your child participants (Danby et al., 2011) and therefore you will need to take measures to ensure that they are relaxed and comfortable. Building a rapport with the child can be helpful and as we have mentioned previously this can be done over a series of visits prior to the interview. Although we have mentioned these earlier we remind you here of some of the practical ways you can build rapport:

> For example… You could volunteer in their school classroom, at their sports club or music lessons.

- Spend time with the child (if you can) in a setting familiar to them prior to the research starting.
- Spend some time with the child and their parents together (if you can).

> For example… You could spend time with them at their home, at the park or other setting that is safe to get to know the child a bit better. This will give you a chance to ask the parents some questions that might help you later when interviewing the child.

- At the start of the interview (or prior to it if you can do multiple visits), ask the child simple questions about their life.

> For example… You could ask how old they are, what they like to do at the weekend, or ask them for information about their pets. In other words, ask them general questions so that they get used to responding to you.

- Allow the child to ask you some questions about you and try to answer them honestly.

> For example… Give them some space to be the interviewer for a while so that they can experience this role.

- Try to wear clothes that are not too smart.

> For example… Avoid a suit as this may make you look like an autho-rity figure such as a teacher which in some situations may be disadvantageous.

- Sit at the same level as the child during the interview so you do not tower above them.

> For example… You could both sit in bean bags or on cushions on the floor.

- Use visual aids such as photographs, pictures or even videos at the start to get them talking. It is useful if you have some information from the parents about what they like to base this on.

> For example… If the parents tell you that the child likes dogs then you could find some pictures or videos of dogs to get a conversation started.

- You could spend some time prior to the interview engaging in tasks to get the child talking to you.

> For example… You could both make name badges and use coloured pens and glitter (obviously the age of the child will make a difference).

However, building up a rapport can be time consuming and one meeting is unlikely to be sufficient, particularly as children tend to be wary of unknown adults (Deatrick and Ledlie, 2000). If your participant is anxious or tense during the interview, then it is unlikely that you will get the best out of them. While there are some strategies for overcoming this anxiety, it may simply be the case that the child prefers to have a familiar adult with them while talking to you and for many topics this is unlikely to compromise the data. Furthermore, the child may need help to find the words to express themselves as children often look to adults for cues and assistance, and the parent is well placed to do this (Irwin and Johnson, 2005). Ultimately offering the child the choice is ethical best practice, and you need to think about how this might affect your interview. For an example of this in research practice see Box 5.1.

▬ Box 5.1 ▬

Research case example of offering children a choice

We conducted a recent research study involving interviewing 11 children aged 8–10 years old who had both educational difficulties and mental health problems. The purpose of the study was to explore the issue of multi-agency working and communication between schools and specialist mental health services. The original plan was to interview the children in their homes on their own. However, at the first interview it became clear to the interviewer that the child was keen to keep his parents in the room and when given the choice, elected to have his mother present. The research team decided it was good ethical practice to offer all participants this choice and notably 9 of the 11 children elected for one of their parents to be present. Please see O'Reilly et al. (2013b) for more details of the project.

- What effect do you think this had on the study?

In your research diary write down a couple of issues that you think our research team faced.

O'Reilly, M., Vostanis, P., Taylor, H., Day, C., Street, C., and Wolpert, M. (2013). Service user perspectives of multi-agency working: A qualitative study with parents and children with educational and mental health difficulties. *Child and Adolescent Mental Health*, 18 (4): 202–209.

Interestingly having the parent in the room during the interview had little obvious effect on the trajectory, content or style of the interview. In seven of the nine cases the parents barely made an utterance during the whole interview, electing to sit near the child as a comfort but not actively contributing anything to the child's responses, even when they struggled to articulate themselves. In one case the child was very anxious and the parent made occasional comments during the interview to explain the anxiety and help the child with the responses, but this was fairly minimal. In one interview however the parent actively contributed to many of the questions and the style of this interview became much more like a paired interview than a child one.

Nonetheless in all of the interviews, given the nature of the children's mental health difficulties, having the parent present had a calming effect, facilitated rapport, encouraged the child to engage in the interview and ensured that the interview flowed without difficulty. Because of this the interviewer was able to conduct a lengthy interview with each child, ask all of the questions on the schedule and ascertain reasonable answers from a 'hard-to-reach' sample of children. Thus, the parents' presence was a positive aspect of the child interviews. However, we cannot be completely certain that the children did not hold answers back from us that they may have given if their parent was not in the room, although in this context it is unlikely. However, overall the advantages appeared to outweigh the potential disadvantages.

FAMILY INTERVIEWS

An alternative to interviewing children (and possibly their parents separately), is to conduct a family interview. This means that you interview all (or as many as possible) family members in one sitting, which allows you to ascertain the views of all members of the family, as well as capturing any tensions that exist. Traditionally, researchers used interviews with a single family member who represented the whole family (Uphold and Strickland, 1993) and yet families represent more than just a set of individuals and are more than the sum of their individual members (Åstedt-Kurki et al., 2001). If you are choosing to conduct your interviews with families, then it will be important that you have a clear working definition of what constitutes a family. This in itself can be problematic as it is difficult to develop a clear definition of the family. There have been many varying definitions of the family and the literature contains many attempts.

> For example… The family has been defined as a social unit that is biologically or legally related, shares a reality and is committed to the security and socialisation of its members as well as sharing labour to provide collective support (Daly, 2007).

We suggest you turn to Box 5.2 and try the exercise on defining the family before you go any further with the chapter.

■ Box 5.2 ■■■

Activity on the family

If you are going to do family interviews for your own research it is important that you have a definition of the family. Take time out now to write down your own definition of what a family is. It is essential that this is developed through an engagement with the literature and so it is useful at this point to search different disciplines to see the differences in definitions. We advise you have a look through some of the developmental, sociological, anthropological and psychological literature in doing this.

If you are choosing to interview the family unit together then the family will become your informant and this will give you data that reflects the persons, relationships and actions of the whole family. By focusing on the whole family through an interview it can be possible to discover the shared family experiences and the meanings they attach to those experiences. There are some benefits to think about when interviewing a family together:

- The use of a family interview enables all perspectives to be heard in an open environment and in this way other family members can become aware of other's perspectives.
- The family interview can facilitate opportunities to construct meanings of the research topic and this may reflect their lives more accurately.
- During a family interview the family may play out their expected roles so this may provide an opportunity to be explored depending on your research question; for example, a father or mother may speak for the family and not think that others in the family may have a different perspective or anything to add. This can be an opportunity for you to observe family dynamics.

It is important to remember that interviewing families together does pose some specific challenges for the interviewer and these need to be carefully managed.

- It is important that you respect the privacy of individual family members and remember that there may be some information that some members are privileged to know while others are not (Dale and Altschuler, 2006).
- When interviewing the family, you may need to facilitate the child in taking an active role as children's ability to participate in family interviews can vary and they generally do not talk on the same level as adults (Åstedt-Kurki et al., 2001).
- There is potential for scapegoating, family disagreement and conflict during the interview. The interviewer should acknowledge and respect the disagreement and where possible take steps to reduce the tension by changing the topic, but this may depend on the research question (Donalek, 2009). It is important that the interviewer does not take sides in the disagreement or form an alliance with any one member or subgroup (Eggenberger and Nelms, 2007). Sometimes the situation is best neutralised by making an observation such as 'Things seem to be getting heated, would a break be helpful?'
- The reliability of the interview will be dependent upon the willingness of the family members to express their thoughts and feelings in front of other members of the family. However, they may be keen to give a positive image of their family life (Åstedt-Kurki et al., 2001).
- Interviewing families will take considerable skills because as well as managing the process, the interviewer may need to attend to differing needs and enable all voices to be heard.
- With interviewing families potential safeguarding issues may arise. Some parents may demonstrate limited understanding of appropriate child/parent boundaries and

venture into areas that are not appropriately discussed in front of children or they may be very negative about a child. This has happened in other areas of family practice such as in family therapy (O'Reilly and Parker, 2014b; Parker and O'Reilly, 2012). In such situations a break or terminating the interview may be needed.

> For example… If you are researching the impact of a child's illness on their family, the child may feel exposed and/or blamed.

- Practically, interviewers need to have a range of skills to include all participants and to have strategies to manage one member of the family taking over.
- It can also be difficult to conduct an interview and make field notes or observations of what else is happening in the room – as a researcher you may be looking at the person talking and miss a rolling of the eyes by the teenager! The extent to which this is relevant for your research will depend on the research topic.
- It can be difficult to maintain and protect confidentiality as several members are privileged to hear the information discussed and may speak about it without the other family members' consent. It will be important to establish boundaries and emphasise their importance.

For an example of family interviews see Box 5.3.

■ Box 5.3 ■

Research case example of family research

Undertaking interviews with the whole family can be a complex and challenging endeavour, but when done well can achieve some interesting and rich information about the child and their place within the family unit. A good example of family research was conducted by Eggenberger and Nelms (2007). In their study they conducted family interviews to elicit information from families regarding the hospitalisation of a critically ill family member. Using a phenomenological framework, they conducted 11 family interviews over six months which included a total of 41 individuals, five of which were aged 13–18 years old, and two were 21–22 years old. They audio-recorded their semi-structured interviews and these lasted between 60 and 90 minutes. The authors reported that the families included in their study wanted to tell their stories and did not perceive the research as a burden. The families felt that it was useful for them to gather together and describe their experiences, talk about their emotions and thoughts and they were happy to express their views. The authors gave particular attention to the involvement of the adolescents in their study and found that these young people were anxious to be included and played an active role in the interview. They openly expressed their views, comforted adult family members, and did not seem unduly distressed by the experience. The adolescents in the study thanked the researcher for the opportunity to be involved and saw the benefits of a constructive dialogue.

- Often adults are concerned about the potentially distressing effects of including children and young people in research, especially if the topic is sensitive. What are your personal thoughts on this, particularly taking into account Eggenberger and Nelms' study?

THE GROUP INTERVIEW AND FOCUS GROUP

There are of course many similarities between a group interview and focus group and the procedures for conducting either with children or young people have much in common. Often researchers and textbooks treat the group interview and focus group as synonymous, as indeed the focus group is a type of group interview. However, there is a small difference. Focus groups tend to be relatively unstructured (although they are guided by the moderator) whereas the group interview tends to be more guided by the research agenda and list of interview questions on the schedule. In some ways this reflects the difference between semi-structured interviews and unstructured ones. Thus in a focus group the role of the researcher (or moderator) is to stay in the background, just to ensure that the boundaries are kept and that the talk stays on topic. However, in the group interview the interviewer plays a much more active role in ensuring that the questions on the agenda are addressed. This difference should be kept in mind as we discuss focus groups and group interviews together in this section.

As previously mentioned interviewing children and young people may be challenging and the possibility of interviewing children in groups can help the researcher in their collection of data, but brings its own issues. Of course you will have to carefully moderate the group interview and ensure that your research agenda is followed or you can conduct a focus group and allow the children to direct their conversation around a central theme. Importantly, whether you are conducting a group interview or focus group you will need to take care not to allow particular children to dominate the conversation. A major factor for both is the pre-existing relationships and potential dynamics between group members. However, using group interviews or focus groups allows you to explore how the children interact with one another and allows the children to reflect on the different ideas posed. It may also provide additional data such as how children use cues from others to discuss sensitive or difficult topics.

> **Important point**: You will need to be clear whether you are conducting a group interview or a focus group and you need to be clear why you have chosen that option.

If you decide that group interviews or focus groups are a more appropriate form of data collection than one-to-one interviews, then you will need to consider how to ensure that the group interview is effective. As with adults, you need to carefully consider how issues of power and hierarchy may manifest themselves during the group interview and you will need to consider how you will maintain the privacy of your group members. Importantly, the power differential can be reduced in a group interview context as the context is more natural when several children are together as opposed to when interviewing them individually (Eder and Fingerson, 2001). You will need to think carefully about why you consider the group interview or focus group more appropriate than the one-to-one interview.

> **For example…** Group interviews can provide a mechanism for revealing consensus views or they can be used to verify research ideas/data gained from other methods and thus enhance the reliability of the children's responses (Lewis, 1992). Furthermore, Lewis (1992) noted that the supportive group environment can mean that children are able to talk about more 'risky' issues that they may have not otherwise voiced.

Now turn to the activity in Box 5.4 to think about the type of interview you feel is most appropriate.

━━ **Box 5.4** ━━━━━━━━━━━━━━━━━━━━━━━━━━━━━

Activity on types of interview

To this point we have considered whether you interview the child alone, with a parent present, as a family or in a group. Think about your own research project. From what you have read so far, which of these options is most appropriate for your own work and why? Write down your answer in your research diary.

SINGLE OR MULTIPLE INTERVIEWS

An important choice you will need to make during the planning stage is how many interviews with each child you should conduct. While a single individual interview can be appropriate and useful, there is a case for conducting more than one interview per child. There are several reasons why a researcher might choose to conduct multiple interviews with each child participant.

First, it is well-known that most children (and even adults) have a short concentration span. In the context of interviewing participants and especially children, it may become evident that after a short while they are losing their concentration. It may therefore be more productive to build in short breaks and to conduct a series of short 20 minute interviews rather than trying to get them all into one long interview. Of course you might be able to make the interview longer by building in engagement techniques and keeping their interest through activities. However, several interviews may be logistically more challenging and financially prohibitive.

Second, as we have already mentioned it is important to build up a rapport and trust with each child participant and this can take time. It is helpful to spend some time with each child participant before you get to the important questions on your schedule. As your relationship with the child or young person grows and develops you can start to ask the more important, more sensitive, or more in-depth questions as the child will hopefully feel more comfortable in answering by this point.

> For example... In the early stages you might ask about school experiences, in the middle stages you might ask about peer relationships, and in the later stages you might ask about the child's bullying experiences.

Third, the interviewer may assume that there is shared understanding of the topic with the child but this may not be the case (Danby et al., 2011). Conducting more than one interview provides an opportunity to clarify any issues where you suspect that the child has misunderstood you in the previous interview, look out for contradictions in responses between interviews and raise anything important that has shown to be problematic previously. It is important to remember that if the researcher is an

> For example... The child might not confess to hitting their brother during the early interviews, but in the later ones may allude to it subtly and you can pick up on the sibling rivalry carefully.

adult, the child is likely to search for preferred responses to your questions (Danby et al., 2011). By conducting a series of interviews you can slowly work to overcome this issue.

Fourth, the use of multiple interviews provides an opportunity to combine different formats to achieve a rich and interesting overall data set. It is possible to combine individual interviews with group interviews (Eder and Fingerson, 2001) and you may choose to conduct some group interviews to ascertain some general issues, and follow up more specific issues with children individually. This will give you a different perspective on the same problem. Furthermore, you may choose to interview all family members separately and then follow up with a group family interview. This will allow you to explore some of the issues raised by individuals with the group (permissions pending).

SAMPLING

During the planning stages of your research and before you can recruit or carry out your interviews, it will be necessary to consider the issue of sampling, in terms of the type of sampling strategy you intend to use and the size of the sample you need for your research to achieve the quality standards. Sampling is an important aspect of any project, and historically some categories of children tend to be excluded (we referred to children's vulnerabilities earlier in the book). When making your sampling decision it is important to try not to exclude particular groups of children simply because they are difficult to reach, particularly if their inclusion is central to the study. However, you may only have limited time to do your research if you are undertaking an undergraduate or master's level project and it is important to not overcomplicate your sampling.

If you are doing quantitative structured interviews, then your sampling strategy is dictated largely by the design and quality markers for this approach to research. If you are doing structured interviews with children or young people, then the likelihood is that you will ultimately be performing some form of descriptive and inferential statistics later on from the data so that you can make general conclusions. For this to work it will be important for you to randomly select your sample of participants. This is a technique where your target group is selected from a larger population. In other words, each individual child participating in your interview is chosen by chance and all members of that population are selected at random and have an equal chance of being selected.

If you are interviewing from the qualitative tradition, then you have a range of sampling options. The sample of children or young people that you choose to interview will represent the broader range of individuals. In qualitative research there are up to 24 different sampling techniques that you can choose to employ (Onwuegbuzie and Leech, 2007), but for this chapter we list the three most popular below:

- Convenience sampling – this is a popular sampling strategy in qualitative research. While it is potentially the least rigorous technique as it selects the most accessible participants, it is the least costly (Marshall, 1996). Thus, in your work you may simply select children to interview who are known to you through your work or personal life.

- Purposeful sampling – this is probably the most common type of sampling strategy that involves the researcher making an active selection of participants who have the potential to provide rich information related to the purpose of the research (Patton, 1990). Thus, in your work with children, you may purposively select children with particular characteristics, ages, experiences and so forth that suit your research agenda.
- Snowball sampling – this is a technique that involves building up a sample from existing participants' recommendations of people who might be approached (Blaxter et al., 2001). This can be particularly useful when the population is difficult to identify through other means (O'Reilly et al., 2013a). Thus, in your research you might ask the parents or teachers of children you have already interviewed to recommend others who might be willing to participate.

Inclusion and exclusion criteria for sampling

When selecting your sample, it will be important to ensure that you have clear inclusion and exclusion criteria before you start. Importantly the inclusion and exclusion criteria will influence the type of sampling procedure that you choose to employ. It is essential that you are as specific as you can be regarding your criteria.

In other words, you are defining the characteristics that those children must have if you are to include them in the project so that you can answer your research question.

It is very important that exclusion criteria are defined clearly so as to facilitate later recruitment.

> Important point: Remember that the inclusion criteria are those markers that you specify must be present for that child or young person to be included in your research as an interviewee.

> Important point: Remember that the exclusion criteria are the criteria that disqualify possible children and young people from being included in the interviews.

> For example… You may decide that you only want teenagers in your sample as this is the most appropriate age group to address your research question. Thus you would have inclusion criteria of participants aged between 13 and 18 years old (however you will need a clear definition of what you mean by 'teenager') and an exclusion criteria of children who fall outside of that boundary. If you look back to our earlier example in Chapter 2 on the example research question of young offenders and the justice system, teenagers were the most appropriate age group due to the typical age of offending behaviour. While not exclusively the adolescent age group, a higher percentage of teenagers than younger children engage in offending behaviour.

Sample sizes

Once you are clear regarding your sampling strategy and your inclusion/exclusion criteria, you will need to think about sample sizes. This is a fairly straightforward issue for quantitative structured interview studies as there are statistical calculations that can help determine sample size. For a quantitative interview study if the results are to be generalised the sample will need to be representative of the population from which it was drawn. So, in order to ascertain the size of the sample that you will need you will have to conduct a 'power calculation', with power referring to the probability that your study is able to illustrate a difference. If you intend to do this, then we recommend that you ask for some help from a statistics expert. Alternatively, you might look at the following book:

- Cohen, J. (1989) *Statistical Power Analysis for the Behavioural Sciences* (2nd edn). Hillsdale, NJ: Erlbaum.

> **Important point:** It is advisable to seek some expert statistical advice from your institution to ensure that this is carried out properly.

There are, however, tensions for qualitative research regarding the number of children who need to be interviewed. The tension for qualitative research is due, at least in part, to its iterative nature, the unpredictability of the process and the ongoing debates regarding quality markers in this approach.

When deciding how many children you need to interview it is important that the number of children included is sufficient to address your research question. In qualitative work there is no universal agreement regarding how many this should be as each methodological approach has its own quality criteria and this will guide your approach to sampling. Typically, qualitative researchers only need small samples of children to satisfy the needs of the project, but some studies will need larger numbers than others. So in qualitative research small sample sizes are acceptable and preferred (Tuckett, 2004) and these can be as low as 1 or 4 participants, although more commonly tend to include approximately 12 participants per group. Recruiting too many participants to the study can lead to an excessive volume of data, with it being considered inappropriate to question more participants than are needed as this uses up their time for no benefit to the study which raises ethical issues (Francis et al., 2010).

The qualitative community has thus proposed a marker for sampling adequacy which is now commonly used, particularly in interview research. There are various different terms used for this marker – see Table 5.2 for the range – with the original being 'theoretical saturation' which was developed in the grounded theory approach (Guest et al., 2006). This notion of theoretical saturation refers to when all the categories are fully accounted for, the variability between then has been explained, the relationships between them are tested and validated and thus the theory can emerge (Green and Thorogood, 2013).

Table 5.2   Terms for saturation

Terms used

- Data saturation (Francis et al., 2010)
- Thematic saturation (Guest et al., 2006)
- Simply the term 'saturation' (Starks and Trinidad, 2007)

While there is some difference in the use of these terms, they generally refer to the continuation of data collection until nothing new is generated. In other words, the data collection continues until there are no new emergent patterns within the data. It is important to recognise that while this is a sufficient marker for many qualitative methods and particularly those that use semi-structured interviewing, it is not appropriate for all of them (O'Reilly and Parker, 2013). For example, unstructured interviews by their nature allow the participant to lead and thus it is possible that new things will keep on emerging infinitely. Additionally, some approaches such as conversation analysis have different ways of determining sampling adequacy, which is more to do with the phenomenon of interest that the number of cases.

> Important point: It has been argued that the sampling adequacy marker of saturation is not 'satisfactory' for all qualitative methodologies, and that not all sample sizes reported in studies should be judged against this criteria (O'Reilly and Parker, 2013).

ACCESS AND RECRUITMENT

When you have decided on your sampling strategy it will be necessary to turn your plans into actual interviews and to do this you will need to recruit children from the relevant population. Recruiting children or young people can be complex as the population is smaller than adult populations (Tishler, 2011) and may also be less accessible, because of perceived vulnerabilities. The recruitment phase of your project will need careful attention and after you have located your sample and screened against your inclusion/exclusion criteria, you will need to communicate effectively with a range of different people to recruit successfully.

Gatekeepers

Given that the sample is children, it is highly likely that you will need to communicate with one or more gatekeepers to facilitate your recruitment. When we say gatekeepers we mean those individuals who have some authority to grant you permission to access a particular group (Piercy and Hargate, 2004).

> For example... Head teachers (principals) will need to be communicated with to allow you to carry out the research in their schools.

It is fairly typical in many settings for gatekeepers to hold some responsibility for making decisions on behalf of children (Heath et al., 2007), with some of this responsibility being to protect children from potentially intrusive research (Heath et al., 2004).

> For example... Doctors will need to be communicated with to allow you to carry out research in their surgeries.

> For example... Social workers will need to be communicated with to allow you to carry out research with children in their care.

It is probable that for you to be able to carry out your interviews you will rely on the goodwill of gatekeepers. A central aspect of recruitment will be your relationship with the gatekeeper(s) and the rapport you build with them (Emmel et al., 2007). You will probably have to work hard to prove your professionalism and illustrate that your interview study is worthwhile. In order to

> Important point: Be careful not to exploit the people you know who may serve as possible gatekeepers for recruitment, by using your relationships with them to achieve recruitment.

achieve this, you will need to have a clear idea of what the potential benefits of your study are to the population generally, and if there are any benefits for the children recruited specifically. You will need to be able to explain this to the gatekeepers clearly.

While gatekeepers play an important role in protecting children in their care, there are some practical challenges when recruiting through gatekeepers:

- Gatekeepers may silence or exclude children from participating without actually consulting them (Alderson, 2004).
- Gatekeepers might be overly helpful and may only recommend children who they think will be cooperative, and thus this may potentially eliminate some interesting cases for your research and bias the data collected.
- Gatekeepers may screen the sample and not allow you access to children who may say negative things about their institution or who they view as too vulnerable to be interviewed.
- Gatekeepers may potentially base their decisions on models of children's competence, the children's developmental age, and fears/confidence in parental reactions (Heath et al., 2004).

It is important that you respect the gatekeepers and their views and if a gatekeeper does become a barrier to your research then there are some strategies you can implement to help you meet this challenge:

- Remember that institutions have schedules, rules and regulations (Freeman and Mathison, 2009). There are periods when they are particularly busy, when they break for lunch, and when they are closed for the holidays (O'Reilly and Parker, 2014a).

What you can do: Offer to fit around their schedules and agree specific times and dates in advance. Be mindful of the holiday periods or exam periods by finding out in advance when these are likely to be. This demonstrates that you respect their rules, but also commits the gatekeeper to set a time frame.

- Gatekeepers have time pressures and other demands on their time and resources (Heath et al., 2007).

What you can do: It is important that you do not become a nuisance to the gatekeeper so try to be patient. Give them time to respond to you and bear in mind that a few days might feel like a long time to you but it is not to them. Always be polite in your communication and acknowledge that you understand that they have many commitments and demands on their time.

- Institutions have a public face and may be concerned about being scrutinised (Heath et al., 2007). The gatekeeper may be concerned to protect the institution from negative exposure.

What you can do: Be mindful of this and make sure that you are clear about what you will do with the information you gain from the children. You may need to do some work to emphasise the confidentiality and anonymity elements of your research project and ensure that no value judgements are made (O'Reilly and Parker, 2014a).

- Gatekeepers tend to be cautiously protective of children (Heath et al., 2004). This is because they are responsible for their safety and wellbeing and it is reasonable to be cautious when they are approached by someone they do not know.

What you can do: You will need to demonstrate what steps you are taking to protect the children from any possible harm (see Chapter 8 on ethics). Furthermore, if you are doing research as a representative of an organisation, such as a University, then you can make this known as the reputation of that organisation may help the gatekeeper feel more at ease. Furthermore, you can assure them of the process of ethics approval (most people have to have approval before they can begin a project).

- Gatekeepers might not understand your interview study. If you are doing qualitative interviews then they may not know what qualitative research is (Mander, 1992).

What you can do: It will be essential that you take your time in explaining your study to gate-keepers and that you answer all of their questions. It is useful to put together a sheet of information for the gatekeeper which explains the aims and purpose of your study, the nature of the study, and the commitment required of the gatekeepers and the children participants.

- Remember that your research project will not be their priority (O'Reilly et al., 2013a).

What you can do: Although you think your interviews are important, it will be necessary to indicate the potential benefits of your research to help them understand this importance. It will be necessary to recognise that they have other demands on their time and try to illustrate how children's participation in the research might be beneficial. A clear rationale in lay language will be helpful here.

- Gatekeepers may be wary of participating in research at some inconvenience with no discernible or direct benefit to them.

What you can do: Ensure that you commit and then deliver the findings that are relevant and potentially useful to them. Developing a partnership with key organisations to identify potential benefits to them can facilitate your project. For example, we have engaged in two major research projects with schools and in return for their participation have provided training in child mental health. That has been mutually useful in that schools have received training in an area that helps them support their pupils and as mental health staff we have promoted child mental health which is relevant to our roles.

It may be the case that you are simply denied access by an institution and you will need to remain patient and professional throughout the process. It may be that you have to find an alternative way of accessing your sample. It is important not to be too dependent upon a single institution for your recruitment if possible. It may be the case that you need to completely change your strategy for recruitment and think of ways of accessing your sample without involving institutions (for an example see Box 5.5 below).

■ Box 5.5

Research case example of recruitment and access

Campbell (2008) wrote an article to describe the recruitment and ethical challenges faced in undertaking research with children. The project used a qualitative approach to explore children's perceptions of themselves and their rights following parental separation. Recruitment proved to be very difficult and it was eight months before the first interview happened. In particular negotiating with gatekeepers made recruitment more challenging and the original recruitment strategy had to be abandoned in favour of a more direct approach. In the original recruitment approach meetings were set up with counsellors and mediators and they were asked to identify possible families. Unfortunately, this led to no referrals from any of the participating organisations. A variation on the strategy was then implemented and gatekeepers were asked to contact parents to gain permission to pass on their contact details so that they might be contacted directly by the researcher; again no referrals were made. Thus the strategy was abandoned and a more direct initiative employed. This direct initiative was a snowballing technique whereby one contact who was known to the researcher asked others in their network if they might be interested in the project. This led to several referrals to other mothers and ultimately children were then asked for consent to participate.

In the article Campbell outlined possible reasons for the lack of referrals through organisational gatekeepers, which included:

- The daily work pressures of those representatives of community organisations.
- Some service providers felt that they had not been adequately informed or consulted about the research.
- Some service providers had concerns about the mental health and mental wellbeing of the children.

We recommend you read this article as it contains lots of useful information about issues of recruitment and communicating with gatekeepers.

Campbell, A. (2008) 'For their own good: recruiting children for research'. *Childhood*,15(1), 30–49.

Recruiting through schools, health settings, the community or the internet

Children spend a lot of their week in school and this is a common place for researchers to recruit children for interview studies. It may seem obvious to approach local schools as a way of identifying and accessing your required sample. However, recruiting through schools can be particularly challenging as these are busy places with their own priorities. It is important to remember that there will be several layers of personnel in the school with a principal/head teacher in charge. This person may in turn have to liaise with school governors and/or other bodies who regulate them. So you may need the consent of many individuals before you can approach parents and ultimately the children.

If you decide to gain access through a school then it will be necessary that you understand the characteristics of the school, that you identify a gatekeeper with authority to communicate with, and that you clearly convey the benefits of your research (Rice et al., 2007). Additionally, it will be important to think about the type of school that you aim to recruit from. Schools with younger children attending are likely to have more personal relationships with parents and have fewer children in the school, but are more likely to have concerns about vulnerability and competence. Schools with older children attending will generally be larger institutions with more staff; children will have multiple teachers and are likely to have greater demands on their time for exams and so on.

It is a good idea to research the school before you approach them. Try to find out as much as you can. It will be important that you select a school that can provide you access to the type of sample you require to address your research question. First you will need to make contact with the school. It is usually best to do this in writing or by email. At this point give essential information about the project and it is a good idea to offer to go and meet with them; you will need to be flexible to suit their schedule. The contact person will probably usually be the head teacher or principal, but it may not be depending on your research topic. Furthermore, head teachers are usually very busy people, so it may be useful to identify a key person within the school with whom to communicate. This person can then liaise with the head teacher for you. Dogra et al. (2013) contacted the special needs teachers with responsibility for mental health as their project was about mental health and once they were on board they took on the task of engaging their colleagues. Remember to explain things clearly at that meeting and do not forget to leave printed documentation (such as a sheet of information) behind about the project as well as your contact details. It would be useful at that meeting to ask the head/principal to nominate a contact for you to communicate with and to help you inform parents and speak to the children. We provide a useful activity in Box 5.6 on gatekeepers and suggest you do this before going any further.

▬ Box 5.6 ▬▬▬▬▬▬▬▬▬▬

Activity on gatekeepers

Think about who your gatekeeper is for your project and take 10 minutes now to brainstorm some questions you might want to ask the gatekeeper and think about why those questions are important. Also, make a list of all the important things about your project that they need to know. Use the lessons learned from the Campbell (2008) article to help you with this.

Depending on the nature of your research question you may choose to recruit your sample through health settings instead of schools. It can be particularly difficult to recruit children and young people from clinical settings as their health status is likely to add a layer of vulnerability. Individuals experiencing chronic illnesses, mental disorders, disabilities, or injuries are considered to require additional protection from gatekeepers and clinical professionals will rightfully take their duty of care very seriously.

Similar to recruiting from schools, recruiting through clinical settings will require communication with multiple gatekeepers at different stages of the process (Coyne, 2010). These professionals will consider the vulnerability of the child and their family when you make a request to interview children and they will probably ask you a lot of questions about your intentions. These health professionals will have a great deal of knowledge about the child's condition and the family's situation and therefore they are well placed to help you identify suitable children for interview, but they will want to protect the most vulnerable from the 'burden' of participation (Coyne, 2010) and may at times be protective and not ask families their wishes.

Recruiting though institutions is not your only option. You may choose instead to recruit through the community, which may be your own or one unknown to you. Remember that a community is a unit of people of any size and what it shares is common geographical location; furthermore in some cases communities may share the same values and beliefs, but this is not necessarily the case. Communities can be small or large but consist of individuals who identify with one another, so you may have local communities, religious communities, virtual communities, organisational communities and so on. If you are a member of a particular community, then you may have insider knowledge about who to approach and you will be a familiar face which can help. This may have disadvantages as well as advantages.

For example… You may be a member of your local village hall leisure group and be involved in organising local activities for the village population. In this situation you are part of a local community and it is likely you will have local contacts that can help you with recruitment.

You do have to be careful however not to be coercive. People you know are far more likely to want to help you and may push others into helping too. Alternatively, recruiting from a community that you do not belong to can be more challenging and again you will need to identify an individual gatekeeper to help you make contact. It will be necessary to have a single individual who will communicate with the community members for you and introduce you to relevant people.

You need to be aware that the help from the community gatekeeper whether you know them or not will influence the research process. You may need to think about the language of that community and you will need to think carefully about the best way to engage members. The members of that community may be suspicious of your motives, worry about what you are going to say about them or generally distrust people with authority. See Box 5.7 for a research example.

■ Box 5.7 ■

Research case example

The second author (Dogra) undertook a local project to explore Gujarati children's view of mental health services and approached some community leaders (Dogra et al., 2007). Some of the community leaders felt that the interviews should be undertaken with them as they knew best what their community thought and it was unnecessary for us to interview children. This led to a change in our recruitment strategy and we recruited through one neighbourhood centre led by an individual who felt the children should be given an opportunity to speak for themselves. In this context the gatekeepers saw speaking for the community as their role and perhaps also had a vested interest in upholding their role as 'the expert' of the community.

Dogra, N., Vostanis, P., Abuateya, H. and Jewson, N. (2007) 'Children's mental health services and ethnic diversity: Gujarati families' perspectives of service provision for mental health problems', *Transcultural Psychiatry*, 44(2): 275–291.

A more popular contemporary way to recruit children and young people is to recruit through the internet. Often researchers turn to the internet to recruit vulnerable populations when they encounter barriers from institutions (Cook, 2011). This method of recruitment is less well-established than other methods and there is a concern about the representativeness of online samples (Koo and Skinner, 2005) so some care will be needed. Reaching children through the internet might not be as straightforward as you think as there is an overwhelming amount of information posted online so you will need to think about how you target your sample. This will be particularly important if you intend to recruit through online communities, through social media and networks as you will need to consider issues of privacy and confidentiality.

One way to recruit is by using email as often children have an email address and it may be possible to obtain email addresses through community gatekeepers, or parents.

When you do make email contact to recruit it is useful to include a hyperlink to the project website so that both child and parent can find out more information about your study (Koo and Skinner, 2005). There are also other things you can do to increase the likelihood of a response to your email as outlined by Meho (2006):

> **Important point:** Remember that you will need the parent's permission to email the child before you make contact.

- Make sure you include a key message in the subject line.
- Be professional.
- Be clear about ethics.
- Be succinct in your request.

Remember also that it helps to use their name in the email as they are less likely to view your email as spam and try to send individual personal emails rather than a group one. We provide an example in Figure 5.1 below.

You could also try to recruit through online discussion boards which can be helpful for accessing particular groups of children. You can (usually with permission) post a link to your project website so that children and their parents can access the information. Some of these groups will have membership lists and this can help you to establish a sampling frame if you can secure access (Wright, 2005).

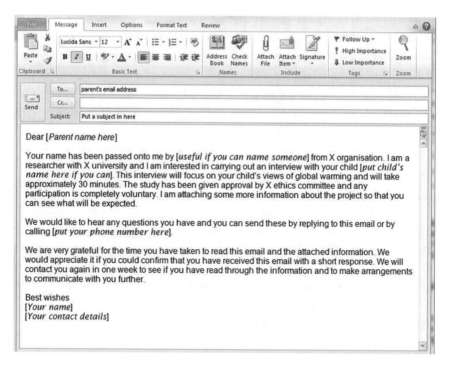

Figure 5.1   Example email

INVOLVING CHILDREN AS STAKEHOLDERS IN THE RESEARCH PROCESS

> **For example...** In some of our own research on autism spectrum disorder we included a stakeholder group that included an adult diagnosed with the condition, as well as parents of children with autism and professionals (see O'Reilly et al., 2014). These stakeholder groups helped us to understand what it was like to work with or live with a child diagnosed with autism and to better appreciate what kinds of information parents with children newly diagnosed might need. This helped us design our interviews for parents about the diagnostic process.

Changes in the way we view children and childhood, and the promotion of children's rights has meant that research communities now take more seriously children's views, not just by engaging them as participants, but by actively involving them during the research process as advisors (Clark, 2005). Over time the notion of the 'stakeholder' in research has become more popular and tends to refer to a person or organisation that has a legitimate interest in the project. In the research context stakeholders can play an important role in facilitating the design and implementation of the research.

The researcher's perspective about children will influence the part children play as stakeholders. Whilst there has been a growing demand for the better engagement of children in the research process, the involvement of children as valid stakeholders has been more challenging partly because of the paternalistic attitudes many still hold. Even when young people are engaged as stakeholders it can be difficult to ensure that the diverse range of children's perspectives are afforded a hearing. Einarsdottir (2007) concluded that research with children is important as it can give valuable information to better shape the improvements we make for children. It is arguable that they should be involved in most if not all projects that are about them. This may need different ways of thinking about the research process but may provide more meaningful research that is relevant to those it is about because it actively involves them.

There is now a much stronger emphasis on listening to and consulting with children and young people. By either including children in your stakeholder group, or having a separate child-led stakeholder group (sometimes referred to as a service-user or patient group when related to health or social care services topics) you can check any uncertainties you have about your research design, ask for practical advice, practice interview questions and test any aspects of the research design. By involving children actively in this way the views of the children can guide action, address the issues of power, and shape the agenda of the researcher (Clark, 2005).

It is important when including a stakeholder (or service-user) group in your research not to do this in a tokenistic way; rather their inclusion should positively influence the content of the research (Trivedi and Wykes, 2002). It is easy to consider the stakeholder group as simply a check-box exercise to satisfy a supervisor or funding body, but if done properly it can really positively influence and shape your research. If you are going to draw upon a stakeholder group in your research, then it is important to listen to their perspectives and make changes to the research process on the basis of the advice given.

> For example... A PhD student of one of the authors planned to interview adolescents about a topic that could be potentially embarrassing for children to talk about. When she carried out the initial consultation with her adolescent stakeholder group they advised her that she would struggle to ascertain the views of this population just on the basis of one-to-one interaction and would benefit from some participatory aspect to the interview. They also advised her not to pretend to be 'cool' or at their level in terms of linguistics and discourse. On their advice the student created some video-based vignettes so that her participants could speak about their experiences in the third person, using the individual in the vignette as a basis for their responses. This worked very well for the actual interviews.

Of course bringing together a stakeholder group can be challenging. If you are involving adults with a degree of expertise, then they are likely to be busy people and coordinating a suitable time for all to meet can be difficult. If you are bringing together a group of children, then you will have to fit around their schedules and the schedules of their parents. Remember also that you will need to ensure that the stakeholder consultations are driven by child-friendly language and that you develop partnerships with children as they can provide you with important insights into their worlds. This is very important for you, particularly in qualitative research with children and young people as meanings can vary between adults and children and clear discussion might prevent misunderstanding (Clark, 2005).

For many disciplines such as education, health and social care, the purpose of research is to impact on practice. If you want to improve your chances of translating your research findings into something practical and applied, then including a stakeholder group from the beginning of your research can be useful.

Furthermore, engaging stakeholders in the research process of doing research with children and young people can maximise its potential impact on the academic conversation, but also on practice, policy and the children who participate in the research (Robb, 2014). When thinking about children as stakeholders it is important to ensure that the diversity of children is considered. Unless researchers actively ensure the encouragement of children from diverse backgrounds with diverse characteristics, research with children may focus on those who are most accessible.

> For example... Having a stakeholder group that includes representatives from related organisations can play a positive role in affecting change and implementing evidence in practice (Rycroft-Malone et al., 2004).

CHILDREN AS CO-RESEARCHERS

A key theme that has run through this book has been the idea of empowering children through research; that is, of giving them a 'voice' so that their views are represented. However, up to now this has been written in a way that has been rather general. We pause here to consider in more detail what this means and why it matters. Arguments have been presented in the literature stating that the child's voice refers to the extent to which researchers and practitioners are prepared to listen to children and the ways in which those voices can be successfully heard (Komulainen, 2007). However, this is not straightforward. Consider the quotation below:

> The oft-heard phrase 'giving children a voice', for example, suggests that voice is a gift, attainable only through the generosity of adult others. The assumption that 'giving children a voice' in research will address inequalities in child-adult power relationships thus presents something of a paradox since participative opportunities for children and young people are, indeed, in the gift of the adults leading the projects, who control not only what can be talked about but also the methods employed. (Bucknall, 2014: 72)

> Important point: If you are going to involve children as co-researchers then it is important that you question what the ethical, methodological and philosophical issues are (Kellett, 2005).

The point being made here is that it is the responsibility of adults to empower children and allow their voices to be heard, as it is rather difficult for children to take this initiative for themselves or create the opportunities to do so. Furthermore, in order to achieve this, children need to be involved meaningfully in the research process to ensure that the data is rich and complex (Grover, 2004).

One of the recent initiatives in research with children has been to actively involve children as co-researchers in a project. This is quite a new endeavour and there is little research done by children, arguably as children cannot carry out research alone, as they need adult support and guidance (Kellett, 2005). Kellett noted that it must be questioned whether drawing upon children as active researchers is realistic.

Involving children as co-researchers is not a simple thing to do and therefore it is important that you are able to define what children as co-researchers means. The very notion of children being active in the process of the research from beginning to end has come from changes in views of children and childhood, which led to an emphasis on listening to children (Kellett, 2005). In turn this led to changes in how children were involved in the research, with arguments emerging that children can be more than simply participants and could actually be actively involved as researchers (Niewenhuys, 2001).

> Important point: A barrier for children working as researchers is that they tend not to have much in the way of research skills or knowledge of methodology (Kellett, 2005).

While it is not always possible to involve children as researchers at every stage of the project, for practical reasons, it can be beneficial to involve them at as many points as possible. They can be particularly helpful when you are planning your research.

> For example… In designing the project you might find it helpful to involve children in developing and refining your research question, getting their advice on the practical side of the methods of data collection at the point of proposal and on the usefulness of your plans for dissemination (Shaw et al., 2011).

Shaw et al. (2011) also recognised that children can be active researchers in the data collection process. They noted that children can collect data from their peers or from other children to whom they are not known. However, they did caution that some topics of investigation may not be ethically appropriate for children to be doing the interviews.

> For example… It may not be appropriate for children to interview other children about subjects such as child abuse or bereavement.

SUMMARY

In this chapter we have introduced you to some of the most important practical factors to consider when planning your interview study with children and young people. There are many issues to review at this stage and these decisions will affect the trajectory, style and content of your interviews. In this chapter we have considered the potential impact of having the parents/guardians present while you interview the child. We have provided some practical advice and examples about this. Additionally, we have considered the issues at stake for interviewing children as part of their family or in a group. We have demonstrated that this can be particularly useful in certain contexts and can produce important and interesting data. We have also reviewed the important issue of sampling. Sampling strategy and sample size are important factors to consider for interview research and we have discussed some of the ways in which you might address this. The chapter concluded with a discussion of stakeholder and service-user groups and involving children as co-researchers, and we reported the value of including such consultation throughout the research process from inception to dissemination and application.

RECOMMENDED READING

On recruitment

Campbell, A. (2008) 'For their own good: Recruiting children for research', *Childhood*, 15 (1): 30–49.

On interviewing children

Eggenberger, S. and Nelms, T. (2007) 'Family interviews as a method for family research', *Journal of Advanced Nursing*, 58(3): 282–292.

Irwin, L. and Johnson, J. (2005) 'Interviewing young children: Explicating our practices and dilemmas', *Qualitative Health Research*, 15: 821–831.

Shaw, C., Brady, L.-M. and Davey, C. (2011) *Guidelines for Research with Children and Young People*. London: NCB Research Centre.

On sampling

Francis, J., Johnston, M., Robertson, C., Glidewell, L., Entwistle, V., Eccles, M. and Grimshaw, J. (2010) 'What is adequate sample size? Operationalising data saturation for theory-based interview studies', *Psychology and Health*, 25(10): 1229–1245.

O'Reilly, M. and Parker, N. (2013) '"Unsatisfactory Saturation": A critical exploration of the notion of saturated sample sizes in qualitative research', *Qualitative Research*, 13(2): 190–197.

6

THE USE OF PARTICIPATORY METHODS

━━ LEARNING OUTCOMES ━━━━━━━━━━━━━━━━━━━━━━━━━━━━

By the end of the chapter the reader should be able to:

- Employ different communication strategies with both children and parents.
- Recognise the different participatory techniques and their strengths and limitations.
- Appraise the potential benefits of participatory methods with children.
- Question the usefulness of participatory methods in relation to power.

INTRODUCTION

Interviewing children and young people can be a challenging endeavour and therefore some researchers decide to include participatory methods to facilitate engagement, put the participants at ease, and encourage more in-depth responses. We open this chapter with a broad discussion of some of the pertinent issues when communicating with children in a research interview and provide some advice for facilitating this process. We introduce you to some of the common forms of participatory techniques that are used by researchers and provide some practical hints for their usage. Alongside this we consider the age-appropriateness of certain techniques and reflect on both the developmental and chronological relevance. In so doing we provide a rationale for why qualitative interviewers particularly might choose to adopt such techniques when interviewing children and young people. We also provide some of the critiques that have been aimed at the use of participatory methods. The chapter concludes with some consideration of the issue of power, an issue that has run through previous chapters and is an inherent difficulty for researchers interviewing children and young people. Arguments have been made that participatory methods are able to reduce the power differential and we explore how this might be achieved in practice.

COMMUNICATING WITH CHILDREN

To interview children and young people effectively you will need to think more broadly about your communication style. As we mentioned earlier in the book, it is now considered good practice to involve children in decisions that affect them (UN Convention on the Rights of the Child, 1989) and this has been adopted in research where it is seen as important to involve children and provide opportunities for them to express their views (Willmott, 2010). You will, therefore, need to think about communication at all stages of the project. When doing so you will need to actively reflect on the child's chronological age, their cognitive ability, and their communication abilities, and be confident that what you are asking them to do is within their capabilities.

Communication is a social process and dependent on the relationship between the parties involved in that process; so it is an integral part of building your relationship with your participants (McPherson, 2010). You need to remember that children's right to speak is often restricted and they are used to petitioning adults in order to be able to join the conversation (Pantell et al., 1982). It is therefore crucial that you communicate with children in such a way as to allow their voices to be heard and affords them a degree of empowerment (O'Reilly and Parker, 2014a). This will usually need to be an active process that you facilitate. Children may require several opportunities before they have the confidence to speak. Previous experiences may mean that they are reluctant to believe that their contributions are truly valued.

Typically, we do not have a culture of listening to children and neither is there a universally accepted set of procedures for engaging them in the research process (Munford and Sanders, 2004). It is important that you respect their autonomy but at the same time understand that this is constrained by their development. By the time you actually get to meet with the child, you are likely to already have been through a long process of communicating with a range of gatekeepers (see Chapter 5) and it can be tempting to see the child's consent as a mere formality as adults will have given their consent. If the child declines to be interviewed or shows signs of dissent it might be tempting to try to persuade them; however, it is essential that you respect their wishes and do not put pressure on them to participate. Remember that the child will not know you very well and they may be anxious in your company. Furthermore, they may view you as a figure of authority and you will need to take steps to ensure that their freedoms are respected. It takes skill to recognise when the child truly does not want to participate or when they are anxious about doing so because they do not fully understand the expectations or the rules.

There are several practical ways in which you can improve your communication with the child, and ultimately your interview:

• Introduce yourself.

Even if you have met with the child previously, it will be important that you remind the child who you are, why you are there, and what the interview will be about. It will be helpful to let the child know how to refer to you and first names can help reduce the power issue, although some children may not feel comfortable addressing adults by a first name. Make sure that you know the name of the child you are interviewing in advance of the meeting and give them the chance to tell you how to address them (Willmott, 2010).

- Avoid using technical jargon.

It can be easy to forget who you are talking to, especially with older children, and you may use words or phrases that the child does not understand. They may find it too embarrassing or intimidating to ask you what you mean. Try to avoid using long or technical words and phrases, explain more complicated concepts and provide opportunities for them to check the meaning. It is also useful to ask them if you have made sense in which case you place the onus on your explanation being suitable rather than their ability to understand.

- Be polite and professional but warm and friendly.

Remember that the participant is helping you with your research and is there voluntarily. You need to keep the communication channels open during recruitment and do your best to be as available as possible for consultation. Send email, telephone, or postal reminders if necessary but be careful not to be pushy. When sitting with the participant, be polite and friendly. Give them lots of opportunities to talk about themselves and answer any questions that they have.

- Be patient.

It is important that you recognise that research with children and young people is time-consuming and that you will need to put in the time and effort with the gatekeepers and the child in advance of the interview.

- Be mindful of coercion.

Remember that it is possible that the parent or other gatekeeper has persuaded the child to participate in the research. You will need to be certain they are opting in of their own free will and that they recognise that they can withdraw. Also, be watchful for any signs of distress or dissent.

- Be aware of any communication difficulties that the child might be experiencing.

Remember that some children may have problems with communication and it is useful to ascertain this from teachers or parents before you meet the child. It can be helpful to talk to parents about helpful strategies to engage the child in conversation and you may need to think about using alternative communication methods such as voice output devices or multisensory references (Benjamin and MacKinlay, 2010).

- Help the child feel comfortable.

You will need to pay attention to the environment you are interviewing in and make sure there is comfortable seating and lighting. Consult with the parents to ensure that the child has no medical conditions or allergies if you intend to provide refreshments so that these can be carefully selected, and also seek parental consent to do so prior to providing them. While you might think that offering sweets/candy is rewarding, parents might have a strict sugar or treats policy or it may undermine an ongoing behavioural programme.

- Offer reassurance.

Some children might be anxious about talking to you so offer some reassurance and praise throughout the interview. However, be careful not to reassure too frequently as this can become counterproductive. Encourage them to expand on their answers and remind them that they are doing well and are helping you.

> Important point: The success of your interview will depend on your communication strategy with each child. You need to be mindful of the individual differences between your participants and take care to communicate with them on a level that they can understand without being patronising.

COMMUNICATING WITH PARENTS

Remember that rarely will you be able to access your child interviewees without communicating with the parents first. Most countries stipulate that legally children under a certain age (16 years in the UK) are not fully autonomous and decisions about them have to involve their parents who often have the final say about the decisions (Heath et al., 2004).

> For example... Some parents may be anxious that allowing their child to participate in the research will mean that they miss out on important lesson/academic time that should be spent in the classroom (Rice et al., 2007).

> Important point: Remember that the parent/guardian is a crucial gatekeeper for almost all research with children projects, so remain professional, friendly and polite at all times, and be flexible with your time and approach.

It will therefore be essential that you communicate effectively with parents.

Importantly, the more supportive the parents are of your research then the more likely it will be that the child will participate and engage in the interview. However, parents have the power to shut down the child's involvement in the project and can deny you access (McPherson, 2010). It is necessary that you handle any communication with parents sensitively and professionally, be careful not to be rude or pushy. It will be important that you build a rapport with them and this may take some time. You will also need to reassure the parents that there will be no detrimental or lasting effect on their child's welfare due to participation.

It will be important that you think about when the data collection will take place and what this means for the child. Communicating effectively with the parents should mean that you can find a mutually convenient time and place to interview. It can be helpful if you communicate with the child's parents during the preparation of the interview as they can help you with key design decisions and may help you to identify potential problems before they arise.

PARTICIPATORY METHODS

Undertaking interviews with children can be challenging and each age group brings with them a set of different types of challenges (as discussed in Chapter 2). It can be difficult to make the research sufficiently interesting so as to engage the participant in the interview and it is fairly common for researchers to employ additional methods to facilitate the interview progress. It will be important that you give serious consideration to which types of participatory methods you might use, how you might use those methods to facilitate engagement, and to what extent you use them throughout the interview.

There are many different types of participatory methods available and there is a broad literature on participatory methods, participatory action research and engagement of children in research. There are a whole range of different types of approaches you could adopt and we list some of the most common ones in Table 6.1.

Table 6.1   Examples of participatory methods

Method	Description
Arts and crafts	This is the use of arts and crafts activities such as painting, drawing, creating pictures, using different materials and so on to encourage the child to talk about themselves or describe events. The activity can be used to relax the child or to communicate about a topic.
Photography	This is when the researcher asks the child to take photographs around a particular theme and then uses the pictures as a basis for asking questions.
Vignettes	This is when particular hypotheses or scenarios are played out either visually as film, or as a written text. This gives the possibility of talking in the third person.
Poetry	This is when the child is asked to express themselves by writing poetry, or using existing published poetry to raise a subject to talk about in the interview.
Dance	This can be used to occupy the child and get them moving about and relaxed. The child can express themselves through dance, or just use it to relax and promote discussion.
Storytelling	This is when the researcher tells the child a story that has some features that will resonate with the child, or asks the child to tell their own story as a point of discussion.
Video clips	Existing video clips from the internet can be shown to the child as a basis of discussion in a similar way to vignettes. With the right resources the child could be asked to film aspects of their life and this can be used as a platform for questions in the interview.
Toys and games	Toys and games can be useful for younger children as they are familiar with these and can help them to relax while you ask your questions.
Emoticons and emojis	This is the use of faces with different emotional expressions in visual form.

> **Important point:** Remember that whichever technique you use you will need to adapt and tailor it to the individual child.

Clearly there are a wide range of participatory techniques and the table itself does not provide an exhaustive list, rather it presents an overview of some of the more common strategies used by qualitative interviewers. If you decide that it would be beneficial to utilise a participatory method, then we direct you to the recommended reading at the end of the chapter to help you further. We now provide an overview of the more common participatory methods in turn.

Using emojis

A simple and often-used participatory technique has been to use faces that express a particular emotion. These faces usually have a simple and clear emotional expression that is recognisable to the child. See Figure 6.1 for an example.

The use of such visual participatory methods is a simple and clear way to encourage children to talk about how they are feeling about something. A smiley face can be used to indicate that the child is happy about something, and an unsmiling face can be used to indicate sadness. More extreme versions can be used as faces can depict a grin or have tears coming from the eyes. Additionally, the face might show a worried or angry expression. This kind of technique can be particularly useful if you are exploring more sensitive topics and are helpful for eliciting feelings (Hill, 1997). They help the child convey how they feel without having to articulate it into words. Some schools already use this technique in their pedagogical activities so their familiarity may increase their usefulness (Due et al., 2014). Of course it will be essential that you do not use abstract images, particularly with younger children, and the emotional expression on the face should be clear and not ambiguous. With older children you may be able to use more challenging emojis which convey more complex emotions as well as ambivalence.

Figure 6.1   Emojis

Using video and other digital technology

There is a wealth of possibilities for incorporating digital media into your interviews. This can be a particularly useful participatory method as many children are familiar with the computer and the internet. You can select YouTube videos online and use them as a basis for discussion. This can be especially helpful for more controversial subject areas where you could download a political speech, clip of film, comedian sketch or documentary segment and use that to ascertain the child's views of that issue or event. Additionally, computers offer a range of applications or software that can allow the child to be creative and express themselves through an alternative medium.

> For example… Using photo-editing software you could have a discussion about the child's body image, as they distort a picture of themselves and describe their thought processes.

Alternatively, you can use digital technology to create a film, music video or collage of artistic representations on the computer. The child could create their own podcast about a particular issue and you can ask them questions about what they talked about on the podcast. You could encourage the child to write you a blog and then use that as a basis for your conversations. See Box 6.1 for an example of research using technology.

> For example… Watching a film clip on bullying can provide a third party platform for the child to talk about their own bullying experiences.

> For example… Playing a video game for 15 minutes with the child can help you build a rapport and break the ice before the interview starts.

▬ Box 6.1 ▬

Research case example of using technology

A study by Levy and Thompson (2013) which sought to engage young children aged 5–6 years explored the use of a specific participatory technique. The authors agreed that including children's voices through research was essential, but noted that including children of this age was challenging. They explored the use of technological participatory methods as a way of engaging children in a project about confidence in reading. In this they provided a forum for the young boys to create their own information DVD on the subject. The young children were helped by older children (aged 11–12) and this 'buddy partnership' was a successful way of eliciting children's voices for the project. It was agreed that the older children played a crucial role in the research and encouraged the younger children to be actively involved in the DVD creation. When the DVD was completed they distributed it to all the children and teachers involved in the project.

Levy, R., and Thompson, P. (2013). 'Creating "buddy partnerships" with 5- and 11- year old boys: A methodological approach to conducting participatory research with young children'. *Journal of Early Childhood Research*, DOI: 10.1177/1476718X13490297

Photography

Photography is being increasingly used in research with children as asking children to take photographs provides a mechanism to appreciate their personal experiences and elicit useful information from them. Such visual participatory methods are a particularly helpful way of exploring the perspectives of children (Clark, 2011). Photography can promote a particular form of visual storytelling and can promote motivation to be involved in the research as children can become excited by the use of cameras (Drew et al., 2010). If you provide each participant with a disposable camera it can help those who find it more difficult to express themselves to stay involved in the project, and this can promote social inclusion (Aldridge,

> **Important point:** Remember that disposable cameras are generally not digital and you may have to pay to have the pictures printed.

2007), or alternatively they could use their mobile phones as the majority of smart phones have a camera function now.

The use of photography is an area that is showing promise as it has potential to yield a range of information as well as generating discussions that provide insights into children's lives (White et al., 2010). Additionally, photo-elicitation is a way for the researcher to encourage and foster a trusting relationship with their participants and to help the child make meanings of their social world as they discuss the pictures that they have taken (Bruce et al., 2009). Using cameras in this way can help you to improve your communication with the children involved in your study and can be an interesting way to involve children in your interview. When using cameras and asking the children to take photographs try not to restrict the children too much in terms of what they can take pictures of or how many to take, but it can be useful to give them some guidance (Drew et al., 2010). The photographs that children take could be a story in themselves.

Remember that using cameras and asking the children to take pictures will invoke additional ethical sensitivities (as the subjects of photos may not have consented for their photograph to be taken) and the boundaries of this will need to be agreed. Furthermore, if you want to include the children's pictures in your dissemination strategy then you will need consent to do so and you may need to deal with the issue of preventing their faces (or anyone else's) being in the picture (te Riele and Brooks, 2013).

Vignettes

Vignettes have been a long-standing participatory technique used with both adults and children to form a platform for discussion in focus groups and interview research. Vignettes can be particularly useful when interviewing children and can be in the form of a written text, as a pictorial representation.

> **For example...** You could use a vignette in the form of a cartoon strip or as a dramatised video-clip whereby a specific scenario is acted out for the purpose of the research.

Through the vignette the researcher is able to present a particular story for the participant and the child is asked by the interviewer to respond to the presented situation by imagining what they think the third party should do, how that third party might have done things differently, and how that third party might have felt.

Children often do not feel confident talking about themselves and the use of a third party reference in the form of a vignette can provide them with some space to explore their experiences and draw parallels with the individual represented in the vignette (Barter and Renold, 2000). It also provides them with the opportunity to imagine alternative scenarios and options. When designing your vignette, it will be important that you choose a scenario that will resonate with the child, and characteristics that the child will recognise (such as a character that has a similar background, culture and age of the children). You may need more than one vignette so that you can select the most appropriate one for your participants or give children an option to use the ones they find appealing. Be careful when designing the vignette not to make it too complex and ensure that it contains sufficient information for the children to discuss. Remember that the characters in your vignette do not necessarily need to be children as they could be cartoon characters or animals which may appeal to younger children. You could also include some pictures to make the written vignette more interesting.

Arts and crafts

The use of arts and crafts is a participatory technique that is familiar to children as they are regularly engaged in such activities at home and at school. This can be an especially useful technique for engaging particularly young children or children with more limited verbal abilities. Asking the child to draw pictures around a theme and the use of glitter, glue and paints can be exciting for the child and you can encourage a narrative alongside the creation of the picture. Asking the child to draw pictures or engage in artistic techniques such as wool/pasta shapes, glitter pens and glue can foster an environment of trust and improve communication in the interview (Horstman et al., 2008). Often they can be easily drawn into providing a running commentary on what they are doing which may be of relevance to the research question. Helpfully the physical act of being creative can take away the focus on you as a researcher and therefore provides a more child-centred way of sharing the child's experiences (Driessnack, 2006). Do not forget though that it is important that the creative outcome is accompanied by the child's narrative and that you do not impose your own interpretation on the drawings. If they do not talk while they carry out the activity, build in some time for them to explain their work to you to give it depth and meaning.

> Important point: Remember that arts and crafts are no longer restricted to the physical form of pens/crayons and paper. There are also digital means for creating art work on the computer or tablet and some children may enjoy this opportunity to be digitally creative.

THE IMPORTANCE OF PARTICIPATORY METHODS

From the range of participatory techniques available it is evident that they can be a useful addition to your interview research. If you are going to include them in your data collection, however, it is important that you have a clear rationale for doing so. Using participatory techniques has become more popular in the last couple of decades and the underpinning assumption of them is that they engage children in research in a more meaningful way (Coad and Lewis, 2004). Although the origin of participatory methods lies with research with disadvantaged adult populations, there has been a significant increase in their usage in child research (Liegghio et al., 2010).

There have been several arguments proposed that illustrate why and how participatory methods are favourable with children and young people:

1. By employing participatory techniques in your research you will provide a mechanism to allow the child to shape the research agenda and you will give them some control over your project (Thomas and O'Kane, 1998).
2. This type of research thus has some potential to empower children as they are able to take some control over the activity (Waller and Bitou, 2011).
3. Arguably such methods are more ethically acceptable than other methods due to their ability to allow children a 'voice' in the research (Gallagher, 2008).
4. Using participatory techniques may provide a way forward for children to talk about more complex and/or abstract issues (Thomas and O'Kane, 1998).
5. This is particularly important with more vulnerable populations and using participatory methods provides them with more meaningful participation as it allows them to participate as collaborators who hold some power and influence the research decisions (Liegghio et al., 2010).

You may find it useful to reflect on the advice given to you in this chapter by considering the vignette in Box 6.2.

▬ Box 6.2 ▬

Vignette – Karolina

Karolina is a social work student training in social care. For her studies she is expected to undertake a small research project and has decided to interview children who are looked after by the State about their experiences of being fostered or living in children's homes. Karolina is aware that engaging these children will be challenging because of their vulnerable status, their history and the problems they are likely to have encountered previously. She decided to only include adolescents aged 13–16 years old in her sample. Karolina is considering using arts and crafts to engage her participants more in the interview as a way of helping them relax.

- What might be the benefits and challenges of using this with adolescents who are in the care of the State?
- Would an alternative participatory method be more appropriate and why?

Take a few moments to write down your answers to these questions.

Possible answers can be found at the back of the book.

QUESTIONING PARTICIPATORY METHODS

From reading the chapter so far it may look like participatory methods are a very good idea for your interview project and we have provided you with some of the arguments in favour of using them. However, it is necessary to take a critical position when making your decisions and to be aware of some of the counter-arguments that have been proposed in the literature.

For example, Horstman et al. (2008) proposed some cautions when applying these methods in practice:

1. The mere usage of participatory techniques does not in itself guarantee that the child can express their views and opinions and you will need to facilitate this.
2. It is important that you do not make assumptions that the participatory technique will be enjoyed by the child. The child may dislike drawing, may not be familiar with the computer, or may not understand the vignette. It can be helpful to consult with parents and teachers prior to the interview. Children often lack confidence in their artistic ability so may not find drawing or arts and crafts as enjoyable as you might expect them to.
3. For some children the use of arts and crafts may give the impression that the topic under discussion is not serious as art is often a fun subject especially for younger children.
4. It can be useful to have different participatory methods available at the time of the interview to allow the child some options to choose their preferred method.
5. Remember that whatever participatory method you choose to use needs to be 'age appropriate' according to the chronological and developmental age of the child.
6. It is important that you are flexible and do not use the participatory method just because it is available. Be mindful that it may not be necessary as the child may engage fully and communicate with you effectively without additional techniques.

It is easy to assume that participatory methods facilitate participation when this is not automatically the case. It depends on how they are applied. It is important that you do not take the use of participatory methods for granted. Instead you should engage in critical reflection of these approaches and think about how you might usefully use them in practice (Punch, 2002). No use of participatory techniques is going to replace the skills of the researcher in building rapport with the child, and realising when that child might need some reassurance or encouragement.

> **Important point:** Remember that your personal view related to children's position in society will also affect your judgements and decisions about participatory methods.

POWER

An underpinning assumption of participatory methods is that children need to be empowered by adults, and that these techniques provide a mechanism for them to exercise their autonomy (Gallacher and Gallagher, 2008). However, the activities will not necessary empower children, rather it is your discussion with the child that actually provides them with the chance to create meaning related to their experiences and it is this shared engagement that promotes empowerment (Waller and Bitou, 2011).

> **Important point:** Remember, power is not a fixed concept but is fluid and shifting (Christensen, 2004). Thus, the nature of your relationship with the child will influence the emergence of asymmetry in your interactions.

Nonetheless there is some potential to promote empowerment through the use of participatory techniques where applied appropriately. It will be important that you give the children some control over the activity and encourage them to tell their stories alongside it. Remember that in society there exists an unequal power differential between adults and children, and children spend considerable amounts of time in personal and institutional contexts being told what to do by adults. As an adult entering the child's world you need to be self-aware of these hierarchical differences that your respective age categories create (Holt, 2004). Be aware that you hold power in the process by virtue of your role and your power to make most of the decisions (Etherington, 2001).

As an ethical researcher it is important to redress the unequal power balance by ensuring that the children are respected and listened to (Flewitt, 2005) despite the fact that it can be time consuming. You can facilitate this by putting more emphasis on children as active social agents and not simply passive subjects (Woodhead and Faulkner, 2000). Remember to value each child participant and encourage the child to communicate in their own way (Horstman et al., 2008).

Managing the issue of interviewer power and asymmetry

Some of the power differentials are related to the power difference between children and adults, and some are related to the research subject and research investigator relationship. Lewis and Porter (2004) argued that researchers ought to consider if there are ways of shifting the power relationship to greater equality for example by using peers. Whilst this may seem like a good solution it would be erroneous to assume that different power dynamics are not set up if peers are used.

The first step to addressing power may be to ensure that the child is really willing to participate in research and has truly assented if consent has been given by their parents or carers. It is worthwhile checking in a sensitive way if they are worried about withdrawing from the research. If they feel that they truly have a choice and choose to participate not only will your research apply good ethical standards but also the data is likely to be of a higher quality. Even though children should have had access to information about the purpose of the project it can still be useful to check this out with them. Again it may give them some control over the process and thereby reduce the power differential.

Thomas and O'Kane (1998) suggested that it can be a helpful strategy to give the child as much choice as possible over how they participate in the research whilst remaining true to the objectives of the researcher and meeting the obligations to funders. This may mean offering children some choice over the research interviews and allowing them to some extent to direct the course of their interviews within the overall themes of the research. Taking this one step further it may mean offering children appropriate opportunities to make choices and have some control over aspects of the interview such as where it takes place and if they wish for others to be present (again being mindful of the research objectives and the need to preserve confidentiality as appropriate). The structure of the interview should be such that it is weighted in favour of enabling the interviewee to give their perspective (Hiller and DiLuzio, 2004). The research interview is not a normal conversation in that it is set up in a particular way and the sample is picked for specific reasons. This reason can be used to balance the asymmetry that exists in the research process.

Thomas and O'Kane (1998) advocated the use of participatory methods and argued that children may be more skilled at using drawings as a way of expressing themselves. Others such as Kirk (2007) and Kortesluoma et al. (2003) argued that assumptions may be made about what is fun for children. However, the major advantage of participatory methods, as long as they are selected by the child and flexibly approached, is not only that they give the interviewee greater control over the agenda and more time and space to talk about the issues that concern them, but also it creates an atmosphere in which there are no right or wrong answers and even some opportunities for children to interpret and explain their own data (Thomas and O'Kane, 1998). The authors also concluded that they found it fun to use the techniques in research – this should not necessarily mean that they were fun for the participants.

For some topics undertaking research with groups may help balance the power between researcher and participants. Cashmore (2006) raised the issue that children's active consent should be sought and it should be clearly explained that it is their right at any time to refuse to continue or answer any questions. However, even if this is the case it can be unclear to what extent children feel able to refuse or withdraw once they have engaged in the research process. It is unclear to what extent children or for that matter some adult research participants understand the conditions surrounding continuing consent. It is therefore important that researchers are aware that because of the power imbalance children may be reluctant to withdraw. Therefore, they need to actively provide the child opportunities to withdraw from the research.

Kirk (2007) summarised the following strategies as ways of managing the power differential between adults and children in research:

- Using methods that allow children to feel part of the research and which give them maximum opportunity to provide their views.
- Being responsive to children's agendas.
- Involving children as part of the research team. This can be a useful way of giving the children some control over the research process.
- Checking on children's willingness to participate throughout the interview.
- Rehearsing with children how to decline participating or answering particular questions.
- In interview studies giving children control over the recording device.

It is also worth noting that sometimes the most vulnerable children are the subjects of research and their experiences (for example, being in care, having experienced abuse and so on) may mean that they feel even less empowered than their peers. This places an even greater responsibility on the researcher to consider the above factors. Take a few minutes now to do the activity in Box 6.3.

■ **Box 6.3** ■

Activity on personal goals

What are your strengths in interviewing young people?

What are the areas you need to work on?

Set yourself one or two specific learning outcomes and also identify how you might meet them.

You may find it helpful to revise your action plan after reading the next section.

SUMMARY

In this chapter we have provided you with some useful and practical ways of thinking about communicating with your child participants and their parents. Communication is central to interview research, not only in the interview, but also during the planning and recruitment phases. This communication practice is potentially facilitated by participatory methods and in the chapter we have provided you with some information about the most common techniques. We have illustrated the value of using this type of approach, but have also cautioned against investing in the technique without critically reviewing its purpose. We concluded the discussion by bringing in the important issue of power, which is intrinsically related to participatory discussions.

RECOMMENDED READING

On power

Christensen, P. (2004) 'Children's participation in ethnographic research: Issues of power and representation', *Children and Society*, 18: 165–176.

Gallagher, M. (2008) '"Power is not an evil": Rethinking power in participatory methods', *Children's Geographies*, 6(2): 137–150.

On participatory approaches

Levy, R. and Thompson, P. (2013) 'Creating "buddy partnerships" with 5- and 11- year-old boys: A methodological approach to conducting participatory research with young children', *Journal of Early Childhood Research*, DOI: 10.1177/1476718X13490297.

Waller, T. and Bitou, A. (2011) 'Research *with* children: Three challenges for participatory research in early childhood', *European Early Childhood Education Research Journal*, 19(1): 5–20.

7

THE STRUCTURE AND FORM OF AN INTERVIEW: THEORETICAL BACKGROUND

▬ LEARNING OUTCOMES ▬

By the end of the chapter the reader should be able to:

- Recognise the importance of cultural considerations in interviewing research.
- Appreciate the importance of safeguarding and identify their role in safeguarding as a researcher.
- Critically assess the stages of an interview and the interview process.
- Evaluate the pertinent factors about the interview when interviewing children and young people.
- Understand the relevance of transference and counter-transference in the interview setting.
- Recognise the role of defence mechanisms in the interview.
- Appraise the difficulties of using interpreters in interviews with children and young people.
- Know how to set up the interview.

INTRODUCTION

Many factors influence our communication styles so it is important to be aware of how some of these factors can interplay with each other to impact on the research interview process. In this chapter we begin by examining cultural considerations and safeguarding before we review well established stages of the interview process and how each of these might be facilitated. Observations and field notes of the interview are also discussed. We consider concepts, such as transference, counter-transference and defence mechanisms, that may influence the interview and are potentially important to consider when the research covers sensitive areas or is close to the researcher's own experience. Understanding these mechanisms may also help the researcher understand the position of the young person they are interviewing and be sensitive about how to manage the interview. Additionally, we introduce the issue of using interpreters before moving on to practical issues such as setting up the interview to ensure optimal data collection and experience for the young person and researcher.

CONTEXT SETTING

Coles (1986) suggested that children formulate their own perspectives about their social, political and cultural contexts that are not simply reflective of their parents' ideas. It was argued that if children had greater access to a public voice through research for example, they would be able to contribute to the social structures that concern them. However, it is worth questioning whether children can play an equal role in some of these debates, particularly as Irwin and Johnson (2005) argued that the standards and principles taught on most courses about conducting 'good' qualitative interviews have been largely derived from research with adults. Their own experience of undertaking research interviews with children was that some of these principles could not be so easily applied. They found that there is relatively little in the literature on practical guidance for qualitative interviews with children especially for 5–12 year olds.

While there is now a growing literature that considers interviewing children for research, there is only a little practical guidance available for qualitative researchers, particularly for interviewing these younger age groups. Much of what we know practically about engaging children and young people in interviews has come from interviewing children in other contexts, for example in clinical practice (for good examples see, Dogra and Leighton, 2009; Instone, 2002) and in forensic settings (for good examples see Lamb et al., 2008; Yuille et al., 1993). Of course researchers need to be aware of the different contexts but they also need to recognise the transferability of skills, and the research guidance is growing as interviewing children and young people becomes more popular. Before we discuss the structure of the interview and some techniques to ensure a high qualitative interview, we will consider cultural and safeguarding aspects.

CULTURAL CONSIDERATIONS

For this section we will use culture in its broadest sense as defined for example by the American Medical Association (1999). The definition used is:

> Culture is defined by each person in relationship to the group or groups with whom he or she identifies. An individual's cultural identity may be based on heritage as well as individual circumstances and personal choice. Cultural identity may be affected by such factors as race, ethnicity, age, language, country of origin, acculturation, sexual orientation, gender, socioeconomic status, religious/spiritual beliefs, physical abilities, occupation, among others. These factors may impact behaviours such as communication styles, diet preferences, health beliefs, family roles, lifestyle, rituals and decision-making processes. All of these beliefs and practices, in turn can influence how patients and health care professionals perceive health and illness and how they interact with one another. (AMA, 1999: 25)

This definition was developed for a health context, but is used here as it is sensitive to individual needs as it allows individuals to identify what is important or relevant to them and does not categorise them according to external characteristics by others. It is probably more effective to have a principle based approach (Dogra, 2003) to ensure that cultural issues are taken on board for all interviews. There are several reasons for this as outlined by Dogra and Baldwin (2009):

- Prevents facts relevant to one individual being assumed to be relevant to others that may appear to be from a similar background.
- Should help to prevent stereotyping of any groups of children and young people.
- Works with the central philosophy that young people and their families all bring potentially unique perspectives which need to be taken into account.

To prepare for working with potentially diverse research samples the following steps have been recommended for clinical practitioners and these recommendations are also useful and translatable for research interviews with children and young people. We present these in Table 7.1.

Table 7.1 Recommendations for working with diverse research samples

Recommendation	Description
Address biases and prejudice	Reflect on your own biases and prejudices to ensure that these do not consciously or subconsciously justify less than quality engagement of all potential research partners.
Check children's understanding	As many factors influence the child and/or the family's understanding of interviews with professionals, at the outset of any interview check the child/family's understanding of what they think is going to happen.
Awareness of roles	Be aware that the family may play out expected roles and it may take a lot of encouragement to ensure that all perspectives are heard.
Ask questions	Do not be afraid of asking if you are not sure – you just need to ask respectfully without judgement (in doing this you also may make it safer for the child and/or their parents to ask questions as you may be modelling interest and curiosity).
Do not be intimidated	Do not be intimidated into avoiding difficult questions just because someone is from a visibly different background. It is worth remembering that all young people have an equal right in the UK and in many other countries to be heard and valued.
Recognise differences	Different families and children will need different levels of explanations and time.

Hiller and DiLuzio (2004) stated that the research interview is usually discussed from the vantage point of the researcher. They identified that the constructivist thinkers have added a new dimension by showing how the research is both collaborative and meaning making. It might be useful to go one step further back and consider how the researcher's own perspectives influence the research methodology and approach. Their own perspectives are a part of who they bring to the interview and how they interpret the data.

SAFEGUARDING CHILDREN

Ensuring children are safe is an integral component of working with children including research with children. Safeguarding legislation is hugely variable with many countries not having specific legislation for this function. Some legislation however, such as the United Nations Convention on the Rights of the Child (1989) (UNICEF, 2015) is universal although its interpretation and application will vary from country to country. Researchers working with children need to be familiar with the legislation and local policies that apply to their work. The responsibility to familiarise yourself with the relevant frameworks is yours as an ethical researcher.

> **Important point**: Safeguarding children is an issue that all those who work with children in any capacity including research need to be aware of. It is your responsibility as an ethical researcher to familiarise yourself with local policies and protocols.

While we talked about children's rights back in Chapter 1, Article 19 of the UNCRC refers specifically to protection from abuse (UNICEF, 2015). In the UK this used to be known as child protection and over the last 20 years it has become increasingly complex. Section 11 of the Children Act (2004) places a statutory duty on key people and bodies to make arrangements to safeguard and promote the welfare of children. Laws have been passed to prevent behaviour that can harm children or require action to protect children. Guidance sets out what organisations should do to play their part to keep children safe (NSPCC, 2015). Although child protection systems are different in each nation, they are all based on similar principles. Another example is Australia where state and territory governments are responsible for the administration and operation of child protection services. Legislative Acts in each state and territory govern the way such services are provided (Australia Government, 2015); for example Queensland has the Child Protection Act 1999 (Government of Queensland, 2015).

When undertaking interviews, the researcher has to be aware of the possibility that the participant may raise issues relating to their physical or emotional safety. If as a researcher you have any concerns these need to be discussed with your supervisor and/ or the safeguarding lead at your organisation. It is inappropriate for researchers to take the lead in investigating concerns but they need to know what to do should this be a possibility and ensure their actions are congruent with local safeguarding policies. We do not propose to deal with this in any further detail here but would like to alert you so you are aware of this issue (Powell, 2011). Safeguarding is a central tenet of Chapter 8 when we discuss research ethics. It is also advisable for researchers to undertake some safeguarding training so that they are aware of the issues and the expectations of them both legally and from their employers.

THE STAGES OF AN INTERVIEW

Whether interviews are structured, semi-structured or unstructured, or any of the other types we have discussed previously, all will have established stages and sometimes formats depending on the nature and context of the conversation. There is always a beginning and an end with the main part of the interview occurring in between. Clearly how an interview starts will dramatically affect the middle and the end. The stages are presented to help you consider important issues but remember that human interactions are complex and this is simply a heuristic to guide you through the principles of interviewing children. Engaging well does not mean the researcher can sit back and relax as the child will be constantly evaluating what is being said, your response to their participation and so on. It might be helpful to think of your own thoughts and feelings when being 'interviewed'. Children may not have the same feelings as you but it should give you an indication of the complexity of the interview interaction.

Engagement

Engagement is the process by which the interviewer establishes a working relationship with the research participants. If the child or young person does not feel engaged or comfortable with you they are unlikely to be as open to sharing their thoughts or views with you. Throughout the book we have emphasised the need for rapport, and building rapport is crucial to engagement. This means that unless they are engaged with you, you may not get all the information you need. Additionally, there is the possibility that the interview can become an uncomfortable experience for both you and the child.

There is much that can be done to increase the likelihood of effective engagement. Some of the suggestions below may sound as though they are basic common sense and in some way most of them are. However, they are often the things that we might forget to do especially when under pressure or feeling uncomfortable or anxious. Appearing warm and friendly but professional at the same time is important in gaining the confidence of children.

During the introduction it is important not just to say who you are, and what you intend to do, but it is equally important to check out with the child what they think is going to happen. It is also important to explain to them at an early stage what information you are obliged to share so no false expectations are set up. Again this would enable them to consider what information they share with you. It is helpful to set some ground rules about what may be okay or not. Whilst it is best to do this early on, it can be better to engage first. Wilson and Powell (2001) suggest that the interviewer needs to make it easier for the child to speak up so you could use statements such as:

- 'Please tell me if I misunderstand what you say'
- 'Please tell me if you don't understand my question ...'
- 'Please tell me if my question is unclear'

Important point: Engaging children properly in the interview will be central to the success of your interview.

It can also be helpful to ensure they are aware that when you are exploring their views there is no right or wrong and that they can say they are unsure or do not know.

The main part of the interview

The success of the main part of the interview itself will depend on how successfully you have engaged with the child and how well prepared you are. This section of the interview may be where you collect most of your data. It is perfectly acceptable to have some side conversations that may not be related to the topic being researched – bear in mind a research interview is a social encounter that takes place in a particular context and both parties are a part of it. Again practice enables this to happen without losing too much time. A child constantly changing topics may also be trying to tell you something important so it can be worth asking if they really want to take part or not (in a sympathetic rather than challenging way).

Endings

Finishing a conversation takes skill. It can be particularly difficult for the researcher if the child wants to continue talking. If the interview has been difficult for the child, acknowledge this and ensure that you do not leave them distressed. Remember to thank them for their time. After the interview, it will be useful to reflect back on your performance and also pay some attention to how you felt doing the interview. This will help improve your interviewing skills, but also help you become more comfortable tackling difficult issues.

Important point: It is essential that you do not leave the child in a distressed state on completion of the interview.

It is useful to note these down in a research diary, particularly if you are undertaking qualitative interviews as these notes about feelings will help you reflect on the process later in the research.

Debrief

There will be some difficult interviews so consider what might have led to this being the case. At times the child may describe events or experiences that resonate personally with you for whatever reason. In these situations, it is even more essential to be aware of the issues of transference and counter-transference discussed below. If the interview is too difficult to continue because of this and you are not able to contain the situation it may be best to terminate it or at least take a break while you collect your thoughts. The research interview may yield stories that are painful and distressing and you should have a range of strategies to manage the situation should this happen. It is an essential part of the qualitative research process that you take field notes and reflect on each interview to note factors that will later provide a better context in which your data is situated.

A debrief may be needed for the child and the researcher. The researcher should debrief the child but it is also useful for the researcher to debrief, and this may need to take place with a peer or supervisor. For debriefing the child, it may be useful to have a definite break so everyone is clear that the interview part is over. Then it can just be useful to ask very generally if the child is okay and whether the interview went as they might have anticipated. This provides an opportunity for the child to share their feelings. If the researcher is concerned the child is upset and might need support after the meeting is over, it can be useful to ask speculative questions.

> For example… You might ask 'I wonder if the interview upset you and whether you would like to share your feelings about it?'

If the child has intimated during the interview they might want help, then asking about this might be helpful.

Of course this might be different for an older child as the information might be given directly to them. The debrief process is about dealing with any after effects of the interview or ensuring actions are in place. This is an ethical approach to interviewing as it ensures that the research process does not leave any distress/issues unaddressed.

> For example… You might ask the child 'During the interview you thought you might need help with that – would you like me to let your parents know about how to get some help?'

THE INTERVIEW INTERACTION

There are some techniques that will facilitate the flow of the interview and are particularly important when interviewing children. It is essential that you show your participants that you are listening and that you are interested in what they have to say. You can encourage them to talk and have an open and friendly body language. We consider the practical techniques you can use now in turn.

Active listening

This is more than just listening to what someone is saying. Active listening is the process by which the listener makes the person who is talking feel comfortable and valued. The listener gives the other person the time and space to be able to say what they need to say. When you have an interview schedule and know the information you want, it can be very tempting to follow your agenda and not really attend to the interviewee. It takes practice to sensitively bring someone back to your agenda but still be mindful of giving them the time to tell their story. To encourage the child, the interviewer can use silence whilst maintaining eye contact to show the child that they can take their time to tell their story and that the interviewer is really interested in what they are saying (see Box 7.1).

■ **Box 7.1** ■

Example of active listening

Child: So I went and told the teacher.
Interviewer: Uhuh.
Child: And she said she was very cross so I got sad.
[Pause (few moments of silence)]

Non-verbal cues from the interviewer are an important component of active listening. When the child is speaking it is important for the interviewer to listen attentively by maintaining eye contact (but not staring or fixing their gaze). Nodding and occasional utterances (such as um, uhuh, as in the example above) to indicate understanding are likely to encourage the interviewee to continue. Indeed, conversation analysis research from child counselling has shown that active listening is a discursive accomplishment and one whereby the adult party displays to the child that they are engaging with what the child has said (Hutchby, 2005). There is also just being in the room and being present with the young person. Cameron (2005) suggested it is unhelpful to mimic the child's vernacular, but sometimes reflecting back what children have said can be very useful. She also warns against using single word exclamations such as 'Great', 'Wow' 'Cool' and so on. Practically active listening is usually subtler than that but it will depend on the topic and context. Silence can be useful as long as while there is silence there is still engagement especially by the interviewer.

Clarifying

It is important that when clarifying what the child is saying the researchers do not lead the child to respond in a way which they might not have otherwise done. If a child is struggling to articulate their thoughts or feelings, it can be all too easy to step in and help them especially if they look to you for help. Sometimes it might be better just to let them take their time but provide reassurance that the struggle is okay and/or praise them that they are doing fine.

For example… 'It's okay. Take your time... You are doing fine' or 'so let me just check with you what I think I have heard you say...'

Using phrasing as shown in the example box ensures there is no right or wrong thing to say.

Reflecting and summarising

Summarising (paraphrasing) is the skill of repeating back what someone has said and is a way of checking that you have understood what has been conveyed. Reflecting is the process by which you consider what has been said and may acknowledge how the person

feels. It is usually best to be speculative rather than presump-
tive given that children, as well as adults, can have a diverse
range of approaches. Saying how someone must have felt may
not enable them to give their own perspective as they may feel
under pressure to conform to social expectations.

> For example... 'that sounds like it was a difficult time' rather than 'that must have been a difficult time'.

Rapport

Earlier in this chapter, and indeed throughout the book, we talked about the importance of engagement and reflected on the need for rapport. This is particularly
important for the interview interaction, and thus we return to it here. Rapport refers to
the development of a relationship where there is a sense of understanding about each
other. In the professional relationship when a rapport is established there is a sense that
both parties are vested in the relationship (in the professional sense) and they are working together towards achieving a goal. Irwin and Johnson (2005) found that building
rapport with children takes time and that researchers should not expect rapport to be
established after one meeting especially in the current context of children being
encouraged to be wary of strangers. They argued that adults more easily understand the
social interaction of building rapport and the etiquette of 'getting to know one another'
whereas young children may be less savvy. They also commented that young children
might not understand the purpose of the research and the relationship that this
context requires. It is up to the researcher to establish a working relationship with the
child and their parents. In some ways Irwin and Johnson may be overcomplicating the
issue. Children, like adults, vary and children at quite young ages can be quite skilled
in engaging.

To undertake research ethically the child needs to understand what is expected of them and
be protected from any harm. It is questionable whether they need to fully understand the
purpose of the relationship or the context of the relationship. Even very young children will
be aware that the nature of relationships varies. Most children will have relationships with
parents that they know (without understanding terminology, such as context and so on) are
different from the relationships they have with teachers. It is also questionable that children
always require more time for rapport to be built up – researchers need to be prepared that it
might take more time but should not assume it will and should not underestimate the social
skills of children. In many situations researchers may not have the luxury of establishing
rapport over an extended period of time so having practice of doing this quickly, but with
sincerity and being child-centred, can be extremely helpful.

Non-verbal cues from the interviewee

Hiller and DiLuzio (2004) identified that the researcher is required to look for non-verbal
cues such as tone of voice, facial expressions and emotional state, deliver appropriate

prompts and use follow up questions and nod, pause or utilise silence. Notably, it is likely that to a lesser or greater extent the interviewee is also looking for some of these cues as we discussed in attentive/active listening. It can take practice to ensure that non-verbal cues are attended to – sometimes this may be at the expense of the research project. However, it would be unethical not to attend to the cues the child is giving you.

For face-to-face and even for live Skype interviews what is not said may be as important as what is said. It is important to be mindful of the non-verbal cues that children give so that you can attend to their needs.

> For example… While talking about how he/she feels when they are getting told off, mid-sentence the child gets up and goes to the window.

In response to this the interviewer will need to provide an appropriate action that recognises that the child has become distracted from the interview as the child is clearly giving a non-verbal cue (see Box 7.2). This may not mean much or it may mean a lot and the interviewer will need some clarity.

■ Box 7.2 ■

Example of response to a non-verbal cue

Interviewer:　I wonder what's so interesting outside …
Child:　　　　I just wanted a look.
Interviewer:　I wonder if that was because it felt too sad to talk about getting told off?
[Child nods]
Interviewer:　Would you rather we didn't talk about it?
[Child shrugs shoulders]
Interviewer:　Shall we take a little break and decide in a few minutes?

> Important point: Children communicate a lot through their non-verbal gestures and it can be important to capture these for the research, but particularly they should be responded to appropriately.

In this way the interviewer has listened to what has not actually been initially said and has queried the reason for the child's actions rather than speculating or assuming. The interviewer has then given the child some space. By suggesting a break there is not a premature end to the interview, nor is the child being asked to continue something which they might rather not. Finding it sad does not mean that they do not want to tell their story, but just that it may take them more time and that they might want to think about the subject in private before sharing more.

Observations as part of the interview process

Certain kinds of research questions can best be answered by observing how people act or how things look. However, observations by the interviewer are an integral part of the interviewing process. There is the possibility that certain characteristics or ideas of observers may bias what they 'see' and also the sense they make of what they see may be coloured by their expectations. If observations *per se* are part of the data collection they may need to be coded. Observations of the interview process and factors in how the interview progressed are important components of data. The use of field notes is essential as not only does this capture the observations made about the interview, they also provide an opportunity for the researcher's reflections. In all cases they need noting as they will help make sense of the interview data and in effect enable triangulation where this is appropriate.

> For example… Rather than saying the child seemed anxious, it would be better to note the actual behaviour.

It is important to note what you see rather than try and speculate.

So, it is quite important for you to monitor the child's behaviour throughout the interview as this will give you some indication as to how engaged the child is in the interview. Try to look for indications of the child's comfort or discomfort:

> For example… A child wriggling around in their chair may be inattentive, may be anxious or may just need the bathroom!

- If the child looks bored, you may have to work harder at keeping their interest by giving them an activity, or asking about something that you know they find interesting.
- If the child is fidgeting, it does not necessarily mean they are bored. They may be too hot, hungry or need the toilet.
- If the child stops looking at you and begins to look to the door or window, they may want something specific or may have seen something they want to look at. It might be worth giving the child a short break.

We return to these issues in more depth in Chapter 9.

It can be helpful to structure the observations depending on the context of your project. You might want to make notes on the following:

- How did the child look?

> For example… Did they look well in that they looked well-nourished and healthy? (That does not mean they were well as not everyone who is unwell will look it but it is a worthwhile observation).

- Was the child appropriately dressed?

> For example… In the context of a project about how children feel about the way they are looked after this might be a much more pertinent observation than in a project on how children feel about a TV character.

- How did the child communicate?

> For example… They might be telling you about how a pet dog knocked them over in a race but have a big smile on their face, which shows you they found the incident funny and it was not a harmful event.

- Did the child present as socially appropriate for their age?

> For example… You may question whether they come across as younger or older than their years and what made you think that.

> Remember: This is of course as dependent on your skills as the child and engagement is a two-way reciprocal process.

> For example… You can observe whether the child seemed happy when talking about positive things or upset when talking about sad things.

- Was the child communicative and did they engage easily?
- Was what the child said congruent with how they said it?

It can also just be helpful to note anything else that strikes you as potentially interesting. If the interviews take place in different settings some observations about the setting might be helpful.

FACTORS TO CONSIDER WHEN INTERVIEWING CHILDREN AND YOUNG PEOPLE

There are a range of factors that are helpful to consider when interviewing children and young people that are largely due to the age group of the participants. We now turn to each of these.

Boundaries

Boundaries are a way of defining your personal space and limits, both physically and emotionally. Physical boundaries are limits around physical contact. It goes without saying that physical relationships with children are illegal and inappropriate. Different people have different levels of comfort around physical contact from unfamiliar people. It is important to be able to offer children comfort if distressed, but be aware that their boundaries may be different from your own. It is probably best to do no more than offer tissues or move closer if someone cries as both will demonstrate that you are attending to the distress but are not running the risk of being misinterpreted.

> Important point: Even taking someone's hand or touching them on the shoulder may be seen as an intrusion by some participants.

> For example… While this is a more extreme example, think about what a hug might mean to a child who has been sexually abused. This information may not have been made available to you as there was probably no need to reveal the information in the context of your interview, which may be on something completely unrelated such as healthy eating.

It is important to be very aware of the cues the child gives you about their comfort levels regarding personal space. Experience teaches you much about when physical contact is acceptable or not.

It is important that you do not make assumptions about the child or their space. The child may feel they have no voice to say what they find comfortable or not so it may only be through their body language that you realise they are uncomfortable.

Emotional boundaries are the limits you set around how much of your thoughts and feelings you choose to share with others. This can be more difficult as children may ask personal questions as they may be less aware of social norms. Being aware of this possibility enables you to be prepared for how to answer any personal questions without snubbing the child or compromising the relationship but retaining boundaries you are comfortable with.

Boundaries are important for your protection and also that of those you are interviewing, so think very carefully before you breach them. As an adult working in a professional relationship with children and their families it is your responsibility to ensure that professional boundaries are maintained. Your research participants may challenge or push boundaries, but it is up to you to ensure you are clear about the limits and to maintain them. When this is looking unmanageable, it is probably best to terminate the interview and reschedule if appropriate. Social engagements with research families are unlikely to be appropriate and given that you may know sensitive information about them, relationships even after the project is completed may be inappropriate given the dynamics. As the adult in the relationship, any breach of boundaries is your responsibility.

Sharing personal information

Sharing personal information may cross some emotional boundaries. It is perfectly acceptable to chat with child participants about subjects other than the research topic and indeed it may be really important to do so to build up rapport and make them comfortable. However, it is advisable to keep conversations non-personal. Sharing personal information in therapeutic contexts can be incredibly powerful but requires skill and experience. However, in the research context the outcomes may not be as expected and knowing how to deal with any fallout from sharing personal information should be anticipated. Sensitive personal information should only be used in a planned manner and not just because you are unable to contain your emotions.

> Important point: Planning ahead what you will and will not share with your child interviewees can help to prevent unintended sharing.

TRANSFERENCE AND COUNTER-TRANSFERENCE

These are terms that are used in clinical contexts and you may have come across them in relation to the theories of Sigmund Freud. However, in the research context there is also some relevance and it can be useful to think of these in relation to your own work. We will define the terms and then consider their application in the research context.

Transference

Transference occurs when a person (usually the interviewee) takes the perceptions and expectations of one person and projects them on to another person (the interviewer). Projecting is when you project your own feelings, emotions or motivations onto another person without realising your reaction is really more about you than it is about the other person. Typically, the pattern projected onto the other person comes from a childhood relationship. This may be from an actual person, such as a parent, or an idealised figure or prototype. This transfers both power and expectation. This can have both positive and negative outcomes. What we read into other people reveals our own prejudices and unfulfilled wishes. Transference occurs on a regular basis and in all relationships, but is particularly useful as a tool to promote understanding as it can provide a good idea of what the child being interviewed might be expecting from you.

In the research context our own experiences and drivers may be leading the research agenda. The process may be strongly influenced by our own experiences and our own personal feelings. That is why there is constant need for reflexivity, particularly for qualitative interviewing. This will be especially true for data analysis as how we understand and interpret what is said may be biased because of our own experiences (see Box 7.3).

■ Box 7.3 ■

Example of transference

Child: You look like my mummy.
Interviewer: I wonder how I look like your mummy.
Child: She is kind and funny.

In reality you may or may not be anything like the child's mother, but the child is setting up an expectation that they are anticipating that you will be both kind and funny. This may be an idealised view of a mother especially if the child has not had such an experience of being mothered by someone who is kind and funny.

Counter-transference

Counter-transference is the response that is elicited in the recipient (usually the therapist) by the other's (usually the patient's) unconscious transference communications. The transference generated by patients may evoke responses in clinicians that they need to be aware of.

Feelings are easier to identify if they are not congruent with your personality and expectation of his or her role. Awareness of the transference–counter-transference relationship allows a more considered response. Understanding this also means that the researcher is able to step back and prevent themselves from feeling overwhelmed by excessive demands from children as they have greater awareness of what might be happening.

For example... In the example in Box 7.3, the child's expectations that you will be kind and funny may draw certain responses (usually emotional, but can be behavioural) from you depending on your own experiences. You may worry that you will let the child down so not carry out the interview you had intended. Your response may be defensive and subtly lead to the child disengaging.

DEFENCE MECHANISMS

These are discussed here as they are important factors that play a part in interactions and although much of Freud's work may now be considered out of vogue except in very specific contexts, understanding defence mechanisms can really help understand human functioning. It is worth highlighting that we all use defence mechanisms and they can be effective coping strategies in the short term. However, over-reliance on them and an unwillingness to explore deeper meanings can impact on relationships and how we feel about ourselves. Freud considered that defence mechanisms are used to deal with anxiety and actions that we may find unacceptable either to ourselves or may be unacceptable socially. There was also an emphasis that at the

Table 7.2 Common defence mechanisms

Defence mechanism	Description
Denial	The refusal to accept the reality of a situation, thought or event. An example of this can be when something that someone does not want to happen has happened, such as bereavement or a relationship break up. The initial response can be a denial that the event has taken place.
Projection	This is placing the feelings an individual has on someone else. So instead of acknowledging that you feel angry, you say someone else is angry because you are unable to own your feelings of anger.
Rationalisation	This is the mechanism whereby we try and explain something logically as the feelings we have may not be feelings we feel are acceptable or logical. An example might be saying that you were justified in being cross with a colleague as they were late for a meeting when the real reason might be that you do not like that person.
Sublimation	This is when the energy from feelings about one issue are channelled into another activity. Being angry with someone at work and then using the aggression when you play sport is an example of sublimation.
Reaction formation	This is expressing the opposite of what you might feel or think because to acknowledge the real feelings or thoughts may be unacceptable (either socially or to yourself).
Displacement	This is placing the feelings for one person (or a situation) onto another person or situation because it may be unacceptable to have the feelings for the original person. This may be being attracted to someone who is unavailable and thereby displacing those feelings onto someone else who may be available. It is also often done when an individual is angry with someone in authority but cannot communicate that so takes out their anger on a peer or someone who is less senior.
Regression	This is when someone reverts to a coping style from an earlier stage of development. A temper tantrum in an adult is a very good example of this.
Repression	Highly stressful events that led to particular feelings are 'locked' away into our unconscious self. They may impact on our response to other situations but we are not aware of this as we do not 'recall' the event. An example might be someone who was bullied at school but repressed the recall of this. In their workplace or other relationship, they may function in such a way that anticipates they may be bullied because of the earlier events.

heart of it lay sexual or violent tendencies. For the purposes of explaining them here, this emphasis is not made. The most commonly described defence mechanisms are outlined in Table 7.2.

It is also important to note that we all use defence mechanisms and they are a useful means of understanding the way we communicate our feelings to others. However, if defence mechanisms, transference and counter-transference are considered together, sometimes what a person is saying is exactly what they are saying. The fact that we are unable to hear this may be because we are using particular defence mechanisms and are unable or unwilling to hear what the person is saying. A child may say they had a tantrum because they were being ignored by their parents when they were expecting to be rewarded for having been well behaved whilst out shopping (rationalisation, if we consider defence mechanisms – the parents did not deliver on their promise so the tantrum was justified). We provide an activity in Box 7.4 to encourage you to think more about defence mechanisms in the context of research.

■■ Box 7.4 ■■

Activity on defence mechanisms

Having read about defence mechanisms, think about when you might have used them in your own life in the last week or so. What are the types of ways in which children may use them in your research interviews?

Consider our answer to this below and think about how it matches up with your ideas:

> A child who does not want to talk about difficult events may be using denial as a way of trying to deal with that event.

> A child who is angry about how school treats him may not have told them that but in an interview about schools may become very angry and hostile with you. They may be using displacement especially if they feel they cannot communicate to the school how they really feel about staff who have told them off.

> A child may tell you they think you are cross with them when what they are really trying to say is that they are cross with you – in this case they may use projection.

USING INTERPRETERS FOR RESEARCH INTERVIEWS WITH CHILDREN

It is beyond the remit of this book to focus on this in detail. However, it is important to make sure that the interpreter is an appropriate person and preferably one that has been trained to act as an interpreter. It is arguable that using interpreters is an important ethical perspective as it ensures including as many people in the research sample as possible. However, we discuss it here as it is often a major practical issue. It is usually not good practice to use children and/or family members as interpreters, except in emergency situations and research interviews would not qualify as emergencies. Temple and Young (2004) explored three questions:

1. Whether methodologically it matters if the act of translation is identified or not;
2. The epistemological implications of who does translation; and
3. The consequences for the final product of how far the researcher chooses to involve a translator in research.

They also discussed ways in which researchers have tackled the issue of language.

There are issues about appropriateness of the content covered but also confidentiality especially if covering sensitive topics. It can be difficult to find trained interpreters, especially for languages that are not widely spoken. There may be concerns that confidentiality will not be maintained. It also takes practice to be aware when the interpreter is interpreting what the child is saying or when they are 'reinterpreting' what the interviewee has said. When using an interpreter, it is important to talk to the child and not just work through the interpreter so for example it is important to say 'Tell me about when you were playing in the park...' rather than saying to the interpreter, 'Please can you ask the child to tell me about when they were playing in the park.' Remember non-verbal language is also important and you can only make sense of this if you communicate with the child directly.

Researchers need to bear in mind that using interpreters carries a cost and unless budgeted for may exclude relevant parties. Consider how you can be as inclusive as possible during the planning stages and also whether there are opportunities to train up volunteers for specific projects although there may be ethical issues of using the community to undertake 'unpaid' work.

SETTING UP THE INTERVIEW

In setting up the interview it is important to consider how diversity factors are managed to ensure that the research is as robust as possible. Research may be targeting specific groups to explore specific issues but it would be wrong to assume homogeneity between groups. No matter how well prepared you are it is best to remain flexible and expect the unexpected. In that way you are less likely to be alarmed when events go off script. This is very common in practice so inexperienced researchers should not be worried if it happens to them.

The setting of the interview

The interview setting may present challenges. If carried out in the home or a public place getting enough privacy for some topics may be a challenge (we discussed this earlier in the book). If any research governance principles are likely to be compromised, it is probably better practice to rearrange the interview than continue in adverse circumstances. It can feel as though the matter is urgent especially if the research is falling behind the time frames set but it is worth asking yourself how you would justify the steps you take. Irwin and Johnson (2005) highlighted that small places are seen as 'intimate' and so may be appropriate for interviews with adults. However, these may make children feel restricted. It is perhaps important not to see a situation as applicable to all children as the variation between them as individuals needs to be kept in mind. The interview setting should if possible allow for breaks as needed. Some children may find it helpful to do other activities as they talk and again it is important to try and accommodate the child's style as that will lead to better data although it may be more challenging for the researcher. Undertaking interviews in a range of settings will increase the likelihood of skills being developed.

As discussed in Chapter 2 the presence of parents may or may not help. The age of the child, the topic under discussion and the relationship between the child and parents are only some of the factors that may be relevant. Rather than having a hard and fast rule it is best to be flexible but be aware of how parental presence may or may not influence the data collection. Often parents may be present for the start of the appointment and once the child has settled may leave. This is often seen in clinical practice (for example, Instone, 2002).

The physical setting

You can ensure the room is set up in such a way that interviewing and communication are facilitated. Try and have furniture that is comfortable for the child and has the interviewer and child approximately level to enable eye contact. Sitting on the floor or on bean bags may be appropriate. The room should not be cold and bland but nor is it helpful for it to be cluttered and distracting. Of course you may have little choice where the interview takes place.

Tools/equipment

For example… You might say, 'When Teddy gets told off for not doing his homework he gets very angry. I wonder if that sometimes happens to you when you get told off'. In this way you use Teddy as a tool for getting the child to open up about how they might feel when they get told off.

In earlier chapters we discussed the need to consider which recording devices might be appropriate. You will also need to consider whether you will facilitate the interview through drawings in which case you will need to ensure you take plenty of paper and coloured pens that are easy for children of all abilities to use (for example felt tip pens rather than colouring pencils) (see Chapter 6). Toys to start the interview process or to help explain points may also be useful depending on your research topic. If you want to explore how the child feels about certain issues, you might want to use a soft toy to give permission for the child to say what they feel.

For example… If you were interested in what the consequences of not doing homework are you might say, 'When Teddy does not do his homework he gets told off. What happens if you don't do your homework?'

However, be careful that you are alert to the child's cues and especially if they think this technique is ridiculous. One of the authors has had a child as young as three respond that the toy is not a real person!

Sometimes this technique can just be a fun way of finding out a little about the child.

> For example... Using toys to externalise feelings may be helpful with sensitive topics.

If using material that requires internet access, making sure this is available will be essential, otherwise you may waste your time and that of your participants. If particular books or video sketches (on a computer or accessed through the internet) are required to engage children with the topic under research, ensure they are available when needed.

Davis (1998) stated that the key objective for researchers is to use tools that enable children to be active participants in the research process and which offer them the maximum opportunity to put forward their view. Kirk (2007) expressed caution about the enthusiasm within children's research to develop and use fun, child-friendly activities. Assumptions are often made about children preferring to communicate through pictures and stories leading to techniques such as sentence completion exercises, story writing and taking photographs or video recordings. Punch (2002) argued that many of these novel techniques have not always been scrutinised and that they have been frequently adopted with insufficient critical reflection. The premise for this is that somehow children are more difficult to engage with. The rationale for the premise may be making assumptions about children rather than checking out what the skills or abilities of any particular child may be. There are also perhaps assumptions made about what is fun for children and any tools or activities should perhaps be selected by children themselves. There may be an over reliance on tools as though these can replace the need for the researcher to acquire the skill of working with children.

Cameron (2005) highlighted that many imaginative (and imaginative based) techniques have application for interviewing children for research purposes. With most children it is useful to have books, pictures, pen and paper, and some toys to hand. However, do not assume that younger children will want to colour and older children will just want to talk. Drawings can help relax some children and free them up to talk (Ivey and Ivey, 2003). Some (for example Henderson, 2000) have suggested that drawings and art can provide a window to the subconscious – this is probably best left to those specifically trained to do this and researchers should avoid this.

SUMMARY

In this chapter we began by looking at cultural considerations and safeguarding before reviewing well established stages of the interview process and how each of these might be facilitated. The importance of observations and field notes of the interview was highlighted. We considered concepts, such as transference, counter-transference and defence mechanisms, that can influence the interview and may be particularly important to consider when the research covers sensitive areas or is close to the researcher's own experience. We also briefly covered the use of interpreters before moving on to practical issues such as setting up the interview to ensure optimal data collection and experience for the young person and researcher.

RECOMMENDED READING

On questions

Cameron, H. (2005) 'Asking the tough questions: A guide to ethical practices in interviewing young children', *Early Child Development and Care*, 175: 597–610.

On challenges

Irwin, L. and Johnson, J. (2005) 'Interviewing young children: Explicating our practices and dilemmas', *Qualitative Health Research*, 15: 821–831.

On interviews in practice

Lamb, M., Hershkowitz, I., Orbach, Y. and Esplin, P. (2008) *Tell Me What Happened: Structured Investigative Interviews of Child Victims and Witnesses*. West Sussex: John Wiley and Sons.

8

ETHICAL ISSUES WITH RESPECT TO INTERVIEWING

━━ LEARNING OUTCOMES ━━━━━━━━━━━━━━━━━━━━━━━━━━━

By the end of the chapter the reader should be able to:

- Recognise the importance of being an ethical researcher.
- Recognise the position of the child in the interview.
- Review the ethical dilemmas that occur in interview research.
- Consider the relevance of capacity, consent and assent.
- Critically assess the principle of consent.
- Evaluate the importance of confidentiality and anonymity.
- Evaluate the importance of protecting data.
- Critically assess how to protect children from harm.

INTRODUCTION

The focus of this chapter is to consider the positioning of children, the application of the principles of consent and capacity, and the relevance of confidentiality and anonymity in conducting ethical interview research with children. We identify the potential challenges when there is a discrepancy between a project that has ethical approval and the actual experiences of the researcher. Structures to safeguard children and researchers are just that, but do not absolve the researcher of constantly having to be mindful about the need to continue to think about the application of ethical principles and the impact of this. This chapter does not focus on the technical aspects of ethics committees and ethics approvals, which are the same for research involving interviews as other data collection methods and are discussed well in general research with children texts (e.g., Fraser et al., 2014; O'Reilly and Parker, 2014a; O'Reilly et al., 2013a). However, it is worth recognising that ethics committees may have greater concerns about the need to protect child participants from potential harm than research involving adults and thus we provide some general information about the role of the ethics committee briefly in this chapter for context. We also discuss the importance of protecting data and protecting children from harm.

ETHICAL ISSUES

It is important to consider the ethical issues that arise from doing interview research with children and to pay attention to the reasons why there are ethical frameworks in place to safeguard children in this context. In other words, the benefits and risks of the work need to be balanced. Even if the risks are minimal it is still important to consider these in advance of your project, and because children are considered to be a vulnerable group by ethics committees, your project will come under greater scrutiny. In the context of interview research there are four major ethical issues identified by DiCicco-Bloom and Crabtree (2006) and these are listed in Table 8.1.

Table 8.1　Four major ethical issues identified by DiCicco-Bloom and Crabtree (2006)

Issue	Description
Harm	It is necessary to reduce the risk of any unanticipated harm.
Protection of information	It is important to protect the information given to the research by the interviewee.
Informing	It is crucial to effectively inform the interviewees about the nature of the study.
Reduction of risk	It is essential that researchers take steps to reduce the risk of exploitation.

The first and last of these identified ethical issues relate to protecting children from harm, the second to confidentiality and the third to informed consent. Before you begin reading the chapter it is worth thinking about why ethics are important. Consider the vignette in Box 8.1.

■■ **Box 8.1** ■■■■■■■■■■■■■■■■■■■■■■■

Vignette – Mia

Mia is planning her undergraduate human geography project where she is interested in children living in poverty. Her intention is to interview children who live in particularly poor socioeconomic areas of her home city about their needs. She intends to recruit children aged between 11 and 16 years. Mia has planned a supervision session but believes that all she needs to do is ask the children if they are happy to be interviewed.

- What should Mia really do?

Take a few moments to write down what you think Mia should do.

We provide some possible answers to this at the back of the book.

Before we consider the core areas of ethical concern we will return to the positioning of children again which we first introduced in Chapter 1. This is because your views, as well as the views of ethics panels, will influence the way in which ethical principles are implemented in practice.

THE POSITIONING OF CHILDREN IN RESEARCH

Christensen and Prout (2002) identified four ways of seeing children and childhood which have been considered relevant in research involving children:

1. The child as an object.
2. The child as subject.
3. The child as social actor.
4. The child as participant and/or co-researcher.

The authors argued that these perspectives co-exist and researchers often combine different perspectives, but may fail to think through the ethical implications of how children are positioned in their own work. They argued that the most traditional and common approach historically was that of the child as an object. This approach views children's worlds through adult priorities and perspectives. This approach also takes the position that children are unable to understand the research fully so have little active part to play in it. Often adults are trusted to be able to speak for children and the research is carried out with parents, teachers or other adults in the child's life.

Viewing the child as a subject moves away from treating the child as the object of the research and instead accepts that the child is a subjective individual. The focus here may be on ensuring that the child's developmental stage is appropriate for the research and affords the child some level of autonomy in decision making, but still sees the adult perspective as important and treats the child's view with some caution.

> Important point: Positioning the child as an object of research advocates the view that adults know what is best for children.

The third approach extends the child as subject to see children as social actors with their own experiences and understandings. Children are seen to act, take part in, change and become changed by the social and cultural world they live in. In this approach the research approach makes little if any distinction between research with children and adults. The methods employed are those that suit the needs of those involved in the study, the research aims and the specific social and cultural context of the research.

A developing and fairly contemporary approach is viewing children as active participants in research as in societal life. Furthermore, this has influenced the perspectives that children can be involved in the research process as researchers, as we discussed in Chapter 5. This is underpinned by adherence with the principles of the UN Convention on the Rights of the Child (UNCRC) and children's participation rights, and has been referred to as a rights-based approach to research. The UNCRC highlighted that all activities that affect children's lives need children's active involvement and this includes the research interview setting. We introduced the notion of children's rights back in Chapter 1 and we recommend you return to this information now if needed. We also suggest you now undertake the activity in Box 8.2.

▬ Box 8.2 ▬▬▬▬▬▬▬▬▬▬▬▬▬▬

Activity on positions of children

It is worth pausing for a moment and thinking about which of these four positions of the child you hold personally. As we noted at the beginning of the book, the way the researcher positions the child can have an impact on the way research is conducted. Importantly the researcher's view of the child can also impact on the implementation of any ethical principles. It is therefore important that you question which position you hold, why you hold it and how it may impact on your own research study. Take a few moments to write down your initial thoughts in your research diary.

Christensen and Prout (2002) argued that the perspective on children that a researcher works with has important implications for their research practice. This is consistent with the authors' perspective that the researcher needs to understand their own perspectives and views about the relevant factors related to any research topic as these views may obviously or subtly influence the decisions made about how the research question is framed, the methods used, analysis and interpretation of data as well as ethical practice (compare this with the issues of transference and counter-transference discussed in Chapter 7). These changing and developing views of children and their place in research add new complexities and uncertainties to the research process because a new set of factors need consideration. This also means that the research practice does not inherently employ particular methods or ethical standards for working with children but ensures that the practices used are in line and consistent with the children's experiences of their everyday lives.

> For example… In the research interview it is likely to be helpful to use language that has relevance for the child.

The approach then taken by the researcher influences how they approach the ethical issues we now turn to in this chapter. However whatever position one may hold, it is important to ensure that as a researcher you comply with the research governance frameworks of the context in which you work.

ETHICAL DILEMMAS THAT WARRANT ATTENTION

Duncan et al. (2009) stated that ethical dilemmas are unavoidable in the research setting, but often they can be pre-empted and researchers can take steps to prepare for these. They noted that qualitative research is particularly susceptible to ethical dilemmas for several reasons, including:

1. It is not always possible to predict all possible questions and responses.
2. The nature of the relationship between researchers and interviewees is amenable to sensitive disclosure.

3. The process of qualitative research can make it difficult for participants to voice concerns or withdraw.
4. The participant identities are usually known to the researcher.

Indeed, the very nature of qualitative research invokes different kinds of ethical sensitivities for the project than quantitative research might. While the general ethical principles remain constant, such as respecting autonomy, promoting beneficence, ensuring non-maleficence and advocating justice, the implementation and the tensions that surround these principles manifest differently in qualitative research. In their work O'Reilly and Kiyimba (2015) identified five key ways in which qualitative research necessitates particular ethical attention and these are outlined in Table 8.2.

Table 8.2 Ethical issues in qualitative research (O'Reilly and Kiyimba, 2015)

Ethical issue	Description
In depth nature of the work	Qualitative research is in depth by its nature and often aims to elicit personal and potentially sensitive information from participants.
The role and impact of the researcher	In qualitative research the researcher is the research instrument and is central to the whole process and an unbiased or neutral administration of data collection tools is not possible (Connolly and Reilly, 2007).
Qualitative research is iterative and unpredictable	Qualitative research evolves through circular stages and research questions become modified and recruitment may become extended. Essentially therefore ethics themselves should also be treated as an iterative part of the process.
Increased visibility of participants	Qualitative research nearly always uses audio- or video-recordings and typically quotes participants in dissemination. Thus there are ethical risks invoked in keeping the identifiable data safe and minimising the risk of deductive disclosure.
Data management	Often qualitative researchers will have collected a great deal of personal information and the onus is on the researcher to use that material appropriately and to not gather more data than is necessary.

When considering these issues in relation to interview research with children there are further challenges and considerations that the researcher must think about both before the project starts and during the research process. Duncan et al. (2009) noted that qualitative research with children adds further dilemmas as:

1. Young people have limited life experience to deal with the challenges posed.
2. Consent is often required from young people and their parents.
3. Issues of competence can complicate assumptions about informed consent.
4. The power differential between researchers and participants is significant.

They concluded therefore that the ethical risks related to qualitative research with young people is substantial and so careful consideration of the issues is needed. Guilleman and

> **Important point**: Ethical research practice with children is especially important and interviewers need to be mindful of the ethical dilemmas and challenges that can occur.

Gillam (2006) raised the concept of 'ethical mindfulness' which involves the recognition of ethically important moments, giving credence to moments of discomfort and being reflexive. They argue that as ethics is 'grey', sharing stories may be the best way of enhancing ethical practice.

ETHICAL ISSUES THAT NEED CONSIDERATION

It is essential that you review the ethical issues that are pertinent to your own project and ensure that you acquire the relevant approvals from appropriate bodies. The review process by an ethics committee for assessing risk of harm is an inherent part of contemporary ethics (Shaw and Barrett, 2006). As we noted in our introduction to this chapter, it is not our intention to discuss this in detail as it is well documented elsewhere. In brief and for context, ethics committees are made up of individuals who have a range of knowledge, experience and expertise and it is this body that assesses the risks and benefits of the proposed research (Alderson, 2007).

As is the case for all types of research there are broad ethical issues that need to be considered when conducting interviews with children and young people, and these are:

- Informed consent.
- Confidentiality and anonymity.
- Protection from harm.
- The impact of power differentials between the researcher and participants.

Each of these will be discussed in turn. The issues that pertain to each of these factors will be covered in the specific section. For all the factors it is noteworthy that most ethics committees view children as vulnerable and incompetent to make decisions about themselves so often assume a more paternalistic approach.

Harden et al. (2000) argued that it is this uncritical acceptance of the Piagetian view of children as not being fully cognitively formed that leads to this perspective (note that we discuss Piaget's theory in more detail in Chapter 9). However, it is important to critically reflect on this and consider that if the Piagetian view is not accepted, then in turn children's research is not viewed as different and it may be that power issues are more relevant which also creates tensions. However, as researchers we need to ensure compliance with research governance principles as they exist in the context in which we are conducting our research. Our own perspectives will influence our work but whatever our views, we cannot ignore the legal and governance frameworks, or the guidance of ethics committees who have the charge to approve or reject our ethical research proposals.

> **Important point**: Ethics committees act in the best interests of the child and often take a perspective that is protective of children; that of paternalism. This means they act in ways which is presumed to be for the child's own good.

Ethical research requires that researchers consider the many variables present in children's lives beyond just their developmental and cognitive ability. However, it is important for researchers not to assume that a particular characteristic (such as gender) will have the same meaning for participants. In an attempt to avoid making assumptions about one issue, researchers may make assumptions about another.

> **Important point:** Remember that the ethics committee has the power to end a project if they refuse to give ethical approval (McGuinness, 2008).

James et al. (1998) argued that age is a social variable rather than a natural variable. In practice the context of the research and the way children are viewed will be more important. Hill (1997) argued that the Piagetian model has led to a developmental age of seven or eight being considered the age at which children may be usefully interviewed. It is arguable that the topic is as big an indicator of potential usefulness as the child's age. It has been noted that many studies of black children have failed to take into account ethnicity as white researchers have been used. It is a huge error to assume

> **For example…** Kirk (2007) suggested that children with health problems may mature quickly and their experiences increase their understanding. However, this view may be taken because it fits with the researcher's perspective rather than reflecting the reality of there being diversity in the maturity at which children with health problems mature. The nature of the health problem in itself may be a significant variable.

that 'black' researchers would inherently engage young people better just on the basis of shared skin colour. Black children will have a diversity of different backgrounds and it is also incorrect to assume that only potentially minority groups have culture. Authors such as Mahon et al. (1996) have argued that matching interviewer and interviewee on basis of gender would be appropriate, but again the assumptions behind this rationale may lead to bias or take the research in a particular direction.

Kirk (2007) concluded that researchers who work with children have to deal sensitively with ethical issues particularly with the process of obtaining informed consent and to providing information in an understandable way to potential participants. Kirk then noted that because health related research often uses Piaget's developmental model, it lacks reflexivity. However, if Piaget's model is used flexibly then the research process can use it and still be reflexive and understand how the researcher perspective influences the research process. We will now consider each of the major issues in turn beginning with the matter of consent.

CONSENT

Informed consent is a fundamental principle of ethical research practice and recognises that potential participants are only involved in research with their consent unless there are exceptional circumstances where this may not be necessary. However, the researchers would need to provide any ethical approving body clear and justifiable reasons as to why this was appropriate. All research participants, regardless of their age, need to have the capacity to provide their consent, and understand the information given to them so that they are able to reach an informed decision. The key elements of capacity to be able to consent are presented in Table 8.3.

Table 8.3   Key elements of consent

Element	Description
Understanding information	The individual should be able to understand the information that is presented to them.
Information retention	The individual should be able to retain the information given to them.
Balanced decision	The individual should be able to weigh the information in a balanced way and come to a decision based on this (i.e., they have capacity or competence to give consent).
Communication of decision	The individual should be able to communicate their wishes and decisions (note that this can be through any means and not just verbally).

If an individual cannot fulfil the above criteria, their capacity to give consent is questionable. To be valid consent needs to be freely given without fear of repercussions for declining and without any coercion or pressure. Alderson (1992) considered that bioethics defines competence as a set of mechanistic skills and questions how expert in the above skills people really need to be to be able to consent. As Horsman (2008) identified:

- There will be children who do not have the capacity to consent
- Those who are assumed to have the capacity to consent and
- Those who may have capacity to consent but where this needs to be established.

Consent where the child does not have capacity

> For example... Young people with intellectual disabilities may not have the capacity to fully understand the information given to them or be able to balance the risks and benefits to their welfare in relation to their participation in an interview research project. However, it is important not to make assumptions about capacity based on this.

If a child is not legally competent, consent is required from the person with parental responsibility. However, this does not mean the child should not be involved and even toddlers can be consulted about their wishes. Having the skills to engage and communicate with such young children was covered in Chapter 6. Good ethical practice would mean that every attempt is made to obtain their views. In these cases, where the child is not legally competent (typically those under the age of 16 years in the UK), then assent is taken from the child (this is discussed in further detail shortly).

Children over the age of 16

The default legal position is that all adults (i.e. people aged 16 years and older) are assumed to have capacity to make their own decisions, to consent to or refuse to participate in research unless there is evidence to the contrary. However, there will be some young people (aged 16–18) who do not necessarily have capacity to consent.

Children under 16 who are competent

In the UK consent issues in the health arena (usually in relation to refusing or accessing treatment) have informed research processes. There is no age of assumed ability to consent under the age of 16, but there is an expectation that the researcher obtaining consent has the skills to decide if the individual child is competent to consent. For children under 16 in most research circumstances, irrespective of whether the child can consent or not, parental consent is nearly always required before the child can be approached. If the child does not have a parent, then a legal guardian or representative of the stage may need to fulfil this role. In healthcare although young people would be encouraged to involve their families, young people can if they have capacity consent without parental involvement. Obviously the exception would be if there were any safeguarding issues. While healthcare and treatments represent a different setting from interview research, the field of research has often learned lessons from this arena and thus it can be helpful to have a broader understanding of consent issues in your work. Additionally, much of the ethical frameworks that researchers rely on for conducting interview projects have been heavily influenced by research in health and its related history.

> Important point: It should not be assumed that children in particular groups such as those with a learning disability or a health problem do not have capacity.

The circumstances for each individual child need to be considered. Children may have capacity to make a decision about one issue but not another so again capacity and consent need to be seen in the context of wider issues.

> For example… Alderson's research in 1995 assumed that school aged children were competent and the onus was on parents who disagreed with their children's participation to prove incompetence. It is unlikely that such an approach would be acceptable in the current climate.

Cashmore (2006) raised the issue that for researchers to determine if a child has capacity to consent may raise a potential conflict of interest as the researcher has a vested interest in the child participating in their research. There is a further complexity as there is considerable variation in the understanding of, and attitudes towards the issues, as well as the skills they may have.

> For example… Ethically if a child is disengaging, the options open to them should be made clear. Remember that the child may need to be reminded that they have the right to stop the interview or withdraw from it.

Cashmore (2006) also presumed that if a child has competence their parents' consent is unnecessary – our own experience in England indicates that this is not the position held by ethics committees. In the case where parents have consented most researchers would accept child assent, but some researchers such as Carroll-Lind et al. (2006) obtained children's written consent after explaining the research. Cashmore (2006) questioned that even when researchers explained that the child can stop the process, it can be difficult to ascertain how able children feel in practice to withdraw from participation. This leads her to suggest the need for continuing consent throughout the interview process. Thus the researcher needs to be continually aware of the cues the child is giving as this may help identify if the child really wants to participate or feels under pressure to do so.

When there is disagreement between child and parent

Interestingly in principle, in the clinical context children can agree to have treatment if their parents do not consent, but they cannot override their parents if their parents wish them to have treatment which they do not agree with. In research, of those parents who do not consent to their children's participation, children may not have the opportunity of deciding whether they want to participate or not. This is because typically ethics committees do not permit researchers to approach children unless the parents have provided consent for the researcher to do so. Turn now to Box 8.3 for an activity on how to approach children.

━━━ **Box 8.3** ━━━━━━━━━━━━━━━━━━━━━━━━━━━━━━━━━

Activity on your opinions

What is your opinion on this? Think about how not approaching children might have implications for treating a child as an individual with rights and autonomy.

───

Parental consent: opting in or opting out?

It is not uncommon for researchers to write to parents about projects and ask for them to opt out of research, especially in projects that involve large scale surveys where recruitment can be complicated by an opt-in policy. The assumption therefore is that as long as parents do not opt out, the children themselves can be asked to actively consent to their participation. This gives children the opportunity to make a decision for themselves. Notably, however, it is increasingly the case that ethics committees are asking for parents to actively consent, which means that an opt-out approach cannot then be utilised.

For example... In a large survey to explore prevalence of mental health in specific ethnic groups we used a 'passive consent' approach for parents so that they had to opt out (see Dogra et al., 2013). Once parents had consented we required children's assent to continue. Parental consent was not in itself sufficient.

The rationale for this opt-out design is that it enables children to be more empowered so that unless parents have a real reason not to allow them to participate they do so passively. This means that children's voices are deemed important but the parental perspective is also recognised as necessary and valuable. To make sure the parents receive the information so they can make a decision it may be important to consider how the information is sent to them. It is important that those parents genuinely do have the opportunity to opt out if they really do not want their child to participate. It is therefore important that the researcher is certain that they have received the information and perhaps it is not best practice to send the information via the children. Getting active parental consent may not only be impractical but it may also mean that children who are competent to decide whether or not to participate simply are not asked as their parents have not responded. This can hardly be deemed child friendly or allowing children to have a voice about the issues that are of interest to them. This may be heightened for particular issues.

> For example... Carroll-Lind et al. (2006) used passive consent by parents for their research in New Zealand exploring children's experience of violence to ensure that children had an opportunity to participate and were not prevented from doing so because of the consent procedure.

Carroll-Lind et al. (2006) stated that while most ethics committees insist that the active consent of the children's caregivers is sought, there is increasing acceptance about the importance of allowing children to describe their views of what has happened to them. Gatekeepers may have their own reasons for preventing children from participation. It is questionable whose interest ethics committees are serving when the conditions they set are unrealistic and paternalistic rather than focusing on what is ethical research. Miller and Boulton (2007) argued that research ethics committees in protecting potential participants from undue pressure or coercion to take part in a study have also played a role in distorting recruitment. This in turn raises questions about who participates in research and if we are not careful we may in practice be researching a select minority.

> For example... If the research is about topics that may provoke greater parental anxiety, such as research about sex, drugs, mental health and so forth, then there may need to be more attention paid to the consent process.

ASSENT

When parents have consented, it is ethical practice to gain assent from children. Assent is approval by the child of the consent agreed by their parents/carers (as defined by the Free Dictionary, 2016). There are two key types of assent which are express and implied:

- Express assent is manifest confirmation of a position for approval.
- Implied assent is that which the law presumes to exist because the conduct of the parties demonstrates their intentions (i.e., the child completes the questionnaire).

> Important point: Note that active assent is different from acquiescence which is passive consent in a context where acquiescence is granted because there is an inability or unwillingness to oppose the consent granted. Ethically it is debatable if acquiescence is appropriate.

It is better practice to gain express assent rather than assume implied assent or implied consent. Note also that not all children are able to assent, or may verbally assent but show signs of disinterest or distress. In these cases, dissent can be the marker for non-participation and it is the responsibility of the interviewer to look out for this. The challenges therefore may be how to ensure that children understand what their participation in the research might mean for them and that there are unlikely to be any immediate or direct benefits to them (Kirk, 2007).

Mahon et al. (1996) highlighted that consent/assent is not a once only process as even if someone has consented or assented to participate they are entitled to change their mind or withdraw from the research. Furthermore, consent and assent should be thought of as an iterative process, and there are various opportunities throughout the process to check this (see for example, O'Reilly et al., 2011). This means that the researcher needs to constantly check the young person wishes to continue. It is important to recognise that the nature of qualitative research may make it harder to withdraw as the child may find it hard to tell the interviewer they do not wish to continue. This is in contrast to survey completion in which they can choose to omit some questions or just not finish the questionnaire.

When considering children's ability to give consent or assent, Alderson (1992) argued that adult views are shaped by experience and their own perspectives about children and childhood rather than by training or a clear rationale. She divided adult views into a range of categories which included:

- Libertarian – who argue that children should be able to exercise adult rights as soon as they are able to do so.
- Protectionists – who believe professionals should intervene to define and protect children's interests.
- Parentalists – who assume that parents/carers should decide for the child until they reach maturity.

Alderson further suggested that developmental maturity was one of several factors that influenced children's ability to consent. Parental estimations of their child's competence work well when there is child and parent agreement but not necessarily so when there is disagreement.

CRITICALLY CONSIDERING THE CONCEPT OF INFORMED CONSENT

Miller and Boulton (2007) suggested that the concept of 'informed consent' is a socially constructed concept and so subject to change. They considered that there is a growing mismatch between increasingly standardised ethics procedures and the complexity of qualitative research. They used their own experience as researchers of over 35 years to illustrate how ethics approval has changed over their working lives. They argued that ethics committees have tried to deal with an increasingly uncertain and changing world by tightening research ethics. There is almost a naïve expectation by ethics committees that the ethics process can anticipate and ensure mechanisms to deal with whatever may happen. They considered that social scientists borrowed from medical research which was required to have consent. Social scientists developed a system of self-regulation in contrast to medical research which established the principle of external regulation to act in the interests of research participants in the context of scandals such as Nazi research on human subjects. Miller and Boulton (2007) considered the various factors that have led to social science research also becoming increasingly regulated and these are outlined in Table 8.4.

Table 8.4 Factors leading to increased regulation (Miller and Boulton, 2007)

Factor	Description
Trust	There has been a decline in the trust placed in scientists and researchers, and this has been influenced heavily by the discipline of medicine and the scandals associated with it such as the Alder Hay hospital organs scandal.
Consumerism	There has been a growth in consumerism and our attitudes towards participants and research has been influenced by this change.
Professional dominance	There has been a challenge to professional dominance and a greater expectation of transparency and need for information.

These three factors have in turn led to a greater voice for participants in the research process. When aligned with the aforementioned consideration of children's rights in the research process and their rights to make decisions for themselves this has influenced important changes in the way in which children participate in interview research and the ethical issues that surround it.

Whilst Miller and Boulton (2007) agreed that interviews can and should be guided by good ethical motives and practice, each research encounter will be unique as will the understanding and practice of consent within it. They presented early examples of establishing 'genuine rapport' based on a sense of solidarity with the research participants but appear not to recognise the assumptions that the approach was based on.

Miller and Boulton (2007) argued that their own 'moral responsibility' has often guided their research practice rather than the verbal consent that was initially obtained. They did not however identify that the moral positions of researchers may differ. There may also be a difference between when the research topic is one that has been developed by the researcher or where the researcher

> **For example...** A researcher may make an assumption that a mother would inherently understand another woman, and particularly another mother.

may simply be carrying out funded research. That is not to say that morality is dependent on the position or role held but what drives the researcher may be. Miller and Boulton discussed the increasing recognition of the need for researchers to be more open and reflexive. They argued that even when formal consent is obtained it can be difficult for research participants to fully know what they are consenting to as different situations may emerge. Duncan et al. (2009) argued that the nature of qualitative research means that researchers may be recipients of unsought information. Qualitative research invariably involves humans who perhaps are more complex than other research variables. The research setting and the skills of the researcher may encourage disclosure as the researcher may create a comfortable and safe environment. Even if the research is thoroughly explained and it is clear that it is not a therapeutic process, participants may find it conducive to sharing more than they might otherwise have intended.

Miller and Boulton (2007) felt that changes in technology change the nature of the relationship between researcher and participant as the process of recruitment through email gives a false sense of an established relationship. They argued that this raises new questions about what the researcher is consenting to when they use an email to establish a research relationship as they may find themselves becoming part of the participant's social emails. They consider that the issue of using email to recruit may be a problem. Miller and Boulton (2007) concluded that while informed consent is often conceptualised as a one-off act and written consent may encourage that view, in practice informed consent includes weighing up risk, privacy and protection, safety and potential harm, trust and responsibility and demonstrating that this has been done in a systematic and auditable way. They called for better education for members of ethics committees and researchers as to the nature of qualitative research and the ethical frameworks within.

CONFIDENTIALITY AND ANONYMITY

A decision you make which has implications is whether you have the parent or guardian present during the interview, and we discussed the practical aspects of this in Chapter 5. Although participants may consent/assent to their involvement in the research it can be difficult for them to know what they are actually consenting to ahead of the interview. For children this is further complicated as in their interview they may disclose information that suggests they or another child may be 'at risk' (Kirk, 2007). In many countries including the UK, Iceland, New Zealand and Australia there will be a legal expectation that the researcher has to inform a relevant agency about the potential risk so that appropriate investigation can be conducted (we discussed safeguarding children and related policies earlier in the book). Thus, it is essential that any limits to confidentiality and what that means for the child in terms of safeguarding should be transparently outlined in advance of the interview, and again at the point of consent. It may be the case that the researcher is obliged to break confidentiality if child protection issues are raised.

Good practice in research would mean that at the outset the limits of confidentiality should be made clear as should how the information shared will be managed. If confidentiality does need to be broken there can still be a conversation about how this might happen. There is unlikely to be a dilemma about breaching confidentiality in clear cut situations where the risk is immediate and serious. The ethical dilemmas are more likely to arise when the risk is less clear or subtle.

However, the research interview should not become an investigative interview about potential harm or risk and it is important that the interviewer does not interrogate the child. In such cases the researcher should discuss with colleagues and junior staff need to raise the issue with their supervisors. The most ethical stance may be to weigh the pros and cons and then reach a conclusion and be able to justify the position taken and how it was reached.

For example… If the child reports being afraid of someone this in itself may not constitute an immediate risk, but without having more information it may be difficult to judge what action, if any, to take.

Interviewees may share information that might jeopardise their position in a particular system (DiCicco-Bloom and Crabtree, 2006) or make them identifiable through what they say. In the first instance there is a need to ensure that the information remains anonymous and protected from those whose interests may conflict with those of the interviewee.

> For example... Research taking place in a school about how a subject is taught may mean children identify poor teaching practice. Having that attributed to a particular child may jeopardise that child's position in that school.

In practice, even if a school commissioned the research, they should only receive anonymised data – children are less likely to be honest if they fear reprisal or being connected to a particular view. In the second example the researcher may need to consider what and how that information is shared. If anonymity has been granted it should be honoured. Sometimes even if young people waive their right to anonymity information should be carefully dis-

> For example... An interviewee may describe a particular incident which may because of the information provided mean that their identity could be deduced.

closed. The full implications of their identity being known may not be clear to the young person (O'Reilly et al., 2012). This is because it is impossible to consent for every possibility and Morse (2007) argued that qualitative research may carry greater risks than are perhaps realised as participants may be vulnerable and disempowered and yet the research context is an intimate one.

Interviews are unlikely to take place completely anonymously, in the sense that the interviewer is present and knows the identity of the child. There is unlikely to be anonymous data so it is likely that the researchers will know who provided the data and therefore have the responsibility of acting on any information which may need to be shared. This is in contrast to surveys which can be completed anonymously although children may have the option of self-identification. Knowing the participant boundaries can also complicate boundary issues and place the researcher in a position where they may need to act on information or advise the participant to seek advice or help. We recommend you now try to address the questions in relation to the vignette in Box 8.4.

▬ Box 8.4 ▬

Vignette – Pierre

Pierre is a psychology student studying for his BSc. For his undergraduate dissertation he has interviewed 12 children aged 11–15 years about exam stress and how they cope with it. The interviews generally went well but in one of them, the child hinted that they coped with stress by hurting themselves. However, when Pierre tried to explore this further, the child laughed and changed the subject. The child refused to answer any more questions about that and Pierre moved the interview on through other questions. Now that the interview is over Pierre is unsure what to do as he is concerned that there may be safeguarding issues but fears he may have misinterpreted the child or be overreacting to a 'throw away' comment.

- What should Pierre do?

Take a few moments to write down what you think Pierre should do.

A possible answer to this question can be found at the back of the book.

WHOSE DATA AND HOW CAN DATA BE SHARED?

In most countries there will be legislation and/or guidance about how research data should be managed. The protocol should clearly state how the data will be stored, who has access to it and why (given that information governance principles state that people should only have access to data because they need to for a specified reason). Researchers can be reluctant to destroy data especially as it is evidence of the research undertaken but it can be useful to review the data held on a regular basis and ensure that data is destroyed when it should be. It is also important to note that data stored on computers needs to be completely wiped and not just deleted when computers are changed.

An interesting ethical question is to whom does the research data belong? Researchers will often feel that it is their data, and institutions may argue it is theirs, whilst funders may believe they own the data. Some would argue that those who participated own it. As with most ethical issues there is no one single right answer. There is an argument that this may depend on the context as some data will be more personal than other data. For an example of when this becomes problematic see Box 8.5.

▬ Box 8.5 ▬

Research case example of problematic ownership

Cashmore (2006) gave an example of her own research in which children shared their views about their involvement in custody and access decisions following parental separation. Parents consented to the children's participation and children were assured confidentiality. A parent subsequently sought access to the interview data through a subpoena but this was declined by the courts on the basis that the information gathered was for research and not part of an assessment for court purposes.

However, note that this is not always the case and there have been instances whereby courts have put in place a subpoena for research data. A good example of this was the case of Boston College whereby interviews were conducted with the Irish Republican Army (IRA). In this case, as is usual in research, the individuals interviewed were assured of their confidentiality (Zezima, 2011) and yet recently in a USA appeals court it was mandated that the college must release some of the interviews (Giglio, 2012).

In terms of ethical research, it is worth identifying the benefits and disadvantages of any potential decision and bear in mind how key ethical principles may be affected. There are potentially important limitations to anonymity and confidentiality and these must be thought about carefully. There is no doubt that researchers have a responsibility to disseminate their research and share the findings to influence change where needed, but protecting the identity of the participants is important. However, it is also worth noting that there have been some tensions around the automatic provision of anonymity (Kelly, 2009) with some arguing that the automatic concealing of participants' identity without consulting them on the issue is in itself disempowering (Bass and Davis, 2002). This has led to some debates regarding whether participants might be given choices with regards to the concealment or revelation of their identity (Giordano et al., 2007). Of course when it comes to interviewing children there are more complexities within this debate than with adults. O'Reilly et al. (2012) explored whether data should be anonymised or not and whether young people should be given the option of having their contributions made public by asking a sample of children for their opinion. This is outlined in more detail in Box 8.6 below.

■ Box 8.6

Research case example of issues in anonymity

In a recent study (O'Reilly et al., 2012) children were asked directly what they thought it meant for their interviews to be anonymous, and were asked what they thought of having their identity revealed in the dissemination process. The children in the study were 8–10 years old and had identified mental health problems. The study highlighted that the children were able to articulate the meaning of anonymity and there was variability in their preferences. Some felt that using their real names was important, whereas others were more cautious. Parents were also generally more cautious, although some felt that identification may have benefits for the research.

O'Reilly, M., Karim, K., Taylor, H., and Dogra, N. (2012) Parent and child views on anonymity: 'I've got nothing to hide'. *International Journal of Social Research Methodology*, 15 (3): 211–224.

It is important to realise that some participants are more cautious in their approach to research than others. Some participants will only consent to participate in research if they are assured they will receive the script of their interview and made aware of how it will be used in dissemination. Children are less likely to make such a demand. The action may depend on the aims of the research. If the research is to identify how young people feel about a new intervention, there is perhaps little need to present the data as spoken and an argument can be made for it to be tidied up before it is presented (that is, the utterance, hesitations and incorrect grammar tidied up). However, if the research question is identifying how comfortable a family is addressing an issue, the hesitations and utterance take on a different relevance. In this case tidying up the data is likely to distort the data in a way which does not help the research outcomes to be met. There is the additional issue of individuals within groups taking different positions and how the waving of anonymity of one may impact on the others depending on what is shared.

While tidying up the script may be less problematic, there is the ethical dilemma of when participants want to change what they have said. As a researcher pragmatism and transparency are often useful tools. It may be acceptable to use the original statement but then say on reflection the participant changed their mind. If the methodology is that participants are to be given their scripts for review, it would seem unethical then not to take their revisions into account or anticipate that there may be changes. We can all regret what we say or how we have said something so it would seem a little strange to assume that what research participants say is unlikely to change. If we take the view that children are social actors and subject to developing and changing as a result of their experiences, it is possible that the research interview will change their perspectives. Between participating in the research interview and receiving the interview they may have changed and would not wish the previous position to be upheld. A way round this would be to state the context carefully and then be transparent about what was changed and why if the data is crucial. If the change is so significant there may be a need to discard the data but again it is important to be reflexive and transparent about this. Most research participants worry that they do not come across as 'stupid' and ill-informed so it is important that the data is not used to undermine individuals but to highlight what is said and to be transparent about the analysis. Ethical dilemmas are more likely to occur when the topics are controversial or highly emotive as both researchers and participants are humans and subject to emotions which are complex.

Pragmatically we would discourage identifying data as the decision to give up anonymity is permanent especially in the digital age. Events and circumstance may define young people for longer than they might want. Public owning of stories may be hard to move past. However, if a child has the ability to consent, the best approach may be to give them the arguments for both disclosing anonymity and for preserving it and then giving them the time and opportunity to discuss this with their carers and/or peers. An ethical approach would need them to be given sufficient time to reach a decision just as is expected for participation in a study. As is often quoted, just because someone does not agree with you, does not make their decision unwise. We are all allowed to make some decisions that appear to others to be foolish.

PROTECTION FROM HARM

A key responsibility of any potential researcher whose project involves working with 'human subjects' or people and especially children and other vulnerable groups, is to ensure that involvement in the project does not cause them harm. However, that does not mean that any project that may raise difficult or sensitive issues should be avoided in case it causes temporary distress. For researchers working with children – who by their very status as children are deemed 'vulnerable' – there are also many additional factors of vulnerability such as being looked after, having been abused and so on. Researchers have an ethical responsibility to ensure that there are processes to support those who participate in their research and may experience negative emotions such as guilt, reliving the experience, or anxiety about letting others down. The challenge is that some of this cannot be predicted as some emotions will be experienced at the time of the interview but some young people may not experience the 'negative' emotions until sometime after the research. The ethical stance may be to warn children about the potential emotions but perhaps also to normalise them.

The rationale is that if talking about the issues in an interview leads to such emotions, the issues are probably relevant and live for the child. The opportunity to talk about them may actually help them realise that they need to address them. Ethics committees are likely to view 'distress' as negative and such events are argued to need to be avoided.

> **Important point**: One of the authors works in clinical practice and would therefore also query whether it suggests that the young person would benefit from further time in a therapeutic context (but not necessarily mental health services) to address the issues.

In the research undertaken by Carroll-Lind et al. (2006) procedures were put in place to assist and follow up with children who chose to disclose harm or other problems in the course of their project. The project was exploring children's experience of violence so it is arguable that the researchers considered the likelihood that there needed to be a mechanism by which children could participate but also be supported. Thomas and O'Kane (1998) took a slightly different perspective. They felt that any disclosure would

> **Important point**: The clinical author would argue that experiencing distress may be the appropriate response and be the start of a healthy resolution of unaddressed issues.

be an inappropriate intrusion into the relationship between researcher and subject, but may be necessary in extreme circumstances of child protection. Thomas and O'Kane (1998) noted that it is important to facilitate children in accessing any support that they may need rather than taking over with decisions. This does however raise some questions about whether research can be carried out without a moral responsibility to those participating in research.

DIFFERENTIALS IN POWER BETWEEN THE RESEARCHER AND RESEARCH PARTICIPANT

This section considers the ethical aspects of the power differential between the research and research participant. Power is an issue that is central to the interviewing process and is a concept that we have visited in several chapters in the book. We return to this issue here in relation to broader ethical concerns in interview research.

There is no doubt that in most if not all societies the position of children in that society is decided by adults and as noted by many (for example Morrow and Richards, 1996) this in turn is reflected in the research process. This applies equally to the stage at which gatekeepers are involved and how the ethics committees decide that children can be approached. The onus and obstacles placed on the researcher may make it so difficult that the ethics committee has in effect reduced the opportunities children have to decide whether or not they want to participate in the research. Ironically most ethics committees are often unaware of these issues as they may place a higher value on 'protecting' children than considering the need to balance between protecting children and equally valuing the need for them to have opportunities to voice their perspectives. As identified above informed consent is a social construct; this applies equally to what constitutes protection, power and how these play out in practice.

SUMMARY

In this chapter we have considered the positioning of children and the ethical issues and dilemmas that may arise. We have considered the practical applications of the principles of ethical research – namely consent and capacity – and the relevance of confidentiality and anonymity in conducting ethical interview research with children. We have also discussed the relevance of safeguarding and managing this ethically as well as the importance of data protection. We conclude that ethical research interviewing requires the researcher to be constantly mindful about the application of ethical principles and the impact of this on the interview process.

RECOMMENDED READING

On consent

Carroll-Lind, J., Chapman, J.W., Gregory, J. and Maxwell, G. (2006) 'The key to the gatekeepers: Passive consent and other ethical issues surrounding the rights of children to speak on issues that concern them', *Child Abuse and Neglect*, 30(9): 979–989.

On anonymity

Duncan, R., Drew, S., Hodgson, J. and Sawyer, S. (2009) '"Is my mum going to hear this?" Methodological and ethical challenges in qualitative health research with young people'. *Social Science and Medicine*, 69: 1691–1699.

O'Reilly, M., Karim, K., Taylor, H. and Dogra, N. (2012) 'Parent and child views on anonymity: "I've got nothing to hide"', *International Journal of Social Research Methodology*, 15(3): 211–223.

On general ethics

Thomas, N. and O'Kane, C. (1998) 'The ethics of participatory research with children', *Children and Society*, 12: 336–348.

9

THE INTERVIEW ENCOUNTER – CHILD AND RESEARCHER FACTORS THAT WARRANT CONSIDERATION AND THEIR INTERACTION

━━ LEARNING OUTCOMES ━━

By the end of the chapter the reader should be able to:

- Recognise the relationship between the researcher and the researched.
- Critically assess the factors related to the child that influence the research process, such as age, intellectual disability, culture, family factors, language and feelings.
- Critically assess the factors related to the researcher that influence the research process.
- Identify the strengths of your interviewing skills and those areas that need development.
- Identify strategies to manage a difficult interview.
- Critically assess the interviewer's communication style.

INTRODUCTION

The focus for this chapter is on those factors that may influence your interview, both from the child and from you as the interviewer. We begin by discussing context and research topics as a way of setting the scene for the core issues at stake for discussion. The key child factors such as age and development, learning disability, cultural and family factors, language and feelings need to be considered in the interview context and these are outlined in relation to research. The interviewer factors that need attention follow. We present the factors separately for ease of discussion and for you to be aware of them although it is essential to remember that there is some overlap. In practice an interview is a highly complex encounter and we cover some situations when it may not go to plan.

We look at the asymmetry of the power relationship between child and interviewer and how this can be reduced. We conclude the chapter by identifying how you can develop and improve your interviewing skills.

CONTEXT

We begin by defining context and as we discuss this further the reason for understanding the meaning of context should become clear. The online Oxford dictionaries define context as:

> The circumstances that form the setting for an event, statement, or idea, and in terms
> of which it can be fully understood and secondly the parts of something written
> or spoken that immediately precede and follow a word or passage and clarify its
> meaning. Furthermore, in context means that information needs to be considered
> together with the surrounding words or circumstances. When something is taken out
> of context some of the information is missing and without the surrounding words
> or circumstances is not fully understandable. (http://www.oxforddictionaries.com/
> definition/english/context)

In considering the context in which the interview is occurring we are trying to account for all the different factors that may influence the process, the outcomes and the way in which the data are interpreted and made sense of. The context of the research will also indicate the generalisability or transferability of the findings. The definition above identifies the circumstances and/or the setting, but emotions are also an important factor to consider.

Irwin and Johnson (2005) raised the point that children may not always understand the context of the researcher–researched relationship. However, arguably it is questionable whether they need to fully understand the purpose of the relationship or the context of the relationship. Even very young children will be aware that the nature of relationships varies. As we pointed out earlier in the book, children of a young age (most anyway) will have relationships with parents, whom they know well and will understand that this relationship is different from the relationship they have with a teacher. Notably, they might not know why it is different or what about it is different, but they will know that it is indeed different. It is important that to engage young children in research, researchers remain mindful of ethical principles, such as having clear boundaries, not making promises and not pretending that the relationship is anything other than a short professional relationship. Evidently the social roles occupied in the interview are important for shaping its trajectory and process.

DiCicco-Bloom and Crabtree (2006) discussed the notion that in attempting to control for the social roles of the interviewer and interviewee, the research process is inherently oppressive. They argued that ignoring social differences neglects the fact that the respective social roles always shape the interview process and that the act of interviewing is invasive. For this reason, reflexivity from the researcher is essential whereby the researcher actively reflects on their role in the process and the influence that this may have.

Notably, the research participants (including children) are part of the active experience and knowledge is produced through collaboration (Hiller and DiLuzio, 2004). Hiller and DiLuzio argued that the research participant is not just a container that empties out relevant information, but a real person who may not have quick and/or ready answers yet may shift their responses depending on the position taken. They took the view that researchers are not neutral or objective, but they themselves are 'biographically situated' and bring factors such as class, race and gender into the equation. This reflects the 'culture' of the researcher as discussed further below. They argued that when the research interview is understood dialogically and when interviewees are encouraged to tell their story, the research interview can have much in common with a therapeutic interview. Both the researcher and therapist must:

- Be encouraged to listen.
- Demonstrate empathy and respect.
- Seek clarification.
- Confront the other with new thoughts.

Ideally interviewees in both contexts experience feeling valued, accepted and understood.

While the research interview's interpersonal dynamics may have much in common with the therapeutic interview the context and expectations are very different. It may be more acceptable to push for a response from a child in therapy to complete an assessment so that treatment can be initiated. Even if the child becomes distressed in the therapeutic context continuing may be necessary. This is however unlikely in the research context and may go beyond the boundaries outlined at the beginning of the interview and the ethical parameters laid out. Notably a context is a culturally and historically situated place and time, a specific here and now; it is the world as realised through interaction (Kortesluoma et al., 2003).

> **Important point:** It is important to remember that the research interview is different from the therapeutic interview, although there are some similarities. They differ in their purpose, but have some similarities in communication and engagement strategies.

After undertaking a literature review of methodological and ethical issues in conducting qualitative research with children and young people, Kirk (2007) concluded that there are similarities and differences between conducting qualitative research with children compared with adults. She considered that often the similarities are overlooked and the differences overstated. Health disciplines, she argued, could learn more about ethical considerations from social researchers, and indeed there is merit in this argument. It is interesting to note however that she did not comment on how social sciences may also learn from clinical contexts in which interviews with children take place on a daily basis. Indeed, there are useful recommendations in the literature for clinicians on how to interview children and some of those core recommendations are useful for the research context, although may require some modification.

There is no doubt that there are differences between the research and clinical context, but how the researcher sets the context of the interview is crucial and the lessons learned from therapeutic interviews can be useful here. Specifically, treating children with respect, listening carefully to what they have to say, reflecting back what they have said and so forth is valuable in the research interview. Staff familiar with clinical contexts, however, may need to watch that they are not as directive as they may need to be in a clinical context and thus it is essential that they consider the impact of having a dual role (researcher/clinician) and the effect that this may have (O'Reilly and Parker, 2014a). It is important that any health professional engaging in research does not simply treat the research interview as they would a therapeutic one.

> **Important point**: It is important to remember that there is a before and after to an interaction, which in itself influences the interaction.

In empirically based social sciences there is argued to be a continuous discussion about how to conduct qualitative interviews that induce informants to share as much and as accurate information as possible while simultaneously respecting their personal boundaries (Solberg, 2014). However, when it comes to children and childhood, the dominant discourse has been about the ethical issues addressing research relationships between children and adults. The focus is not on the quality of the verbal exchange. A key ethical issue is the power inequalities inherent in the relationship between an adult researcher and a child research participant. Two main approaches have developed: the first is participatory research, which serves to engage children and try and ensure the research has their voice as central and to try and share power; the second, which is usually expressed by ethical committees, emphasises the protection of young children and sometimes in very paternalistic ways. This was also discussed in Chapter 1 so you may want to revisit it with context specifically in mind. We suggest you now turn to the activity in Box 9.1.

━━ **Box 9.1** ━━

Activity on your experiences

Before we continue further reflect on your experience of interviewing by answering the following questions. It might be useful to write your answers down in your research diary.

- When have you undertaken interviews with young people?
- How did you find doing them?
- Which ones went well and what went well?
- Which ones were less successful and what made them unsuccessful?

We now turn to both child and researcher factors that may influence the interview process and outcomes as variation of the factors changes the context often in quite subtle ways.

TOPIC

Topic and context are linked. Some topics will be perceived to be more sensitive or have greater potential for distress from the outset and ethics approval committees will already have demanded that researchers anticipate the potential harm that may be caused to those participating and how the researcher plans to mitigate this or deal with it should it occur. However, as the interviewees are largely unknown to the researcher there is always the potential that even those topics deemed 'safe' may have different meanings for some participants. Gatekeepers may make paternalistic decisions and decide which topics they will allow young people to talk about (for example Carroll-Lind et al., 2006). Adults will sometimes feel that their actions are for the best interests for the child without really stopping to consider what factors may be driving their perspectives (that is, their own religious views or beliefs about gender equality may be driving their decision, but this is not reflected upon).

AGE AND DEVELOPMENTAL STAGE

The rationale for considering age and developmental stage together is because the two are linked. Whilst age may give an indication of the developmental stage a child is at, there is considerable variation of the development of children at the same age. It is therefore important not to assume that a child of a specific age will or will not be able to participate. The areas of development that are most relevant are cognitive and social development as these are most significant. However, development such as motor development may be important when non-verbal methods of communication are used as replacement or complementary methods of communication – for example, drawing or playing.

It is usually helpful to consider the following age groups; under-fives, 5–11 years, 11–16 years and 16–18 years. There are several similarities in interviewing those aged 14 and older, but the legal positions of those who are 16 and over are different to those under 16. It is worth familiarising yourself with cognitive child development (Dogra et al., 2009 offers a brief overview suitable for those new to the subject). Other texts offer more detailed accounts (for example, Smith et al., 2015) to help understand how children think and how to modify your communication with them. For the sake of convenience, we present an outline of the stages as described by Piaget (1950) below.

Piaget's stages of cognitive development in children

Piaget (1950) suggested that cognitive development depends on several steps and these are described in Table 9.1.

Piaget, through observations, identified four stages of intellectual (or cognitive) development and these are:

- *Sensorimotor:* Birth through ages 18–24 months
- *Preoperational:* Toddlerhood (18–24 months) through to early childhood (age 7)

Table 9.1   Cognitive development

Step	Description
Assimilation	This refers to relating new information to previous understanding of the phenomenon.
Accommodation	This refers to changing the prior understanding as a result of new information.
Adaptation	This refers to responding to new situations.

- *Concrete operational:* Ages 7–12 years
- *Formal operational:* Adolescence through adulthood

Sensorimotor stage: During the early stages, infants are only aware of what is immediately in front of them. They focus on what they see, what they are doing, and physical interactions with their immediate environment. As they develop between 7–9 months they learn about the permanence of objects (think of how much time can be spent playing peek-a-boo with a nine-month old baby!). This is when more obvious attachment to carers also begins as they are able to remember carers. The first eighteen months of life are when major motor milestones such as crawling, standing and walking are usually attained. Fine motor skills and speech (initially through babbling and then with words followed by sentences) develop.

Preoperational stage: During this stage (toddler through to age 7), young children are able to think about things symbolically. Their language use becomes more mature. They also develop memory and imagination, which allows them to understand the difference between past and future, and engage in make believe. Concepts such as cause and effect, time and comparison are not fully developed (although they will understand concepts such as big and small). In real life think how often children struggle to understand having to wait for something. During this phase, children are also very 'egocentric' in that they view themselves as central to the world. They often think that events happened because they wished for them.

> For example… If they hoped something bad would happen to someone who was mean to them and then that person had an accident they might feel they caused it, or they may believe they caused their parents to separate.

By the end of this stage children can take another's perspective and can understand the conservation of number.

Concrete operational stage: During the period from 7 to 12 years, children begin to show logical, concrete reasoning. They are less egocentric and increasingly more aware of the external world.

> For example… Think back to your school years and when you were asked whether the tall thin jar or the short fat jar held more water.

Hypothetical or abstract thinking is still not present for the vast majority of children, but they are able to understand conservation of mass, weight and volume. They are able to organise objects into series.

Formal operational stage: From about 12 years of age abstract thought develops and concepts such as algebra and science are now possible. Children can think about multiple variables in systematic ways, formulate hypotheses and consider possibilities. They also can ponder abstract relationships and concepts.

Piaget (1950) argued that all children go through the above stages in the same order, but the ages at which they are achieved vary from child to child. Whilst Piaget proposed these as step wise developments it is more helpful to see them developing on a continuum. Piaget's ideas have been of practical use in understanding and communicating with children and are still relevant today. Children may pass through the stages at different times. Piaget's assertion that cognitive development always follows this sequence, that stages cannot be skipped, and that each stage is marked by new intellectual abilities and a more complex understanding of the world have been challenged.

> For example… Children can be presented with a story and can easily identify other possible endings other than the actual one. They are able to see that there are various possibilities other than the one they were presented with.

There have been criticisms that development does not occur in discrete stages, but is a continuous process. There is also the question of social and cultural contexts, which may influence development and learning. Piaget relied heavily on his own interpretations which may have been biased to support his perspective. Keating (1979) reported that 40–60% of college students fail at formal operation tasks, and Dasen (1994) states that only one-third of adults ever reach the formal operational stage; challenging the notion that stages are completed by specific ages. Piaget viewed the formal operational stage as the final stage of cognitive development, and that continued intellectual development in adults depends on the accumulation of knowledge. How self-reflection and ongoing development fits with Piaget's framework is less clear. Whilst these are all valid criticisms the above still provides a useful framework especially for the context under discussion – which is communicating with children – and notably the theory has been a hugely influential one in our understanding of children.

> Important point: While the stage theory of Piaget remains a useful heuristic for understanding cognitive development of children it is important to remember that it is not without criticism.

Instone (2002) suggested that eliciting information from children should generally proceed from less threatening topics such as school or friends to more sensitive issues, such as concerns, fears or risk behaviours. However, for some children, school and peer relationships may not be as safe a topic as the researcher may think and so it is usually better to take your cues from the child as discussed below. The reasons young people participate in research will vary and some may choose to participate as it gives them an opportunity to explore the issue. However, if the research issue is about health issues it is important that the child understands that the research interview is not part of their treatment process, and if it is about educational issues that they understand they are not being tested like they might in a school environment.

Kortesluoma et al. (2003) warned against over simplifying concepts and questions. The art of the interaction is to pitch the questions and conversation at the right level for that particular child. Rephrasing what the child has said can be a useful way of checking that their perspective has been heard. As Irwin and Johnson (2005) identified, a key factor in successfully working with children is having a range of strategies to manage the unexpected. They made some key recommendations including:

- The interviewer should 'go with the flow' if it puts the child at ease.
- Be prepared that some children will ask questions and some will talk more than others during the interview.
- Some children will need more breaks than others and it is important to give these to the child when they need them.

Being flexible and letting the child make some choices can be productive for your research but also help the child have some say in the process.

Taking into account Piaget's work, we will now consider strategies to use with specific developmental stages and remember it is the developmental age that is more important for communication than the chronological age.

Under fives

Infants (children under two) are generally not interviewed due to the issue of verbal communication. There can be direct observations of them alone and/or observations of them with their caregivers (consider the research of Thomas and Chess, 1977, which used this method to develop types of attachment children have with caregivers). This may give you an indication of whether the child is responsive to the parents and how the parents manage the child. You may be able to observe that the child is frightened, there may be indications they are happy or content and so on. However, we can never truly know, as the child's perspective is only approximated through observations.

For children aged from 2–5 years old, play will usually be a significant part of the interview. There are a number of strategies you can use with this age group:

- When talking to them keep it simple.

> For example… When communicating with very young children it is important that you keep your sentences and/or questions short and simple. Use language that they can understand and do not over complicate your questions.

- Check that the child understands.

> For example… Try to check whether the child has understood the vocabulary you have used as within their own family there may be their own terminology that they know and use.

- Do not repeat yourself.

> **For example…** If the child appears not to understand rephrase the question rather than merely repeating. Repeating something they do not understand will not be helpful.

- Games can be very enlightening.

> **For example…** Typical games may be having a tea party, acting out scenarios (using figurines, cars, etc.) and puppet shows.

- Flash cards and prompts can be very useful.

> **For example…** It can be helpful to have picture cards or prompts in simple forms as these can help to encourage the child to chat with you.

However, keep in mind that previous exposure to all these methods will vary in children depending on their parents and how much they have used them in other contexts (refer back to Chapter 6 on participatory methods). Children may appear to have limited skills when the reality is that their skills have not been nurtured. Asking questions using the framework of time is unproductive if the concept of time is not one they have yet begun to understand.

Children 6–11 years

With children aged 6–11 the verbal skills should be improving, although some children, especially the young ones, may still need to be helped and you can use the strategies suggested as above. With this age group it can be helpful to encourage children to read stories and explain how they feel or relate to the characters as this can be a useful way into their worlds.

> **For example…** Children may say 'Elsa and Anna were sad because their parents have gone away' with reference to the Disney film *Frozen*. You might then say 'I wonder when you feel sad like Elsa and Ana.'

To ascertain what priorities children have, asking the children how they might use three wishes can often be very revealing.

> **For example…** You suggest that the child has three wishes and encourage them to let you know what those three wises might be, such as 'I wish I could fly' or 'I wish I had a puppy'. These can be a useful foundation for probing further questions around their lives.

In both of the young age groups discussed, asking children to draw pictures of their families can be an inroad into getting them to describe their drawing. Using jugs to show feelings may be more useful than asking them how they feel. This technique requires the interviewer to draw a jug and ask the child how far up the jug the child's feelings go.

> **For example…** You can say to the child, 'how happy are you today? If we were to fill this jug with your happy feelings how high up the jug would it go?'

> **Important point:** It can be helpful to engage people who know the child, such as parents or teachers, to ensure that the strategies you plan to use will be helpful to use with the child who will be in front of you.

This tends to be easier to use with this age group than a scale. As Christensen (2004) stated it is your responsibility as a researcher to fit into the child's world rather than expecting the child to understand yours.

12 years of age and beyond

For this age group there are so many ways of enhancing communication, but the challenge may be finding the best method that facilitates the research. Most, but not all, young people will be familiar with social networking, the internet and computers. Many are familiar with using the internet for educational and entertainment purposes. They may also be savvier than they are sometimes given credit for. Bone et al. (2015) found that young people said they wanted to use the internet to learn about mental health, but were aware of some of the limitations of information accessed from the internet.

Although most children in this older age group will be able to talk and are likely to have more sophisticated communication skills than younger children, it is important that you do not assume that traditional participatory methods, such as drawings and books, do not have some value. However, it is important to bear in mind that because they are older children the techniques used need to be utilised in a way that does not come across as childish and patronising. Music and films may also be useful tools to encourage them to share their views. Children in this age group may be more aware of the expectations of them. In a research context they may have greater say about their participation. Most are likely to be keen participants.

> **Important point:** Again remember that the legal position of those aged 16 years and over is different.

It is likely that young people in this age group can be interviewed alone for at least part of the interview. It is however appropriate to give them a choice if possible. Young people may show 'bravado' about some issues but it is important to remember that this may just be a way of managing anxiety.

INTELLECTUAL DISABILITY AND PARTICIPATION IN RESEARCH

Individuals with a learning disability may find it difficult to understand new or complex information, learn new skills and/or cope independently. A learning disability is not the same as a learning difficulty as the latter tends to be more specific. Children with mild learning disability or mild intellectual disability (with an IQ of between 50 and 70) may not have their disability identified. Children with moderate (with an IQ of between 35 and 49) or severe (with an IQ usually in the range of 20 to 34) and profound learning disability (with an IQ of under 20) are likely to be excluded from research because researchers may assume that they are unable to participate rather than considering how to make their participation more possible.

Lewis and Porter (2004) provided a range of questions for researchers to consider at every stage of the research process to ensure that the voices of young people with learning disabilities are heard and valued. To communicate effectively with children with learning disabilities they suggest researchers ask themselves the following questions:

1. Is the style of questioning appropriate for the participants?
2. Is the interviewer skilled in the specific skills of interviewing people with learning disabilities?
3. Is it recognised that multiple disabilities may involve difficulties associated with restricted communication channels, for example deafness as well as learning disabilities?
4. Are the implications for exploring views recognised?
5. Has consideration been given to utilising computer-mediated communication to access views?
6. Have narratives been preferred to question formats as much as possible?
7. Has consideration been given to using cue cards for facilitating uninterrupted narratives?
8. Have focused questions been preferred to either very specific or very general questions?
9. Has consideration been given to using various motor activities such as stepping on to a marker to assess a scale of responses?

Other disabilities and/or disorders

Children may have other disabilities or disorders that need to be taken into account. Rather than excluding them from research, ways to include them should be considered although this can be difficult if it incurs expenses as for unfunded or student projects there may be no resources available.

For children with speech impediments different provisions may need to be made available. It can be worth investigating with university, educational and health services' disability officers as to specific modifications or supports that may be locally available. Children with communication interaction difficulties such as autism spectrum disorder may not be obvious so interviewers need to be flexible. Many of the strategies to engage children may be ineffective with children who have autism spectrum disorder as they will often not be interested in what you need them to be. If you are carrying out interviews with groups of children, be aware that children may be self-conscious about themselves in front of their peers. This applies to all children.

CULTURE AND DIVERSITY

We introduced you to issues of culture and diversity in Chapter 7 and return to some of these here in more detail. There are several reasons diversity factors are important to consider as part of the interview research process, which include:

- Increasing understanding of the relevance of diversity factors on expectations of self and others.
- Our perspectives are coloured by our own cultures and experiences.
- Increasing diversity of society.
- Increasing acknowledgement that diversity matters.
- Increasing recognition of the need to ensure inclusion of marginalised and traditionally under engaged groups.
- Legislative frameworks (changed October 2010).
- We may think we are being fair to all but we may be subtly different with people with whom we more easily identify.
- If we do not check our own perspectives, our actions may be made based on assumptions we have made rather than the reality.

> For example… Younger children are less likely to challenge their family's religious beliefs than a teenager may.

In terms of interviewing children, it is important that you need to be aware of their sense of belonging, but also about how their parents view or feel about the issues being investigated and the processes used to explore them. Factors of diversity and their interplay with each other will influence how families' regard the views of children (and whether they even consider the views of children as relevant), participation in research, children being interviewed without parents being present, the topic under research and so on. As we have already discussed, our world views influence everything we do and how we see the world. This applies equally to children. As children grow up they are more likely to form their own views and may challenge the views of their families.

Children, as we discussed in Chapter 8, may need to have confidentiality clearly explained if they are going to give their views about issues which may not be accepted within their family. In other words, children may fear providing you with their views if they feel that their parents or teachers are going to have access to what they have said, and some reassurance may be required.

FAMILY FACTORS

Families, in terms of how they are structured and function, vary enormously and we discussed this in relation to family interviewing in Chapter 5. In many ways families are subcultures of their own. Before we go any further it is useful to reflect using the activity in Box 9.2.

━━ **Box 9.2** ━━

Activity on the family

Think about your own family and how someone from the outside might understand many of the things that are your 'normal'.

Within families, children may have specific roles so to partici-pate productively in a research interview you may need to give them the opportunity to change their roles. There may be guilt they feel that in voicing their views they are betraying their family. Depending on the context even safe topics can become

> **Important point:** As well as parenting, the way in which the family functions may also influence how the children communicate in the interview.

unsafe. Families are our first experience of the social world and our experience of them significantly shapes who we are. How children are parented can influence the way they see themselves and interact with the external world. The role of parenting is to adequately nurture the child and prepare them for adulthood (whether that is independent living or living in an adult role within an extended family depending on the cultural norms and expectations).

LANGUAGE

While language was covered in Chapter 7, it is also important in the context of this discussion. Spoken language is the most common way of communicating. However, depending on the characteristics of the study population different methods may be needed.

> **For example...** Sign language may be appropriate if deaf children are to be included.

Child-centred information should be available in a language and form that children can understand. This may mean their earlier involvement in the design of the research.

Some researchers have also warned against assuming homoge-nisation of any group including those who may fall into a group who, for example have experienced sexual abuse as this can be an imprecise term (see Carroll-Lind et al., 2006).

> **For example...** Carroll-Lind et al. (2006) provided an example of ask-ing children to define emotional violence as their study was about eliciting the meaning of emotional violence for them.

FEELINGS

The emotional state of both the child and interviewer at the time of the interview may be significant factors in how the interview plays out. If the child is angry or upset, you may struggle to have a productive encounter. This may be more relevant for younger children who are more unlikely to be able to put their feelings aside and continue.

If a child becomes distressed or upset, it is important to ask them if they wish to stop the interview. Sometimes they may say they wish to continue, but you may decide to stop it if you feel it is in the child's best interests to do so. It is important not to view this as ignor-ing the wishes of the child, but you as the adult taking responsibility. The child may feel they are obliged to continue because they signed a consent/assent form. There are unlikely to be any research situations in which it would be ethical to continue an interview which was distressing the child. However, a child crying does not necessarily equate to distress. If a child is crying because they are describing something sad, you may need to make a judgement call about whether or not to continue.

Finally, our own state of mind can strongly influence the outcome of the interview. If you have had a difficult day, you need to ensure you have unloaded any issues so that when you meet the child you are able to hear their story. If you cannot attend to the child it may be worth considering whether you should postpone the interview as a poor experience for the child may be difficult to compensate for. Being aware of your own issues and feelings is important so you can recognise the potential impact of these when you communicate with others including your research subjects.

RESEARCHER FACTORS

It is important to remember that the interview is a two-way reciprocal communication encounter. While we have considered the role of the child and the factors relevant to the child that may influence the interview, it is also necessary to bear in mind that you, the interviewer, will also have some bearing on the encounter. It is therefore important to think about the researcher factors that are relevant to the interview.

Experience and comfort

There is no doubt that having experience of interviewing children is likely to lead to greater comfort. However, less experienced researchers may be able to channel other factors – less experienced researchers may be younger so able to relate in ways that may be more difficult for older interviewers. This may be particularly relevant for some topics, for example, sex or drugs where talking to older interviewers may feel uncomfortable for children as it may feel too much like talking to a parent. Children and young people can be incredibly intuitive about false sincerity so it is best not to try and be someone you are not. Make sure the way you conduct an interview is congruent with who you are. If you plan to use a technique you have seen someone else use, it is usually worth letting the young person know so they can give you constructive feedback on whether it has been helpful or not.

MANAGING AN INTERVIEW

Arranging the interview and then preparing yourself for it are two of the main preparation steps of an interview as discussed in Chapter 7. However, the reality of the interview situation can feel quite different from how you imagined and therefore there are areas to consider when managing the interview itself and we deal with these each in turn.

Engaging with the child

As we said in Chapter 7, engagement is a crucial part of any interview. Reading Chapter 7 may give the impression that interviewing is an objective process that can be easily learned. It can be easy to forget that communication is as much an art as it is a science. It is easy to teach novice interviewers in any field the different stages of an interview, but it is less easy to teach them how to modify the interview as it happens, taking into account the verbal and non-verbal cues they may be getting from the interviewee.

There are particular stages of an interview that may be more crucial in terms of working with the interviewee. In the next section we focus on the function of small talk and how it can help bring the art and science of communication together and also help researchers work with diversity in a child-centred way.

The function of small talk

This can serve many functions but it can be awkward and uncomfortable for both parties if done badly. Modifying small talk routines to suit a diverse range of people is an incredibly useful skill to have. Some people are more naturally comfortable with small talk than others. Practice can make us more comfortable and competent even if it cannot make it entirely second nature. Perhaps reading this will encourage you to strike up conversation in a range of different contexts so that you begin to learn how to modulate your responses and how you can begin to recognise when you are making the other party comfortable or not (and sometimes this may be at the risk of increasing your own discomfort).

Small talk is a useful skill through which to engage someone and build rapport. It can be helpful to think of the other person's perspective rather than one's own nerves or discomfort. It is usually best to stick to safe and non-controversial topics such as the weather, their interests, asking about their journey to the interview or what is happening with the rest of the day. However, it is important to have a variety of topics so you can engage with a range of people. The skill is being flexible enough to know when to change gear or topic.

At this point in the chapter it would be useful to look at the personal case example in Box 9.3 where one of the authors reflects on her own clinical practice.

■■ Box 9.3 ■■

Personal case example

The second author (Dogra) is a child and adolescent psychiatrist and writes an example here from a personal practice perspective:

> I see young people ranging from 5 to 18 years old in my clinical practice and they often attend with their parents/carers. Many of them come in wearing football shirts with the football team logo printed clearly on the front. I will often ask about this as a starting point for small talk to engage them in

(Continued)

(Continued)

conversation but do not make the assumption they are necessarily football fans. I might say something like: *'Does the cool football shirt mean you are a fan?'* This gives the young person to engage with a conversation about football if it is of interest but also to just say no if they happen to be wearing it because it belonged to a sibling or was the only clean item in their wardrobe or was the first thing they picked up that morning. Talking about football just because you have a male patient in front of you might go horribly wrong because contrary to popular belief not every male does like football.

The same applies to T-shirts/sweatshirts with names of music groups – some of whom are no longer known to me! The point here is I am taking my cues from the child about what might be of interest to them but not making assumptions about them. Over the years I have learnt how to be me in a variety of ways that fits the clinical role I need to fulfil. In some ways small talk with children can be easier as they are often less constrained by social expectations. However, the small talk also serves a useful function – not only do I find out about what matters to the young person, I am able to ascertain their level of understanding and the language I might need to use to engage further with them.

MANAGING DIFFICULT INTERVIEWS (THE HOSTILE, AGGRESSIVE OR NON-COMMUNICATIVE CHILD)

However well prepared and practised you are there is always the possibility of things going wrong or the interview being difficult. If adults responsible for the child or the young person have forgotten about the interview it may be more productive to rearrange rather than try and squeeze it in if the child feels unprepared. This may of course be more difficult if you have travelled for the interview and making sure the interview is still expected before you set out may reduce this possibility.

As we mentioned earlier in the chapter, the use of drawings and/or play as a way of understanding what is important to children cannot be overstated. Giving them the freedom to choose what they want to draw or asking them to draw something and talk you through it can tell you much about how they understand the world. A drawing early on can also serve as a quick developmental screen – ask the child to draw themselves or a parent and then ask them to write their name on their art work (Dogra and Baldwin, 2009). In a relatively short space of time you will be able to gauge their developmental level, their familiarity with pen and pencil and how they hold a pencil. It is a very good indicator of the level you need to pitch your interview and conversation at.

Hostile children and/or uncommunicative children

A further difficulty is that the child may be hostile or aggressive during the interview. Consider the difficulties of managing a hostile interview in Box 9.4.

▬ Box 9.4 ▬▬▬▬▬▬▬▬▬▬▬▬▬▬▬▬▬▬

Vignette – Cameron

Cameron is doing his MSc in criminology and decided to interview young offenders about family life and their perceptions of the role of the family in their criminal behaviour. Having got through the difficult ethical process and finding a helpful gatekeeper Cameron has successfully interviewed eight young offenders and is on interview number nine. During this interview the young female adolescent begins to get rather agitated and looks unwell. She is sweating slightly and seems to be losing focus. She is no longer answering his questions and has her arms folded across her chest. Cameron continues with his questions, but she starts to pace the room.

- What should Cameron do?

Take a few moments to write down what you think Cameron should do.

We suggest some answers to this at the back of the book.

There may be several reasons for a child behaving in a hostile manner or being non-communicative. They may not feel they really want to participate in the research. Between arranging the interview and meeting the child circumstances may have changed. It is worth spending a little time clarifying whether they are uncommunicative because they do not want to participate in the research at all or just at that particular time. If there is any indication that they are not willing participants it would be unethical to continue. This is because there may be a very fine line between gentle persuasion and coercion. They may be anxious or worried so explaining the research process may be helpful if they do not clearly indicate that they do not wish to participate.

Aggressive children

If a child appears to be becoming aggressive or irritated, it is worth suspending the interview to consider whether it is safe to continue or not. If you as a researcher feel unsafe stop the interview as carrying on whilst fearing for your safety will not result in a good interview (we discussed researcher safety earlier in the book). If potential interviewees have a history of aggression or violence, consider the risks and how to mitigate them ahead of the interview. If you are dealing with young people with such histories, consider where it will be safe to interview them. Interviews at home are unlikely to be a viable solution.

> For example… A child starts to raise their voice. You notice that they also appear more agitated. Rather than continue you might want to say, 'You seem to be getting upset. I would suggest we stop or take a break?' This in itself may deescalate the situation.

> Important point: Remember no research project is worth putting your safety at risk!

DEVELOPING YOUR OWN COMMUNICATING AND INTERVIEWING STYLE

As you develop your interviewing skills, consider which aspects of good practice you have observed that you can incorporate into your style. It is rarely effective to simply 'copy' someone else, as people, including children, can tell whether your communication is genuine or forced. Interviewing is a skill that requires continued refinement even if you are quite experienced. As you learn, you will inevitably make mistakes, but this is an important learning opportunity if you are prepared to reflect and change your practice. It is helpful to identify if the research interview will raise any issues for you and how this might impact on the way you interview.

> For example… If you are interviewing children who have experienced the loss of a parent and you have also experienced this, the interview might be more challenging for you.

Practising talking with children in non-research contexts will help you develop a conversational style which is always a useful skill. It ensures that the research 'subject' is enabled to feel more comfortable and thereby talk more freely. It can also be helpful to talk to children across the age spectrum as that enables you to learn how to more quickly gauge how to pitch your vocabulary at a developmentally appropriate level. If your project aims to collect data from children from a specific age group, then ensure you have had some practice with the relevant age. However, keep in mind that age is a rough guide as to what to expect from children, but there will be a range of developmental levels. The variation may be more evident in younger age groups. As well as developing your interviewing skills, it is important to develop complementary communication skills such as using drawings and toys to facilitate children communicating. Again practice helps.

In clinical contexts practitioners in training are often encouraged to video themselves interviewing (having of course ensured consent from the patient) and identify their communicating skills and areas for development. This can be more challenging in research contexts as projects may be short-term and have limited budgets. However, you can be creative and consider friends and family members who may be able to help. Even in these cases remember to consider consent and capacity issues to ensure the integrity and transparency of the process.

SUMMARY

In this chapter we have explored the importance of the context of the research project and the research interview. We have then considered child and researcher factors that can influence the research interview. The most important child factors for the research interview are age and development but other factors also influence how the child will participate. There is some overlap between child and researcher factors as the culture and feelings of both the parties ultimately influence the interaction that takes place. Children, as adults, are hugely diverse and the researcher increases their chances of a successful interview if they treat each child as a unique individual about whom they are genuinely interested. They are more likely to get a better reflection of the child's perspective if they do not make assumptions but treat the interview as an exploration. The child is more likely to find it a productive experience if through that exploration they have an opportunity to gain insight, share their experiences and perhaps help make a difference.

RECOMMENDED READING

On child development

Dasen, P. (1994) 'Culture and cognitive development from a Piagetian perspective', in W.J. Lonner and R.S. Malpass (eds), *Psychology and Culture*. Boston: Allyn and Bacon.

McLeod, S.A. (2015) *Jean Piaget*. Available at: www.simplypsychology.org/piaget.html (accessed 14 December 2015).

Smith, P.K., Cowie, H. and Blades, M. (2015) *Understanding Children's Development*. Chichester: John Wiley and Sons.

On children and socialisation

Macoby, E.E. and Martin, J.A. (1983) 'Socialisation in the context of the family: Parent–child interaction', in P. Mussen and E. Hetherington (eds), *Handbook of Child Psychology, Volume 4: Socialisation, Personality and Social Development* (4th edn). New York: Wiley. pp. 1–101.

On understanding children

Dogra, N., Parkin, A., Gale, F. and Frake, C. (2009) *A Multidisciplinary Handbook of Child and Adolescent Mental Health for Front-line Professionals* (2nd edn). London: Jessica Kingsley Publishers.

10

ANALYSING CHILDREN'S INTERVIEWS

■■ LEARNING OUTCOMES ■■■■■■■■■■■■■■■■■

By the end of the chapter the reader should be able to:

- Recognise and critically assess the different analytic approaches for interview data with children, including thematic analysis, template analysis, grounded theory, IPA, narrative analysis, DA and CA.
- Evaluate the usefulness of using NVivo as a coding tool for analysis.
- Recognise the need for congruence between data collection methods and analytic approach.

INTRODUCTION

Data analysis is an important part of the research process and interview data can be subject to a range of different analytical approaches. In this chapter we focus on some of the most common approaches to analysis of the interview data and consider how children's voices might be considered throughout this process. We provide practical guidance for conducting this type of work and introduce you to these key approaches. We include thematic analysis, template analysis, grounded theory, interpretive phenomenological analysis, narrative analysis, discourse analysis and conversation analysis (recognising that conversation analysts prefer naturally occurring data and thus analyse naturally occurring interviews). Additionally, we provide some guidance on the use of computer software in assisting with coding, such as NVivo. There are many different approaches to qualitative analysis and these are tied to different theoretical perspectives and we conclude the chapter with some critical discussion of the necessity for congruence throughout the research stages.

THEMATIC ANALYSIS

Thematic analysis is probably the most common form of qualitative analysis used with interview data and is sometimes combined with content analysis. Thematic analysis is frequently used by researchers wishing to provide an overview of the salient issues raised by interviewees, as well as being used by those who are new to qualitative analysis and who are learning the basic skills of coding and reporting themes. Thematic analysis is an epistemologically flexible method and this means that it is compatible with a range of differing theoretical positions. This does not mean that it is free from an epistemological base, but does mean that it can be adapted to suit most of the theoretical positions available in qualitative research (see O'Reilly and Kiyimba, 2015 for an overview of these).

The reason why thematic analysis is so popular is because it is a useful method to organise data in meaningful ways through the identification and analysis of patterns within the data (Braun and Clarke, 2006). This means that you will be able to make some simple interpretations regarding what is going on in your data (Boyatzis, 1998). Thematic analysis is commonly used with child interview data (Joffe and Yardley, 2004) as it can capture the issues that are perceived to be relevant and important from the child's perspective. Furthermore, it is a relatively simple method with a clear strategy for coding and analysis. Thus you will need to strategically code your data and then break it down into key themes that reflect the core concerns of your participants.

> Important point: A theme is a category that captures something important in your data and reflects what your research question was seeking to address (Braun and Clarke, 2006).

There are a series of simple steps you can follow for thematic analysis and these are outlined in Table 10.1.

There are therefore several benefits of using thematic analysis to analyse interview data with children:

- All aspects of the child's narrative can be given full attention.

The coding framework of thematic analysis allows you to give each response in the interview full attention. The whole interview is coded and thus the child's voice is given full attention and nothing important is missed out.

- It is theoretically flexible.

This means that you can identify your personal theoretical position at the beginning of your research and adapt the techniques to fit in with your views of children and childhood.

- It is a useful approach for exploring similarities and differences across participants.

There is a great diversity across child populations and using the coding strategy of thematic analysis will enable you to explore some of the similarities and differences in responses. You are not able to correlate variables but you may be able to indicate if themes are more common in specific groups of your sample.

- It is an accessible and easy to understand approach.

Table 10.1   Practical steps in doing thematic analysis

Step	Description
One	Remind yourself of your research question as this should guide the coding process and re-familiarise yourself with the data by listening again to the actual interviews. As you listen to the interviews you should also read through the transcripts and highlight anything of interest as it arises.
Two	Once you are fully familiar with your data and the associated transcripts it is time to start the coding process. According to Boyatzis (1998) there are three levels of coding: • First order coding – this requires you to code all of the data, more or less sentence by sentence. This is a descriptive level and will result in a great number of codes as the whole data set is subjected to this process. • Second order coding – this requires you to capture larger segments of the data by grouping your first order codes together into more meaningful categories. • Third order coding – this is an organisational level of coding as you collapse your categories into more meaningful themes/patterns. This means you will be identifying the salient issues at stake for the participants.
Three	You now need to make your thematic coding more meaningful and review your research question. Once the three levels of coding are complete you need to consider which of the identified themes are most pertinent to your research question. You are likely to have several general themes identified from the main data set and you will not be able to report them all, so decide which ones are most relevant or useful for the context of your research.
Four	The themes you have identified as relevant to your research question are likely to reflect quite broad issues and so the next step is to identify the key issues within each theme, in other words the sub-themes that are relevant to your analysis.
Five	You are now ready to actually start your analysis. The organisation and coding of the data is central before you can begin this phase. At this point you need to organise your themes and their sub-themes into an appropriate order and identify the analytic narrative that you wish to report. You will need a clear and critical analytical argument to present that addresses the research question.
Six	Once you have organised your analytic narrative and have a sense of the points you want to make, you will need to select quotations that support that argument. Remember that you should not select quotes to be sensationalist or because they appeal, but because the quotes support your argument (that is they are research evidence to support an argument).
Seven	The final step, which should be iterative as opposed to occurring at the end of the process, is reflexivity. As you are developing your coding and analysis it is important to note down your feelings and decisions in your research diary and reflect on the impact you have on the analytic process. This process also ensures that you look at the whole data set and not only those parts that may resonate with you

Due to its identification of salient issues and patterns in the data, thematic analysis is an approach that is easy to understand and thus means that the findings from the interviews will be accessible to a range of different audiences.

It is of course important however to recognise that there are some limitations to this approach and you may need to think about the best ways of mitigating these in your research. Sometimes interviews with children can produce a large volume of data and organising this in a meaningful way can be challenging. It is possible that you may end up with a huge coding framework that is difficult to make sense of and break down into more sensible categories and later into themes. Furthermore, remember that thematic analysis is predominantly a descriptive method that describes the salient issues at stake in the data, therefore any interpretation is merely speculative and it is difficult for you to go beyond description with this approach. We provide some reading in Box 10.1.

■ **Box 10.1** ■■

Reading on thematic analysis

If you plan to use thematic analysis for your interview data, then it is important that you undertake some additional reading:

- Braun, V. and Clarke, V. (2006) 'Using thematic analysis in psychology', *Qualitative Research in Psychology*, 3: 77–101.
- Joffe, H. and Yardley, L. (2004) 'Content and thematic analysis', in D. Marks and L. Yardley (eds), *Research Methods for Clinical and Health Psychology.* London: Sage. pp. 56–68.

We also recommend that you read some research that has used thematic analysis to see how this has been used and reported in practice. We make two recommendations below but it is a good idea to seek out some that explore the research area that interests you:

- Bone, C., O'Reilly, M., Karim, K. and Vostanis, P. (2015) '"They're not witches…": Young children and their parents' perceptions and experiences of Child and Adolescent Mental Health Services', *Child: Care, Health and Development*, 41(3): 450–458.
- Bourke, S. and Burgman, I. (2010) 'Coping with bullying in Australian schools: How children with disabilities experience support from friends, parents and teachers', *Disability & Society*, 25(3): 359–371.

TEMPLATE ANALYSIS

Template analysis is not a single method of analysis and actually refers to a group of techniques that are designed to thematically organise data. Template analysis is a form of thematic analysis and like thematic analysis utilises hierarchical coding, but this type of analysis balances some degree of structure with the flexibility for adaptation to the study at hand (Brooks et al., 2014). Template analysis is a particularly useful approach for interview data, although it has also been used for focus groups, internet blogs, open-ended questionnaires and diary extracts. Template analysis is epistemologically flexible and can be used from most of the different theoretical positions, but does advocate the need for a clear philosophical position to be taken (King, 2004).

When undertaking a template analysis, it is important that you organise your data in a meaningful way. To do this you need to start developing a coding template which summarises the key data (King, 2012). Thus, your analytic process will start with some a priori codes which are expected to be relevant for analysis, and these are refined as you develop the themes. The goal of template analysis is to create a template which forms the basis for the interpretation and identification of relationships between the different themes (King, 2004). The approach of template analysis is therefore flexible in terms of the style and format of the template produced (Brooks et al., 2014).

> **Important point**: Although template analysis has many similarities with thematic analysis it is a different approach (Brooks et al., 2014).

It is important to be clear regarding the differences between thematic analysis and template analysis and we list these below:

- For thematic analysis the identification of themes is driven by the data and this identification takes place after data collection. However, for template analysis, some of the categories are pre-determined by the research agenda (O'Reilly et al., 2013a).
- For thematic analysis the development of the coding structure and themes takes place after an initial coding process, but for template analysis it is usual for an initial version of the template to be produced on the basis of a sub-set of the data (King, 2012).
- For thematic analysis the themes are defined in a late stage of the analytic process but for template analysis the initial template construction will guide further coding and template refinement (Brooks et al., 2014).
- For template analysis a predetermined coding schedule and coding manual are designed, but this is not the case for thematic analysis (O'Reilly et al., 2013a).
- For thematic analysis there are not specified limits to the number of levels of coding, although typically there are only one or two levels of sub-themes, but it is common for template analysis to use four or more levels to capture the rich and detailed aspects of the data (Brooks et al., 2014).

The process of undertaking a template analysis is relatively straightforward and again there are a series of simple steps you can follow which are outlined in Table 10.2, as adapted from Brooks et al. (2014) in their article on the approach.

> **Important point**: Be careful not to produce your initial template too early! You will need to account for your methodological position as some approaches encourage openness and you will need to take longer developing your initial template than if you are addressing a specific question (King, 2004).

There are therefore several benefits of using template analysis to analyse interview data with children:

- It allows you to make sense of data.

This approach to analysis will allow you to organise the interview data in a meaningful way, even if you have carried out a large number of interviews with children and young people.

- It allows you to remain active in the process.

Table 10.2   Practical steps in doing template analysis (Brooks et al., 2014)

Step	Description
One: Familiarity	It is important to first familiarise yourself with your interview data. You should listen to your data several times and become familiar with the participants' accounts. Alongside this read through the transcripts.
Two: Coding	Preliminary coding is required at this point and this is similar to other thematic approaches to analysis. You should begin to highlight parts of the transcript whereby there is a potential contribution to understanding. You may start with some a priori themes that have been derived from your research agenda and the interview schedule.
Three: Organising	The emergent themes from the data now require some organisation into meaningful clusters and these themes need to be defined in terms of how they relate to one another within and between groupings. You will need to include hierarchical relationships with narrow themes embedded within broader ones.
Four: Defining	At this point in the coding it is necessary to define your initial coding template. This is the template developed on the basis of a subset of your data before you can define your thematic structure.
Five: Modifying	Once you have your initial template this needs to be applied to more data and modifications should be made if these are necessary. At this point you need to examine new data and consider whether any of the themes you defined in your initial template can be used to represent it. If the existing themes do not fit with your new data, then you will need to modify your template.
Six: Finalising	While there may never be a final version of the template per se as continued engagement with the data will probably suggest further refinement, practically you will have to make a decision as to when the template has met your needs for your particular project and when it has addressed your research question.

This approach means that you stay active in the whole analytic process which means that you are able to work with a team of researchers in the creation of the template while maintaining a particular role in the template development.

- It highlights important issues.

The use of this approach means that you can tease out the most salient and important issues from the children's perspectives and this can be important in informing policy issues.

- You can go beyond description.

To some extent you are able to go beyond description with template analysis and make some interpretations based on the template that you have created. These interpretations will be important for the narrative argument that you disseminate and for the ways in which you include the children's voices and perspectives through using direct quotations from the data.

It is of course important to recognise that there are some limitations in using this approach and that you are mindful of how these influence your project. Remember that when using template analysis, it can be quite difficult to choose which codes to look for in the data. Selecting appropriate codes, particularly in the initial stages, is crucial to the development of the template. It can be difficult to ascertain this from the literature and your research agenda. Also be mindful that by going beyond descriptions of the data you may open yourself up to criticisms from others. We suggest some reading in Box 10.2.

■■ Box 10.2 ■■■

Reading on template analysis

If you plan to use template analysis for your interview data, then it is important that you undertake some additional reading:

- Brooks, J., McClusky, S., Turley, E. and King, N. (2014) 'The utility of template analysis in qualitative psychology research', *Qualitative Research in Psychology*, 12 (2): 202–222.
- King, N. (2012) 'Template analysis', in G. Symon and C. Cassell (eds), *Qualitative Organizational Research: Core Methods and Current Challenges*. London: Sage. pp. 426–450.

We also recommend that you read some research that has used template analysis to see how this has been used and reported in practice. We make two recommendations below but it is a good idea to seek out some that explore the research area that interests you:

- Ferguson, K. and Heidemann, G. (2009) 'Organizational strengths of Kenyan NGOs serving orphans and vulnerable children: A template analysis', *International Journal of Social Welfare*, 18: 354–364.
- Ray, J. (2009) 'A template analysis of teacher agency at an academically successful dual language school', *Journal of Advanced Academics*, 21(1): 110–141.

GROUNDED THEORY

Grounded theory is a qualitative methodology designed for exploratory investigations (Charmaz, 1995). This approach emerged from the collaborative work of Glaser and Strauss (1967) who aimed to develop an inductive approach with the goal of developing an explanatory theory of social processes in the environments in which they took place. More recently different versions of grounded theory have been developed with an aim to also understand the multiplicity of interaction (Heath and Cowley, 2004). Importantly, grounded theory promotes an iterative cyclical process whereby you need to engage in simultaneous data collection and analysis (Charmaz, 2000). The process of the approach is to identify and integrate categories within the data (Willig, 2008) and to use constant comparative analysis, which means that you have to go back and forth between data to look at the similarities and differences between categories (Charmaz, 2006).

Overall therefore the function of grounded theory is to generate theory, and in order to do this you need to progressively move through your data to identify and integrate categories.

> **Important point:** Remember that in this approach you use the collection of one interview and its analysis to help refine and undertake the second interview and so forth.

Because you continue to collect data at the same time as analysing the data, due to the iterative nature of the approach, you will need to use the marker of theoretical saturation to know when to stop recruiting your child participants. We considered the issue of sampling adequacy and saturation in Chapter 5, and you may find it useful to refer back to that at this point. For grounded theory theoretical saturation means that you have sufficient data to generate the theory and nothing new is being identified from the data.

The process of undertaking grounded theory requires a series of practical steps and these are outlined in Table 10.3.

Table 10.3 Practical steps in doing grounded theory

Step	Description
One: Revisit the literature	The first step you need to take when doing grounded theory is to look at the evidence base on the subject matter. Reviewing the literature should be done concurrently with data collection and analysis. At this stage you should consult the notes you took during the interview (a grounded theory interview style requires that you take notes as you listen to the participant).
Two: Begin your coding	It is expected at this point that you have completed one interview and so coding can now begin. It is useful to take the transcript while you listen to the data and code line-by-line, sentence-by-sentence to identify any important points or issues.
Three: Conduct the second interview and continue coding	You can now undertake your second interview and refine based on what you have discovered so far. It is now important to start coding the second interview and identify important categories and assign labels that are meaningful. You can also start your constant comparative analysis as you now have two interviews conducted. Continue interviewing and coding until you reach theoretical saturation. It is important to record any connections between your categories by writing memos.
Four: Identify the core category	Once you have reached theoretical saturation and have completed coding and constant comparative analysis, you can identify your core category. This is the category that has emerged frequently. Be careful not to try and identify this too early in the process.
Five: Connected categories	It is useful to code for other connected categories to the core categories.
Six: Develop the theory	Develop the theory that has emerged from your core category and write up your findings.

There are therefore several benefits of using grounded theory to analyse interview data with children:

- You are able to immerse yourself in the data.

Due to the nature of the approach and the constant comparative design you can become fully immersed in the data as you go along, becoming familiar with the children's voices.

- The approach provides rich detail.

Because of the close attention to detail, the systematic coding process and the identification of a theory, the project will produce a rich and detailed account of the children's perspectives, opinions or feelings.

- A grounded theory analysis is systematic.

This approach has a clearly demarcated and systematic approach to coding and analysis, meaning that there is a clear method for you to follow.

- Allows for some creativity.

Grounded theory is an approach that allows you some freedom to be creative throughout; this is because it does not rely on prior assumptions.

- It is a mechanism for generating theory.

One of the important aspects of research is that it can pose questions and theories and these can be tested using other methods. It is important to remain inquisitive in research and generate new ideas and new knowledge.

As with other methods of data analysis, there are some limitations to using a grounded theory approach for your interviews. It is quite a complex qualitative approach and if you are new to this then it may feel quite overwhelming and you are likely to benefit from some formal training. Do not underestimate how long it will take you to undertake the open coding process as this can be time-consuming. Also, do not forget that there are multiple approaches to grounded theory with differing theoretical assumptions and slightly varying tools for analysis and we have only provided you with a general overview here. It is therefore advisable to learn more about the different types of grounded theory approach if you plan to use this for your research. You may want to refer to Hussein et al. (2014) for an in-depth discussion of the advantages and disadvantages of this approach. We suggest some reading in Box 10.3.

▬ Box 10.3 ▬

Reading on grounded theory

If you plan to use grounded theory for your interview data, then it is important that you undertake some additional reading:

- Charmaz, K. (2006) *Constructing Grounded Theory: A Practical Guide through Qualitative Analysis*. London: Sage.
- Glaser, B. and Strauss, A (1967) *The Discovery of Grounded Theory: Strategies for Qualitative Research*. Chicago: Aldine Publishing Company.

(Continued)

(Continued)

We also recommend that you read some research that has used grounded theory to see how this has been used and reported in practice. We make two recommendations below but it is a good idea to seek out some that explore the research area that interests you:

- Connors, P., Bednar, C. and Klammer, S. (2001) 'Cafeteria factors that influence milk-drinking behaviors of elementary school children: Grounded theory approach', *Journal of Nutrition Education*, 33: 31–36.
- Karlsen, M., Coyle, A. and Williams, E. (2014) '"They never listen": Towards a grounded theory of the role played by trusted adults in the spiritual lives of children', *Mental Health, Religion & Culture*, 17(3): 297–312.

INTERPRETATIVE PHENOMENOLOGICAL ANALYSIS

Phenomenology is an approach that studies people's experiences (Smith et al., 2009). It is important however to note that interpretative phenomenological analysis (IPA) is one of the commonly recognised ways of doing phenomenological analysis, but that there are other ways. This approach was pioneered by Smith and was influenced by the philosophical work of Heidegger and Husserl. The main aim of IPA is to explore in depth the personal lived experiences of participants to examine how they make sense of their own experiences (Smith, 2004). It emphasises that knowledge gained through research should reflect the participants' perspectives. According to Smith (2004) there are three central characteristics of IPA:

1. It is idiographic, in that it starts with a detailed examination of one case before moving to the next.
2. It is interrogative, in the sense that it shares some constructs with mainstream psychology.
3. It is inductive, in the sense that the techniques are flexible.

Researchers using IPA tend to favour interviewing as the most appropriate method of data collection as this allows for 'thick description' of the participants' experiences (Sokolowski, 2000). However, when undertaking interviews the style must be consistent with the approach and the interviewer is required to 'bracket off' their own assumptions of the world and adopt a detached position (Wimpenny and Gass, 2000).

> Important point: Remember that in the interpretive tradition of phenomenology there is a particular interest in the life-world of the participants.

The process of undertaking IPA requires a series of practical steps and these are outlined in Table 10.4.

Table 10.4 Practical steps in doing IPA

Step	Description
One: Familiarise yourself with the data	You will need to be familiar with your data and the corresponding transcripts so go back and listen to the interviews a couple of times. While you are listening it is useful to write down any ideas or feelings that you have and note down any broad themes that you think are emerging. You need to go through each of the transcripts systematically to look for meanings and make notes in the margins. At this stage this can be quite descriptive.
Two: Identify key issues of interest	You now need to go back through your transcripts and identify issues and quotations that are relevant to your phenomenon of interest. Highlight anything at this stage that looks interesting and identify any similarities and differences between your participants. At this stage you should try to identify any connections between the themes that you are identifying and start to identify sub-themes.
Three: Produce a table	At this stage in the analytic process it is helpful to produce a table of the themes and write down any actual quotes from the interviews that support those themes. The themes you identify should be grounded in the data and any themes that cannot be evidenced should be abandoned.
Four: Identify evidence of the four core concepts	IPA has four central concepts to facilitate the process of analysis and at this point you should go back through the data to explore these: 1) temporality – the experience of time; 2) spatiality – the experience of space; 3) intersubjectivity – experiences of relationships with others and social groups; and 4) embodiment – the experience and connection with one's own body.
Five: Finalise the themes and reflect	You are now ready to develop your final list of relevant themes. These should encapsulate the experiences of the participants and report their life-worlds clearly. You need to develop these themes in a way that addresses the research question and you should reflect upon how your own preconceptions may have influenced the process.

There are therefore several benefits of using IPA to analyse interview data with children:

- There is some creativity to the approach.

IPA has an interpretative element which provides you with some creativity when collecting and analysing the data (Willig, 2008).

- IPA takes an in-depth approach.

The depth of the approach means that you can become immersed in the child's life-world and pursue interesting and important issues that they raise during the interviews.

- IPA is participant-focused.

This approach focuses in on the participant and therefore it provides you with a mechanism for being child-centred and exploring the experiences from the child's own point of view.

- Small sample sizes are sufficient.

The depth of IPA means that you will achieve a large volume of in-depth data from only a small sample of children. However, you then need to be careful about how the findings are applied to a wider context.

- IPA recognises the dynamic influence of the researcher (Brocki and Wearden, 2006).

This approach recognises that the interviewer has an important role in gaining information about experiences from children and asserts that the interviewer plays an active position in the research process.

It is of course important to recognise that there are some limitations to IPA as an approach to analysing children's interviews. The depth of the approach will make it a time-consuming form of analysis (and data collection) and therefore it is important that this is planned for. This depth also means that you may miss out important contextual details, particularly if you are new to the approach so it is advisable that you have an expert available to help you through the process. Although IPA uses small sample sizes so that it can focus on depth, this has been a source of criticism by some and it can be difficult to show transferability of your findings. This is a fairly complex approach to analysis and so it is advisable to undertake some specialist training before considering it for your work. While focused on health research particularly, and not specific to children, you may nonetheless find the review of IPA studies by Brocki and Wearden (2006) useful for learning more about IPA and its advantages. We suggest some reading in Box 10.4.

■■ Box 10.4 ■■

Reading on IPA

If you plan to use IPA for your interview data, then it is important that you undertake some additional reading:

- Smith, J. (2004) 'Reflecting on the development of interpretative phenomenological analysis and its contribution to qualitative research in psychology', *Qualitative Research in Psychology,* 1(1): 39–54.
- Smith, J., Flowers, P. and Larkin, M. (2009) *Interpretative Phenomenological Analysis: Theory, Method and Research*. London: Sage.

We also recommend that you read some research that has used IPA to see how this has been used and reported in practice. We make two recommendations below but it is a good idea to seek out some that explore the research area that interests you:

- Back, C., Gustafsson, P., Larsson, I. and Berterö, C. (2011) 'Managing the legal proceedings. An interpretative phenomenological analysis of sexually abused children's experience with the legal process', *Child Abuse and Neglect*, 35: 50–57.
- Griffiths, M., Schweitzer, R. and Yates, P. (2011) 'Childhood experiences of cancer: An Interpretative Phenomenological Analysis approach', *Journal of Pediatric Oncology Nursing*, 28(2): 83–92.

NARRATIVE ANALYSIS

Narrative analysis was pioneered by Labov in the early 1970s and this approach to analysis focuses on the ways people use stories to interpret the world. Thus narrative analysis is an approach to analysis that recognises that people tell stories and this provides insight into their lived experiences and how they understand their social worlds (Thorne, 2000). Narrative analysis is a systematic approach to narrative data (Riessman, 2008) and sees storytelling as a normative human activity (Crossley, 2000).

Like many of the other qualitative approaches to analysis, there are different types of narrative analysis and Riessman (2008) outlined the four most common:

1. Thematic narrative analysis which focuses on the content of the narrative.
2. Structural narrative analysis which focuses on how the narrative is conveyed and the structural features of the narrative.
3. Dialogic narrative analysis which takes a broad interpretative approach and pays attention to reflexivity.
4. Visual narrative analysis which focuses on images and how they can be interpreted with participants.

Overall narrative analysis sees narratives as interpretative devices that people use to represent themselves and their worlds to others (Riessman, 2008).

The process of undertaking narrative analysis requires a series of practical steps and these are outlined in Table 10.5. However, be aware that there are different types of narrative analysis and each of these follows a slightly different trajectory. Thus, what we present is a rough overview and an oversimplification of the main steps, and not a systematic guide. We recommend that you identify and attend some specialist training on this approach before attempting to use it for your research.

> Important point: Remember that there are many different types of narrative analysis and these each have a different focus and way of doing analysis.

There are therefore several benefits of using narrative analysis to analyse interview data with children:

- There is a holistic presentation of the child's experiences.

Table 10.5　Practical steps in doing narrative analysis

Step	Description
One: Consult the literature	It is important that you are familiar with the literature on both your topic of interest and on narrative analysis before you begin the process.
Two: Identify the stories	You need to go through your interviews and identify the stories that are told. Often the stories will develop naturally during the interview and you need to decide what does and does not constitute a story. There are likely to be many stories told in each interview and you need to highlight all of them.
Three: Reduce the stories	You need to systematically go through each child's narrative to reduce each of the stories they have told to a set of elements that reveal important issues or events in the child's experiences.
Four: Identify the common elements	Looking at the different children's interviews, try to identify the common elements to develop cross-case comparisons (see Garaway, 1996). Look for patterns or themes, as well as contrasts in the data.
Five: Develop the 'story map' for each child	You should now attempt to develop the story map for each story that is part of the research (Richmond, 2002). This means that you need to organise the accounts of the past and present experiences and potential future intentions in relation to the character, setting, events, themes and outcomes (Richmond, 2002).
Six: Be reflexive	Although reflexivity is iterative and should be practised all the way through the analysis, it is important to remind yourself to actively reflect on the process.

A focus on narratives allows you to present the child's experiences holistically as opposed to separating them out or narrowing them down into categories.

- It brings to the fore unnoticed experiences.

By using narrative analysis, you will be able to examine experiences that the child may not be consciously aware of themselves.

- Language is studied in context.

This approach means that language is studied in context which gives you some control over the context and its influence when you are engaging in the analytic process.

- Rich and interesting data.

The focus on narratives and stories means that you will be provided with rich and interesting data which can emerge through the process of interviewing children.

- Narratives are common.

Children are used to telling stories about their lives; it is a natural and common way in which they convey their experiences. As the process is more natural, the data collected through narrative methods may be richer but also more complex.

It is of course important to recognise that there are some limitations to using narrative analysis to analyse your child interviews. Remember that this form of analysis is particularly time-consuming and specialised. You will need some assistance from an expert if you are going to do this form of analysis effectively and you will need to make sure that you have sufficient time available for this phase of the research. As you will be doing your interviews with children their ability to tell stories will relate to their cognitive and literacy abilities, so while children are generally familiar with telling stories about their lives, the scope of this is likely to depend on their chronological and developmental age. Also, there are some potential ethical issues in encouraging children to tell their stories effectively and in depth as it will require some deeper levels of rapport with the researcher and if not carefully managed this can be misleading for some children. We provide some reading in Box 10.5.

■■ Box 10.5 ■■■■■■■■■■■■■■■■■■■■■■■■■■■■■■■

Reading on narrative analysis

If you plan to use narrative analysis for your interview data, then it is important that you undertake some additional reading:

- Crossley, M. (2000) *Introducing Narrative Psychology: Self, Trauma and the Construction of Meaning.* Buckingham: Open University Press.
- Riessman, C. (2008) *Narrative Methods for the Human Sciences*. Thousand Oaks, CA: Sage.

We also recommend that you read some research that has used narrative analysis to see how this has been used and reported in practice. We make two recommendations below but it is a good idea to seek out some that explore the research area that interests you:

- Foster, J. and Hagedorn, B. (2014) 'Through the eyes of the wounded: A narrative analysis of children's sexual abuse experiences and recovery process', *Journal of Child Sexual Abuse*, 23(5): 538–557.
- McAdam, J. (2013) 'Coping and adaptation: A narrative analysis of children and youth from zones of conflict in Africa', in C. Fernando and M. Ferrari (eds), *Handbook of Resilience in Children of War*. New York: Springer. pp. 163–177.

DISCOURSE ANALYSIS

It is challenging to conceptualise discourse analysis succinctly to provide a brief introduction to the approach as there are many different ways of doing discourse analysis (henceforth DA) (for a more detailed account see Lester and O'Reilly, 2016). DA is actually an umbrella term (Harper, 2006) and one that refers to a qualitative approach characterised as attending to talk and text as social practice (Potter, 1997). The basic premise of DA is that through language, speakers or writers accomplish tasks, such as offering advice, inviting another individual, complaining, and so on. DA is characterised by a commitment to studying discourse as social practice and there are some features that are common to the different approaches:

1. There is a focus on language – both spoken and also utterances and the subtle nuances used in conversation.
2. There is a focus on the ways in which accounts are constructed.
3. There is an acknowledgement that there is variability in the ways people construct their accounts.

Before you can consider undertaking a discourse analytic study it is important that you appreciate the different types of DA that exist. There is great diversity in the DA approaches, with approaches operating from different theoretical perspectives and engaging in different practical steps. Some DA approaches attend to the structure of language and consider how this structure functions to create a particular understanding of the phenomenon while other approaches are more descriptive, focusing on the performative functions of language, and other approaches are fundamentally critical (Lester and O'Reilly, 2016). It is therefore not possible to offer a simple description of the 'steps' or procedure for conducting a discourse analysis as this is dependent upon which approach to DA you adopt. Instead of offering a practical table with a process of doing DA, we offer one that outlines the different approaches to DA so that this can inform your understanding of the approach and guide you to other sources for practical procedures. We provide a brief overview of each of these in Table 10.6.

> Important point: Remember that there are many different types of discourse analysis and these are underpinned by different epistemological assumptions.

There are therefore several benefits of using discourse analysis to analyse interview data with children:

- DA is applied to talk *and* text.

DA is an appropriate form of analysis regardless of the type of interview that you conduct as it can be used on talk-based interviews or text-based ones. This means that it is suitable for Instant Messenger and email interviews as well as face-to-face or telephone ones.

- DA is able to generate new insights.

DA is a useful approach for generating new and novel issues that arise from interactions with children.

Table 10.6 Different types of discourse analysis

DA approach	Description
Sinclair and Coulthard's discourse analysis	This has also been referred to as the Birmingham model and was informed by the work of Sinclair and Coulthard (1975) on classroom discourse. They noted that classroom talk followed a fairly rigid and institutional structure. They described their model of DA as a tool for studying classroom interactions but it has since been utilised in other settings. This form of DA uses a ranking scale to describe the nature of the discourse (Sinclair and Coulthard, 1992).
Traditional discourse analysis	While this version of DA is rarely referred to as a specific model of DA, this was an early inception of the approach and was grounded in ethnomethodology and social constructionism, and was bought to academic attention in the works of Potter and Wetherell (1987). This form of DA uses three core concepts:
	1. Interpretive repertories: These are the common sense ways in which people talk about the world. In other words, they are the cultural explanations, arguments and accounts that people draw upon in conversation.
	2. Subject positions: These are the discursive ways of locating one's identity and the identity of others by using adjectives or categories to position people in a particular way (for example, 'good father'). Identity is viewed as fluid and produced through discourse.
	3. Ideological dilemmas: This was a concept developed by Billig and his colleagues (1988) as a way of relating to the fragmented and contradictory nature of everyday common sense. These are used as flexible rhetorical resources to illustrate the dilemmatic nature of interaction.
Discursive Psychology (DP)	This is an approach to discourse analysis developed by Edwards and Potter (1992) and was generated due to an interest in the way mental states are reported, suggesting that mental states are themselves social actions. DP is an approach that has provided a general critique of cognitive theory and thus has focused on the way in which speakers make cognition relevant, such as invoking memory states. DP aligns with conversation analysis and considers the way in which matters in conversation are a social accomplishment.
Interactional sociolinguistics	This involves an analysis of power within linguistic practices and considers the ways in which particular linguistic features are produced for a specific context. This form of DA recognises that common grammatical knowledge may be mobilised in different ways by different ethnic or social groups. This form of approach to the study of language therefore looks at the patterns of language as a system.

(Continued)

Table 10.6 (Continued)

DA approach	Description
Bakhtian Discourse Analysis	This form of DA is grounded in the work of Bakhtin (1981). Bakhtin argued that when people speak they contribute to meaning making in a fluid way and that each utterance is formed in response to another's utterance. Bakhtin noted that language is a mechanism for operationalising the struggles around power and ideology and in this form of DA there is an explicit focus on social conflict and ideology.
Critical Discourse Analysis (CDA)	This version of DA grew from linguistics, semiotics and other forms of DA. For those practising CDA there is a focus on researching social processes and social change and there is an explicit focus on social and political issues. Thus, the primary focus for CDA is in the production of power within social structures. Researchers using this approach are concerned with how language functions to sustain and legitimise inequalities in society (Wooffitt, 2005).
Foucauldian Discourse Analysis (FDA)	Stemming from the work of Foucault, this form of DA analyses how discourse informs and shapes an understanding of the world and has a focus on understanding political and social relationships. FDA focuses on the ideological underpinnings of the dominant discourses that have shaped the ways in which we think about the world (Wooffitt, 2005). Thus, FDA focuses on how people are positioned in society and how they take up or resist these positions. FDA was also shaped by the work of Derrida (1981) who noted that the structuralist notion that meaning is always constructed through a system of signs means that each meaning is constructed in relation to something else.

- All of the approaches to DA are systematic.

Each of the different versions of DA has a systematic and rigorous procedure and so quality is built into the approach.

- Analysis is grounded in the data.

The claims you make about the children and/or phenomenon of interest will be empirically grounded in the data which promotes trustworthiness of analysis.

It is of course important to recognise that there are some limitations to using discourse analysis with child data. It is important to appreciate that not all forms of DA are congruent with interview data that is not naturally occurring. For example, DP tends to favour data that is not generated by the researcher for research purposes, but instead occurs naturally in the world. Other limitations are more conceptual in the sense that the similarities and differences between the different DA approaches can cause some confusion, particularly to those new to the approach. It is a complex method for those new to research to use. We recommend some reading in Box 10.6.

■■ **Box 10.6** ■■

Reading on discourse analysis

If you plan to use discourse analysis for your interview data, then it is important that you undertake some additional reading:

- Potter, J. and Wetherell, M. (1987) *Discourse and Social Psychology.* London: Sage.
- Wooffitt, R. (2005) *Conversation Analysis and Discourse Analysis: A Comparative and Critical Introduction.* London: Sage.

We also recommend that you read some research that has used discourse analysis to see how this has been used and reported in practice. We make two recommendations below but it is a good idea to seek out some that explore the research area that interests you:

- Ghaill, M., Mac, M. and Haywood, C. (2012) 'Understanding boys: Thinking through boys, masculinity and suicide', *Social Science and Medicine*, 74(4): 482–489.
- Heydon, G. (1997) 'Participation frameworks, discourse features and embedded requests in police VA.T.E. interviews with children', *Monash University Linguistics Papers*, 1(2): 21–31.

CONVERSATION ANALYSIS

Broadly speaking Conversation Analysis (henceforth CA) is the study of talk-in-interaction (Schegloff, 1987) and is an approach that aims to identify the ways in which talk is sequentially organised and the way in which members of any given interaction make sense of the talk that is unfolding. For those practising CA there is a focus on the structure of conversational turns, which are referred to as 'turn construction units' whereby the turn is recognised by both speakers as being incomplete until the speaker has finished the turn (Sacks et al., 1974). Thus, the central task of CA is to examine the social organisation of activities that are produced through talk (Hutchby and Wooffitt, 2008).

For conversation analysts it is essential to collect data that is considered to be naturally occurring (Hutchby and Wooffitt, 2008) as this reflects the underpinning relativist ontology of the approach. In CA there is a distinction made between mundane conversation and institutional talk. Mundane conversations are those that occur in everyday face-to-face or telephone interactions whereas institutional talk is that which has an institutional purpose and typically takes place in institutional contexts (Wooffitt, 2005).

> **Important point:** It is argued by many to be only plausible to undertake conversation analysis on naturally occurring interviews due to the ontology underpinning the approach.

The process of undertaking conversation analysis requires a series of practical steps and these are outlined in Table 10.7 and were proposed by Drew (2015). We recommend that you identify and attend some specialist training on this approach before attempting to use it for your research as it is a skilled approach to analysis that requires some expertise.

Table 10.7 Practical steps in doing conversation analysis (Drew, 2015)

Step	Description
One	The conversation analyst must start by considering the fact that speakers are not simply talking, but actually they are engaging in some form of social activity. For you, this social activity will be an interview. So the first step in the process is to make some notes where you identify what the speaker is 'doing' with their talk. Is the child or adult complaining, inviting, justifying, excusing, asking and so on.
Two	For the conversation analyst it is the interaction that is interesting and therefore each speaker's turn is in response to a prior turn. At this point you need to look at how the previous speaker's turn initiated the action in the current speaker's turn.
Three	It is now important that you look at how that previous turn has initiated a particular social action and you should look at how the activity you have identified has arisen as part of the sequence.
Four	It is now important that you examine how the recipient responded to the prior turn of the initial speaker. You now need to look at what the participants are understanding from the previous speaker's turn.
Five	At this point you can identify the social action that interests you. You will have explored the ways that individuals have managed their activities and how that was constructed through what people are saying.
Six	This is a more implicit stage whereby although every interaction is unique, there are systematic properties of the talk and these can be identified by the analyst.
Seven	Now you have identified a social action of interest you need to explore the sequential pattern by collecting a series of cases of the phenomenon of interest to look at the features each case has in common.
Eight	The final stage is for you to provide an account of the identified pattern and this means you need to be clear about what the collection of cases has in common and where and how the pattern arose in the data.

There are therefore several benefits of using conversation analysis to analyse interview data with children:

• Analysis is grounded in the data.

Like with DA the claims you make in CA are grounded in the data. In other words, it is the actual talk of the children and their co-participants that forms the basis of the analytic claims that you make.

• CA has depth.

Because of the micro-approach to analysis the process has depth and you can explore in depth the children's contribution to the interview.

• CA is precise.

The approach is a very precise analysis that explores the details of the conversations.

• CA is systematic.

CA is considered to be a scientific approach to analysis and has rigour. It has its own quality markers and is a systematic and rigorous approach to data.

It is of course important to recognise that there are some limitations of the approach. To enable you to perform your CA effectively you will need to ensure that the recording is of high quality. This may not be a problem if your naturally occurring interview is from the television or newspaper, but if you are recording interviews in natural situations such as child witnesses being interviewed by police, or children being interviewed by social workers then good quality recording equipment will be essential. It is also important not to underestimate the time it takes to perform a good CA. The specialised transcription system (Jefferson method) is highly detailed and you will need to become familiar with it. Furthermore, estimates indicate that one minute of audio-recording will take one hour to transcribe using this specialised system (Roberts and Robinson, 2004), and potentially longer for video-recordings. We suggest some reading in Box 10.7.

■■ **Box 10.7** ■■

Reading on conversation analysis

If you plan to use conversation analysis for your interview data, then it is important that you undertake some additional reading:

- Drew, P. (2015) 'Conversation analysis', in J. Smith (ed.), *Qualitative Psychology*. London: Sage.
- Wooffitt, R. (2005) *Conversation Analysis and Discourse Analysis: A Comparative and Critical Introduction.* London: Sage.

We also recommend that you read some research that has used conversation analysis to see how this has been used and reported in practice. We make two recommendations below but it is a good idea to seek out some that explore the research area that interests you:

- Stokoe, E. (2010) '"I'm not gonna hit a lady": Conversation analysis, membership categorization analysis and men's denials of violence towards women', *Discourse and Society*, 21(1): 59–82.
- Suoninen, E. and Jokinen, A. (2005) 'Persuasion in social work interviewing', *Qualitative Social Work*, 4(4): 469–487.

USING NVIVO

There are now a range of qualitative software programmes available for the organisation of data to assist the coding process of which NVivo is the most well-known. This programme is designed to help you manage large qualitative data sets. However, it is important to recognise that NVivo does not do the analysis for you in the way a statistical programme might; rather it facilitates the coding process (Bryman, 2008).

You will need to make a decision whether to use NVivo or a similar programme to organise your data. If you have a small data set and a short time frame, then it is probably not worth doing as manual coding will be sufficient. However, if you have time to undertake some training and your data set is quite large then you might decide to attend a specialised training course to learn the basics.

The function of NVivo is to help you organise your data in a manageable way as by importing your interview transcripts into the software you are able to address the process of coding. You can view the transcripts in NVivo and go through each sentence in the transcript to assign codes (these are called Nodes in NVivo). You can organise the quotations from the transcripts into labelled folders and organise your data into general broad codes and sub-codes. This is suitable for many forms of qualitative analysis that require you to code your data as part of the analytic process. NVivo has many useful functions and will allow you to print out the data that you have assigned to a specific code so you only view that part of the data.

There are some useful resources available to help you learn about this software and two books are recommended below:

- Bazeley, P. (2007) *Qualitative Data Analysis with NVivo*. London: Sage.
- Gibbs, G. (2002) *Qualitative Data Analysis: Explorations with NVivo*. Buckingham: Open University Press.

THE NEED FOR CONGRUENCE

It can be easy to assume that a qualitative interview is a straightforward and generic task. However, as we pointed out in Chapter 3 there are many types of interview and while structured, semi-structured and unstructured are a general heuristic, the picture is actually more complex. Although generic qualitative research is an approach and would generally utilise a straightforward semi-structured design, it is important that you address the issue of congruence in your interview research. Generic qualitative research is that which is not explicitly guided by an epistemology and generally these types of interview studies are restricted to thematic or template analysis because of their epistemological flexibility (Caelli et al., 2003). The style and trajectory of the interview, however, should ideally be shaped by the perspective and approach being utilised. We provide some examples below for clarity:

Example 1… In grounded theory data collection and analysis are concurrent. In other words, as each interview is conducted the analysis is developed further so that the analysis informs the following interview. This iterative process means that interview questions and style may change slightly as data collection progresses. This helps to build the theory. Also, grounded theory requires that you take notes during the interview process.

Example 2… Narrative interviews do not engage in the traditional question and response format per se, as they encourage children to tell their stories in their own words. Refer to Chapter 3 for more detail.

Example 3… Interpretative phenomenological interviews (IPA) require considerable depth as the interview probes the life-world of the participants. Questions are designed to explore temporality and spatiality and are shaped in a way that ensures the core concepts of the approach are maintained. Typically, small samples are used as depth is favoured. Additionally, the role of the interviewer is seen as critical to the interview and interviewers are expected to 'bracket off' parts of the self (Wimpenny and Gass, 2000).

Example 4… Conversation analysis favours naturally occurring data and would draw upon interviews that occur as part of real world tasks, such as news interviews, police interviews and social worker interviews with children.

SUMMARY

In this chapter we have introduced you to the more common forms of data analysis for qualitative interview research with children. In each approach we have provided information about the analysis as well as providing some practical guidance for conducting that form of analysis. Within each approach we have explicated the benefits and limitations. Additionally, we have provided some useful information about computer software and cautioned about the need for congruence. Before you can apply any of these methods you will need to undertake further reading so that you do justice to your data.

RECOMMENDED READING

For this particular chapter we have provided recommended reading within each section rather than putting it all at the end here.

11

REFLECTING AND ATTENDING
TO THE PROCESS

■ LEARNING OUTCOMES ■

By the end of the chapter the reader should be able to:

- Recognise the relationship between reflection, ethics and data collection.
- Recognise the iterative nature of qualitative research.
- Evaluate the relevance of ethics in interview practice.
- Critically assess how the facets of the research come together to form a project.

INTRODUCTION

In this concluding chapter we review the contents of the book to consider how the elements of the interviewing process come together to make a cohesive project. We then move to consider the need to reflect on the interview process and assess how the process may influence the research outcomes including interpretation of the findings as well as dissemination. This is particularly important for qualitative research which typically has reflexivity as part of the quality mechanisms. Thus the chapter will broadly cover reflecting on the interview process and considering the interview in the context of the overall project. The need for the researcher to be reflexive and constantly attend to the ethical and other debates about children and their place in research is highlighted as we revisit some of the essential messages from Chapter 8 particularly and other ethical messages that have been considered in other chapters. The way the data is written up and disseminated is reviewed and this includes the application into practice of the findings from interview research. This can be particularly important for applied interview research and for research conducted to inform a particular discipline.

OVERVIEW OF THE BOOK

We began this book by considering the importance of interviewing children in the research context. Much of how we approach research with children including research that involves interviews is dependent on our views of children and the part they play in society. This is likely to be influenced by many factors and as a reflexive researcher you need to be aware of those factors most relevant to you. These factors and your philosophical position in turn influence the way you design your study and your use of interviews as the research method for data collection.

The book then moved on to consider some of the theoretical aspects of interviews. It is important to consider the type of interview selected and ensure that it is the best method for most appropriately answering the research question. Economic considerations are more likely to be a factor as to whether interviews are carried out face-to-face or whether other methods are employed. Again the question you need to be asking as you make your decision is whether the approach or method used is the best one to answer the research question. We noted that congruence between your perspectives and the methodological decisions you make is important to the overall coherence of your project (O'Reilly and Kiyimba, 2015).

As we mentioned predominantly in Chapter 6 the use of participatory methods is on the increase but they need to be carefully applied and not simply used because of the chronological age of the child participants you are interviewing. Researchers need to be careful not to make assumptions about children and what they may or may not like. Just because one child enjoys using glitter glue and creating pictures, does not mean that the next child you interview will have the same enthusiasm for that technique. Remember that some children may find the use of participatory methods inhibiting rather than encouraging. Children are individuals and good research should be tailored so that their needs are met, enabling them to be effective participants.

The theoretical stages of an interview were introduced. In the research process the flexibility available to the researcher is dependent on whether the interview is structured, semi-structured or unstructured and in Chapter 3 we illustrated that although this is a useful heuristic for conceptualising interviews, there are indeed many other types of interview which do not fit into those neat categories. Indeed, the nature of the interview itself can encourage more reflection on the process (Roulston, 2010).

With children as your participants it is important to bear in mind when planning interviews their development stages as well as various other factors to ensure that the interviews are set up to collect the best data possible. We discussed the ideal context when the researcher can build a relationship with the interviewee over time. In practice this is not often possible. There are many different things that may prevent you from spending so much time with your participants in advance of the interview.

Remarkably although interviews are widely used there is relatively little information on their structure. Thus we also discussed the process of an interview and the potential challenges that may arise. At this stage you should also be considering how you are going to share your findings with your research partners including those that were interviewed. This is important in the process of analysis and the choice of analytic methods you employ. Remember that if you are to feed that analysis back to your young participants it will be necessary to consider the language that you use to do so in order that the findings can be meaningful to that audience.

THE INTERVIEW AS PART OF THE OVERALL RESEARCH

It is important that the research interview is viewed in the context of the overall research. The quality of the interview is crucial for the data collected, but will only be useful if the research question was well defined in the earlier stages of the project. Of course in qualitative research the development of a research question is an iterative process and it is shaped and changed as the project evolves. Remember that this process is not only acceptable but desired, but that the question should drive the decisions made and these decisions should be reflexively revisited.

Interviews can be exploratory to help define the research question for a larger scale project and in these cases should then be part of a pilot project. Researchers should avoid 'fishing trips' – where interviews are undertaken in the hope they will yield something of interest. It is unlikely that projects with unclear aims would receive ethics approval. The interview process needs to be considered throughout but it is only a part of the project. At the planning stage you should already be anticipating the potential issues that might arise throughout the project and how you would address them, including data collection through interviews.

ETHICS IN PRACTICE

The ethics chapter (Chapter 8) discussed the principles of ethical research and the particular challenges that pertain to working with children given the vulnerable status they are usually afforded. This can mean that gatekeepers take on a paternalistic role and in their attempts to protect children from potential harm they actually deny children a voice. The very nature of ethics means that there are very few issues with 'black and white' options, but many grey areas. We highlighted in that chapter the need to be reflexive and to discuss ethical issues widely to continue learning. Even when a project has ethical approval, the responsibility to review whether to continue an interview remains with the researcher. Being an ethical researcher requires attending to the debates about the positioning of children and how this impacts on their potential participation.

In practice researchers can take polarised positions and regard their perspective as child-centred. All positions will have their strengths and limitations. Giving children equal power in a relationship may sound child-centred and aligned with a rights-based approach to research, but it is not if it leaves a child feeling unsafe or uncontained. Evidently it is important to balance children's rights and autonomy with keeping them safe from harm – psychological, emotional or physical. It may sound child-centred to promise the child that you will not betray any confidence and that you will keep everything they say confidential and anonymous. However, this is not legally or morally acceptable if it leaves the child exposed to potential abuse or harm and in some cases the interviewer may have a responsibility to breach confidentiality and inform the appropriate services if the child is at risk. Pragmatically, rarely is it helpful to take an extreme position and different children because of their diverse experiences will take different meanings from the same situations. Interactions between people cannot be predicted with certainty so interview research projects are always going to be prone to throwing up the unexpected. Expecting the unexpected may go a long way in helping you prepare effectively.

REFLECTION AND REFLEXIVITY

All professional practice these days requires some degree of reflection and reflexivity and this applies equally to the practice of research. Dewey (1933) saw reflection as a further dimension of thought, and as such we are in need of education – 'while we cannot learn or be taught to think, we do have to learn to think well, especially [to] acquire the general habit of reflection' (1933: 140). He defined it as 'active, persistent and careful consideration of any belief or supposed form of knowledge in the light of the grounds that support it and the further conclusions to which it tends' (1933: 118). As Vaughan summarised, reflection is 'as much a state of mind as it is a set of activities' (1990: ix). Reflective practice can help bridge the gap between theory and practice, help manage uncertainty and attain critical awareness. The process of reflection helps identify possible solutions to a problem or a dilemma or alternative explanations. It involves conceptualising a situation as a problem and then producing hypotheses to review the situation (during which time more information may be required depending on context). The hypotheses were elaborated and tested.

Schön (1983) developed this further and discussed 'reflection in action'. In the context of having to manage the unexpected he suggested that the problem is reframed and reworked from a different perspective to establish where it fits into existing understanding. It also involves understanding the elements and implications present in the problem, its solution and consequences. Reflection is often viewed as thinking about an experience after its occurrence and considering what occurred, what was learnt and how to incorporate the new learning into 'knowing in action'. There is a tendency to focus on this over reflection in action.

Research requires both types of reflection especially when interviews are part of the research method. As you are doing the interview you will need to be alert to whether it is going well or not. Reflecting after the event may provide some useful learning but it is less likely to help with the quality of data collection. As a researcher once you identify the interview is not going well you will need to reflect in action and quickly review what is the problem and how it can be resolved. Like any other skill you can improve reflective skills with practice.

The process of reflection enables you as a researcher to identify what you know and what you need to learn.

For example... You may reflect on your interviewing skills and decide that before embarking on interviewing children some specific training in this would be helpful.

Reflection also helps you understand your own position on various issues and the potential impact this might have on your research. It also should enable you to consider your emotions and how these might influence the process. It is important to be reflexively aware of your own emotional state when collecting the data and when analysing it. We cautioned earlier in the book about staying safe in the field and made some recommendations for protecting your emotional safety. Reflecting on how you feel can help you to manage your emotional state and you can use your research diary to help you do this.

It is also important to consider the effects of the interview on the researcher and as discussed in Chapter 7, the opportunity to debrief as needed is important.

Throughout the book we have highlighted the need to be reflective so that you are constantly challenging your perspectives and ensuring you are aware of how they are being formulated.

Having reviewed the contents and emphasised that throughout the research process reflection is a critical component we now ask you to attempt the exercise below. Hopefully this will link all the different components and highlight the part reflection plays. Start now with the activity in Box 11.1.

▬ Box 11.1 ▬▬▬▬▬▬▬▬▬▬▬▬▬▬▬▬▬

Activity on methods

For this activity you are given a research aim and then asked to answer some questions about the method including data collection and ethics.

    Research aim: To explore the views of 13-year-old school children about where they would prefer sexual health education to occur.

1 What type of research method might you use and why?
2 If you decided to interview your participants what kinds of interviews might you use?
3 How might you involve young people in the design of such a project?
4 How would you decide your sample?
5 Who are likely to be the gatekeepers for such a project?
6 What are likely to be the concerns of gatekeepers?
7 What are likely to be the concerns of an ethics committee?
8 What researcher factors may be significant?
9 How might you start such an interview and what aids might you use?

The answers given here are not comprehensive, but illustrate the kinds of issues you should be thinking about. You may arrive at a different conclusion from us, but as long as that can be justified and supports the research question being answered and has ethics approval that would be fine.

1. Qualitative research methods would be best as the project is an exploratory one.
2. If you remember, interviews can be structured, semi-structured or unstructured. In the context of this project semi-structured are likely to be most appropriate – you will be able to ask about issues you may have found to be relevant through the literature, but also provide young people an opportunity to give their perspectives without you having a specific agenda.

You will also recall that interviews can be face-to-face, telephone interviews or use more advanced computer technology. Given the potential sensitivity of the subject face-to-face interviews or Skype interviews where you can see each other are likely to be the best way of carrying out your interviews with children or young people. It could also be argued that not being able to see each other may protect the young person from potential embarrassment. The benefits and disadvantages of each approach would need to be carefully considered. The embarrassment you observe may be an important factor to consider later when you are informing those who want to develop such education. It may be that before any useful education can be delivered potential teachers need to consider how to make the subject more comfortable for students.

It is also likely that you will achieve better data collection through individual interviews rather than through group interviews or focus groups as, given the topic, participants may be even more aware of the reactions of their peers.

Again given the subject you would need to consider whether parent/carer attendance at the interview is likely to give you less honest data.

Given the age of the participants and the topic if you were to undertake group interviews you might want to consider if you have single sex groups or mixed sex groups.

3. You might want to ask young people to comment on the research proposal and also on the interview schedule. Young people may be part of the advisory group. However, remember that the young person is an individual and whilst their views are valid they do not represent the views of 'young people' generally, which are likely to be diverse.

   You might also just want to do a poll to see if the topic is of relevance or interest to young people.

4. The sample for such a project will not be large. Rather than asking a school for example to send letters to all 13-year-old children in that school, you may randomly select one class and then put the names of all of those in the class who have parental agreement to participate and also assent in a hat and select the number you need.

5. The setting in which the project is to take place will determine who the gatekeepers are. Whatever the setting, as the children are 13 years old, parental consent will be required followed by child consent or assent.

   If the project is to be undertaken in a school the gatekeepers will be head teachers and schools (who may sometimes have to seek approval from council or educational boards). If the project is to be undertaken in a hospital you may need to contact the relevant health managers and/or clinicians depending on the scope of your project.

6. The concerns of gatekeepers are likely to be around how they can recruit an appropriate number of children without having time consuming and overburdening processes. The topic is likely to raise some concerns – schools may worry about offending parents or that they are opening themselves up to potential scandal. Parents may feel that encouraging their children to talk about sex might encourage promiscuity or curiosity and prefer not to deal with that. Parents and staff may object on religious grounds on the basis that their faith and/or culture discourages premarital

sex so this is an inappropriate subject to discuss with children. Sharing the interview schedule with gatekeepers may be helpful.

7. Ethics committees are also likely to be worried about parental reaction and so may make parental opting in compulsory rather than letting you work on the basis that parental consent is implied if no response is made. Ethics committees are likely to want to scrutinise even more carefully the information provided about the study and also the interview schedule to ensure there is minimal risk.

8. Given the topic and the perceived risk of child abuse by strangers, male researchers may find it difficult to carry out such research without the presence of a chaperone which might impact on the quality of the data. As researchers our own experience of sexual health education may subconsciously colour our views on the subject so before carrying out this research some careful reflection would be required to ensure that the data is not collected or interpreted with a particular perspective. The age of the researcher may be relevant as younger people may be more comfortable talking to people more similar in age about sex but on the other hand may find it more uncomfortable as the researcher may be someone they might view as attractive. As a researcher you will need to be aware that some young people you interview may be sexually active and how you will deal with that given they are all legally below the age of consent. Some may also have experienced abuse and there may be the chance they disclose this. You will need to have planned for these possibilities but also be aware they may arise at unexpected times.

9. Most 13-year-old young people will be able to converse with you but some may still find it useful to have an activity such as drawing to do when they talk especially if the subject is potentially embarrassing. Using a recent news item or magazine article related to the research topic may be a way to break the ice. Sometimes it is useful just to be upfront and acknowledge that the topic may be potentially embarrassing.

SUMMARY

In this chapter we have pulled together some of the core issues that have been raised throughout the book. We have illustrated that qualitative interviewing projects are iterative and circular and that the research process is one that requires constant reflection and reflexivity so that decisions can be made carefully. In this chapter we have drawn your attention to the ethical frameworks that underpin interview research with children and the careful considerations that need to be made in the project.

RECOMMENDED READING

Dewey, J. (1933) *How We Think*. Boston: D.C. Heath & Co.

Schön, D.A. (1983) *The Reflective Practitioner: How Professionals think in Action*. London: Temple Smith.

ANSWERS TO VIGNETTES

RESPONSE TO BOX 1.4 VIGNETTE – ADAM

Adam is taking a fairly optimistic view of his study in the hope that the views of the children he engages might influence curriculum design. Adam takes a contemporary position that is informed by a rights-based framework through his aim to include children's voices and listen to their views. His aim was to be informed by the children so that he could deliver a teaching programme that was based on child perspectives.

RESPONSE TO BOX 3.4 VIGNETTE – ALICIA

There are several things Alicia needs to consider before making a decision. First, Alicia will need to identify what level of depth she wants to gain from the interviews. If she simply wants a checklist of key opinions, then a structured interview may be sufficient. However, if she wants a richer data set and to allow the young people to express themselves then one of the other types will be more appropriate.

Alicia will need to consult the literature to ascertain how much is already known in this area, and to see whether other researchers have explored teenage victim's viewpoints on criminal justice. If there is already some useful quantitative and qualitative research, then Alicia can use this to help her shape and develop a semi-structured interview schedule. However, if there is very little on the subject she may want to consider an unstructured one. Alicia will also want to think about how much control of the interview she wants to take in order to achieve her objectives. While semi-structured interviews are to some degree participant led and have flexibility, unstructured interviews give the participants more control. Alicia will need to consider her rationale for her choices carefully.

Finally, Alicia may consider the naturally occurring interview. She may seek out media interviews where young people have been consulted on their opinions of the criminal justice system (although these may not exist or may not be easy to find). Alicia could record naturally occurring interviews with social workers or police and victims and see if their opinions of the criminal justice system occur naturally (but this is a risky strategy if the focus is narrow or the topic quite specific as it may not come up in a naturally occurring interview). Of course, Alicia's theoretical position may influence her choice as some methodological and epistemological perspectives critique researcher-generated interviews due to their views of reality. However, the design of the research question is written in a way that lends itself to researcher-generated interviewing, which suggests that Alicia's theoretical standpoint is congruent with that approach.

RESPONSE TO BOX 4.4 VIGNETTE – MANJIT

Possible answers to question 1

Although there are many challenges that Manjit faces by interviewing children in India, the key one would be access. If Manjit chooses to interview those children face-to-face then it will be necessary to travel to India and stay there during the process of data collection. This could prove to be expensive, and difficult if Manjit does not have a budget for this. However, computer-mediated interviewing, which negates the expense and time of travelling, is likely to be inappropriate, as those children who are living in poverty are very unlikely to have access to a computer, unlikely to be computer literate, and unlikely to have access to the internet.

Possible answers to question 2

We would first question whether it is appropriate to use computer interviewing techniques with children who live in poverty. These children, whether in the UK or India, are disadvantaged by their circumstances, and while those children in the UK may have some computer literacy through their education in schools, and may have access to a computer in the school environment, Manjit would then need to undertake the interview on school grounds, rather than at home, and this may make the children uncomfortable. Of course many 'smart' mobile (cell) phones have Instant Messenger capabilities, social networking and text messaging functions, so if Manjit had a budget she could provide the children with a complimentary phone for the interviews as a token of thanks. However, some of these are expensive, and ethics committees may see this as a form of coercion. An alternative would be for Manjit to provide the children with a 'cheap' tablet but this carries similar expense and ethical implications.

An additional issue here is the sensitivity of the topic. There are contentions regarding what constitutes poverty, and this can be slightly different for the UK and India. The children themselves may not understand that they live in poverty and may become distressed during the interview and thus Manjit will need sensible safeguarding measures in place which computer-mediated interviewing may not allow.

RESPONSE TO BOX 6.2 VIGNETTE – KAROLINA

Possible answers to question 1

Given the age group that Karolina is hoping to recruit, arts and crafts might be perceived by some of the adolescents as a little young for them. Although this is a vulnerable group, and a group that may have mental health difficulties or emotional problems, using a participatory method for the sake of it could make things difficult for Karolina. First, Karolina should not take for granted that a participatory method is needed. These are older children and many of them will have reasonable communication skills and be able to converse with her. Second, offering the young people the option of arts and crafts might be a way of allowing them to direct the interview and to opt out of engaging in the participatory tasks if they want to. The use of arts and crafts, if the young person likes the idea and shows willingness to engage, can provide a way of gradually introducing new topics into the conversation and to take the focus away from the immediate interview. This can help with the rapport building. The young person can talk about their drawings or craft creation and this can provide a platform for later topics.

Possible answer to question 2

Although we have noted that it may not be necessary for Karolina to use participatory methods, she may want to have a choice of them available if the interview starts going badly, or if the guardian (foster parent, care home manager) has identified the young person as particularly withdrawn or quiet. It would be useful for Karolina to consult with as many of the people who know the young person well to get ideas regarding how to best engage them in an interview. Also she needs to remember not to treat each young person the same and different participatory methods might be needed for different young people.

One useful participatory technique for adolescents and for those who might be reluctant to talk is to use 'third party' techniques such as vignettes or clips from YouTube or other social media sources. By telling a story about someone else with similar experiences, the young person can relate to that third party and start talking about themselves. For example, video vignettes with actors can be created whereby the actor is given a name and behaves in a particular way that Karolina knows may resonate with the young person she is interviewing. The actor may get angry, or may cry a lot, or may sit quietly in a corner while others around him/her are talking. This depiction of a particular scene in a video can form a basis for questions about the participant's experiences and may feel safer for the young person.

RESPONSE TO BOX 8.1 VIGNETTE – MIA

Even before reading the rest of the chapter we hope it is obvious that Mia needs to do more than simply ask the children if they are happy to participate. The children she is planning to recruit are potentially vulnerable because of their socio-economic status. Furthermore, these children are under the age of 16 years old which means that Mia will need to get the consent of their parents too. Furthermore, some of the questions Mia will be asking relate to what is considered to be an area which may cause the children some distress and therefore it will be necessary for Mia to take steps to prevent this but also to address it if it arises. As Mia is planning to interview children who are all from one geographic location there need to be steps taken to protect the identity of these children from one another, and from other people in the community. They may express some views which cast the local community in a negative way and it is important that their views cannot be traced back to them. There are of course other ethical considerations you may have thought of and reading through the chapter should help you to see the relevance of these.

RESPONSE TO BOX 8.4 VIGNETTE – PIERRE

Safeguarding is always a very tricky issue and Pierre has very little evidence that the child is actually hurting themselves. If he reveals too much information to other people, he will be breaking the child's confidentiality which was promised at the start of the study. However, Pierre should have outlined in a simple way the limits to confidentiality and this should have included the clause that if he was to find that the child was being hurt by someone or they were hurting themselves he may have to disclose it. The real difficulty here for Pierre is that the child hinted at hurting themselves, but did not disclose very much information. Self-harm is also a common behaviour in young people and a maladaptive coping strategy employed by many young people. Self-harm in itself may not indicate mental health concerns or be risky but it is the nature and context that would indicate reasons to be concerned. Often adults want children to stop self-harm more than children might want to. As the interviews are about managing stress it might be reasonable to predict that self-harm as a theme might arise. A way of supporting the child without pushing them may be to say at the end, 'You mentioned self-harm and I understand you do not want to discuss it further with me. However, should you find you wish to do so you may find it useful to contact the school nurse or your GP.' This demonstrates that you have heard the child, are respecting their wishes but also addressing possible concerns. As Pierre is a BSc student in a psychology department within a university his most appropriate course of action is to discuss this with his supervisor without actually naming the child. The supervisor can then check the university's guidelines and consult with their colleagues to make a decision on this.

RESPONSE TO BOX 9.4 VIGNETTE – CAMERON

It is clear that the female participant Cameron is interviewing is becoming hostile toward him and she has lost her focus on the interview. She is displaying non-verbal signs, such as folding her arms and pacing the room. Cameron should have talked to the probation officer or social worker and her parents prior to interviewing her as there may be important things he needed to know (for example, she may have a drug addiction which is causing some of the physical symptoms she is displaying or she may have a history of violent behaviour). Furthermore, for his own safety and for that of his participants, Cameron should have done a basic risk assessment. Nonetheless, in the here-and-now of the interview, Cameron should suggest a break to give the participant the opportunity to rest, stop, or withdraw all together. Cameron should have chosen a location where there were other adults around, such as at the institutional setting or in the home where parents were in another room (again this is not always possible, but is advisable). Either way, Cameron should start to close the interview, stop the recording and, if she is willing, set up a follow-on interview at a later date.

REFERENCES

Adams, C. and van Manen, M. (2008) 'Phenomenology', in L. Given (ed.), *The SAGE Encyclopedia of Qualitative Research Methods,* Volume 2. Thousand Oaks, CA: Sage. pp. 164–169.

Agee, J. (2009) 'Developing qualitative research questions: A reflective process', *International Journal of Qualitative Studies in Education,* 22 (4): 431–447.

Alderson, P. (1992) 'In the genes or in the stars? Children's competence to consent', *Journal of Medical Ethics,* 18: 119–124.

Alderson, P. (2004) 'Ethics', in S. Fraser, V. Lewis, S. Ding, M. Kellett and C. Robinson (eds), *Doing Research with Children and Young People.* London: Sage.

Alderson, P. (2005) 'Designing ethical research with children', in A. Farrell (ed.), *Doing Research with Children and Young People.* Thousand Oaks, CA: Sage. pp. 97–112.

Alderson, P. (2007) 'Governance and ethics in health research', in M. Saks and J. Allsop (eds), *Researching Health: Qualitative, Quantitative and Mixed Methods.* London: Sage. pp. 283–300.

Aldridge, J. (2007) 'Picture this: The use of participatory photographic research methods with people with learning disabilities', *Disability and Society,* 22 (1): 1–17.

American Medical Association (1999) 'Enhancing the "cultural competence" of Physicians', Council on Medical Education Report 5-A-98, in *Cultural Competence Compendium.* Chicago: American Medical Association.

Andrews, R. (2003) *Research Questions.* London: Continuum Books.

Åstedt-Kurki, P., Paavilainen, E. and Lehti, K. (2001) 'Methodological issues in interviewing families in family nursing research', *Journal of Advanced Nursing,* 35(2): 288–293.

Australia Government (2015) Australian Child Protection Legislation. Available at: https://aifs.gov.au/cfca/publications/australian-child-protection-legislation (accessed 19 December 2015).

Bakhtin, M. (1981) 'Discourse in the novel', in M. Holquist (ed.), *The Dialogic Imagination: Four Essays by Bakhtin, M.* (C. Emerson and M. Holquist, trans.). Austin: University of Texas Press.

Barratt, M. (2012) 'The efficacy of interviewing young drug users through online chat', *Drug and Alcohol Review,* 31: 566–572.

Barter, C. and Renold, E. (2000) '"I wanna tell you a story": Exploring the application of vignettes in qualitative research with children and young people', *International Journal of Social Research Methodology,* 3(4): 307–323.

Bass, E. and Davis, L. (2002) *The Courage to Heal: A Guide for Women Survivors of Child Sexual Abuse.* London: Vermilion.

Bauer, M. (1996) *The Narrative Interview: Comments on a Technique for Qualitative Data Collection*, Papers in Social Research Methods (Qualitative Series No 1). London: London School of Economics and Political Science.

Benjamin, H. and MacKinlay, D. (2010) 'Communicating challenges: Overcoming disability', in S. Redsell and A. Hastings (eds), *Listening to Children and Young People in Healthcare Consultations*. Oxon: Radcliffe Publishing Ltd. pp. 151–168.

Berger, R. and Paul, M. (2011) 'Using e-mail for family research', *Journal of Technology in Human Sciences*, 29: 197–211.

Bertrand, C. and Bourdeau, L. (2010) 'Research interviews by Skype: A new data collection method', in J. Esteves (ed.), *Proceedings from the 9th European Conference on Research Methods*. Spain: IE Business School. pp. 70–79.

Bevan, M. (2014) 'A method of phenomenological interviewing', *Qualitative Health Research*, 24(1): 136–144.

Bhavani, K.-K. (1988) 'Empowerment and social research: Some comments', *Text*, 8: 41–50.

Billig, M., Condor, S., Edwards, D., Gane, M., Middleton, D. and Radley, A.R. (1988) *Ideological Dilemmas*. London: Sage.

Blaxter, L., Hughes, C. and Tight, M. (2001) *How to Research* (2nd edn). Buckingham: Open University Press.

Bloor, M., Fincham, B. and Sampson, H. (2007) *Qualiti (NCRM) Commissioned Inquiry into the Risk to Well-being of Researchers in Qualitative Research*. Cardiff: School of Social Sciences. Available at: www.cf.ac.uk/socsi/qualiti/CIReport.pdf (accessed 19 December 2015).

Bone, C., O'Reilly, M., Karim, K. and Vostanis, P. (2015) '"They're not witches …": Young children and their parents' perceptions and experiences of Child and Adolescent Mental Health Services', *Child: Care, Health and Development*, 41(3): 450–458.

Bottorff, J.L. (1994) 'Using videotaped data recordings in qualitative research', in J.M. Morse (ed.), *Critical Issues in Qualitative Research Methods*. London: Sage. pp. 244–261.

Boyatzis, R. (1998) *Transforming Qualitative Information: Thematic Analysis and Code Development*. London: Sage.

Brannen, J. (1998) 'Research note: The study of sensitive topics', *Sociological Review*, 36: 552–563.

Braun, V. and Clarke, V. (2006) 'Using thematic analysis in psychology', *Qualitative Research in Psychology*, 3(2): 77–101.

Brinkman, S. and Kvale, S. (2005) 'Confronting the ethics of qualitative research', *Journal of Constructivist Psychology*, 18: 157–181.

Brocki, J. and Wearden, A. (2006) 'A critical evaluation of the use of interpretative phenomenological analysis (IPA) in health psychology', *Psychology and Health*, 21: 87–108.

Brooks, J., McClusky, S., Turley, E. and King, N. (2014) 'The utility of template analysis in qualitative psychology research', *Qualitative Research in Psychology*, 12(2): 202–222.

Bruce, B., Ungar, M. and Waschbusch, D. (2009) 'Perceptions of risk among children with and without attention deficit/hyperactivity disorder', *International Journal of Inquiry Control and Safety Promotion*, 16(4): 189–196.

Bryman, A. (2008) *Social Research Methods* (3rd edn). Oxford: Oxford University Press.

Bucknall, S. (2014) 'Doing qualitative research with children and young people', in A. Clark, R. Flewitt, M. Hammersley and M. Robb (eds), *Understanding Research with Children and Young People*. London: Sage. pp. 69–84.

Burgess, R. (1981) 'Keeping a research diary', *Cambridge Journal of Education*, 11(1): 75–83.

Burns, E. (2010) 'Developing email interview practices in qualitative research', *Sociological Research Online*, 15(4): Art 8 [online]. Available at: www.socresonline.org.uk/15/4/8.html (accessed 18 January 2016).

Burr, V. (2003) *Social Constructionism* (2nd edn). London: Routledge.

Bushin, N. (2007) 'Interviewing children in their homes: Putting ethical principles into practice and developing flexible techniques', *Children's Geographies*, 5(3): 235–251.

Caelli, K., Ray, L. and Mill, J. (2003) '"Clear as mud": Toward greater clarity in generic qualitative research', *International Journal of Qualitative Methods*, 2(2): Article 1 [Online]. Available at: http://www.ualberta.ca/iiqm/backissues/pdf/caellietal.pdf (accessed 31 May 2014).

Cameron, H. (2005) 'Asking the tough questions: A guide to ethical practices in interviewing young children', *Early Child Development and Care*, 175(6): 597–610.

Campbell, A. (2008) 'For their own good: Recruiting children for research', *Childhood*, 15(1): 30–49.

Carroll-Lind, J., Chapman, J.W., Gregory, J. and Maxwell, G. (2006) 'The key to the gatekeepers: Passive consent and other ethical issues surrounding the rights of children to speak on issues that concern them', *Child Abuse and Neglect*, 30(9): 979–989.

Cashmore, J. (2006) 'Ethical issues concerning consent in obtaining children's reports on their experience of violence', *Child Abuse and Neglect*, 30: 969–977.

Charmaz, K. (1995) 'Grounded theory', in J.A. Smith, R. Harre and I. van Langenhove (eds), *Rethinking Methods in Psychology*. London: Sage. pp. 27–49.

Charmaz, K. (2000) 'Grounded theory: Objectivist and constructivist methods', in N. Denzin and Y. Lincoln (eds), *Handbook of Qualitative Research* (2nd edn). Thousand Oaks, CA: Sage. pp. 509–535.

Charmaz, K. (2006) *Constructing Grounded Theory: A Practical Guide through Qualitative Analysis*. London: Sage.

Children Act (2004) Available at: http://www.legislation.gov.uk/ukpga/2004/31/contents (accessed 4 February 2016).

Christensen, P. (2004) 'Children's participation in ethnographic research: Issues of power and representation', *Children and Society*, 18: 165–176.

Christensen, P. and Prout, A. (2002) 'Working with ethical symmetry in social research with children', *Childhood*, 9(4): 477–497.

Clark, A. (2005) 'Listening to and involving young children: A review of research and practice', *Early Child Development and Care*, 175(6): 489–505.

Clark, A. (2011) 'Breaking methodological boundaries? Exploring visual, participatory methods with adults and young children', *European Early Childhood Education Research Journal*, 19(3): 321–330.

Coad, J. and Lewis, A. (2004) *Engaging Children and Young People in Research – Literature Review*. London: National Evaluation of the Children's Fund.

Coles, J. and Mudlay, N. (2010) 'Staying safe: Strategies for qualitative child abuse researchers', *Child Abuse Review*, 19: 56–69.

Coles, R. (1986) *The Political Life of Children*. Boston: Atlantic.

Cook, C. (2011) 'Email interviewing: Generating data with a vulnerable population', *Journal of Advanced Nursing*, 68(6): 1330–1339.

Corbin, J. and Morse, J. (2003) 'The unstructured interactive interview: Issues of reciprocity and risks when dealing with sensitive topics', *Qualitative Inquiry*, 9(3): 335–354.

Coyne, I. (2010) 'Accessing children as research participants: Examining the role of gatekeepers', *Child: Care, Health and Development*, 36(4): 452–454.

Crossley, M. (2000) *Introducing Narrative Psychology: Self, Trauma and the Construction of Meaning*. Buckingham: Open University Press.

Dale, B. and Altschuler, J. (2006) 'Facing what can and cannot be said: Working with families, parents, and couples when a parent has a serious illness', in D. Crane and E. Marshall (eds), *Handbook of Families and Health*. Thousand Oaks, CA: Sage. pp. 423–437.

Daly, K. (2007) *Qualitative Methods for Family Studies and Human Development*. Thousand Oaks, CA: Sage.

Danby, S., Ewing, L. and Thorpe, K. (2011) 'The novice researcher: Interviewing young children', *Qualitative Inquiry*, 17(1): 74–84.

Dasen, P. (1994) 'Culture and cognitive development from a Piagetian perspective', in W. Lonner and R. Malpass (eds), *Psychology and Culture*. Boston: Allyn and Bacon.

Davidson, C. (2009) 'Transcription: Imperatives for research', *International Journal of Qualitative Research*, 8(2): 35–52.

Davis, J. (1998) '"Understanding the meanings of children": A reflexive process', *Children and Society*, 12(5): 325–336.

Deatrick, J. and Ledlie, S. (2000) 'Qualitative research interviews with children and their families', *Journal of Child and Family Nursing*, 3(2): 152–158.

Del Busso, L. (2007) 'Embodying feminist politics in the research interview: Material bodies and reflexivity', *Feminism and Psychology*, 17(3): 309–315.

Derrida, J. (1981) *Positions*. Chicago: University of Chicago Press.

DeVault, M. (1990) 'Talking and listening from women's standpoint: Feminist strategies for interviews and analysis', *Social Problems*, 37(1): 96–116.

Dewey, J. (1933) *How We Think*. Boston: D.C. Heath & Co.

DiCicco-Bloom, B. and Crabtree, B. (2006) 'The qualitative research interview', *Medical Education*, 40: 314–321.

Dogra, N. (2003) 'Cultural competence or cultural sensibility? A comparison of two ideal type models to teach cultural diversity to medical students', *International Journal of Medicine*, 5(4): 223–231.

Dogra, N. and Baldwin, L. (2009) 'Nursing assessment in CAMHS', in N. Dogra and S. Leighton (eds), *Nursing in Child and Adolescent Mental Health*. Maidenhead: McGraw Hill. pp: 55–68.

Dogra, N. and Leighton, S. (eds) (2009) *Nursing in Child and Adolescent Mental Health*. Maidenhead: McGraw-Hill.

Dogra, N., Vostanis, P., Abuateya, H. and Jewson, N. (2007) 'Children's mental health services and ethnic diversity: Gujarati families' perspectives of service provision for mental health problems', *Transcultural Psychiatry*, 44(2): 275–291.

Dogra, N., Parkin, A., Gale, F. and Frake, C. (2009) *A Multidisciplinary Handbook of Child and Adolescent Mental Health for Front-line Professionals* (2nd edn). London: Jessica Kingsley Publishers.

Dogra, N., Svirydzenka, N., Dugard, P., Singh, S.P. and Vostanis, P. (2013) 'The characteristics and rates of mental health problems among Indian and White adolescents in two English cities', *British Journal of Psychiatry*, 203: 44–50.

Donalek, J. (2009) 'The family research interview', *Nurse Researcher*, 16(3): 21–28.

Drew, P. (2015) 'Conversation analysis', in J. Smith (ed.), *Qualitative Psychology*. London: Sage. pp: 108–142.

Drew, S., Duncan, R. and Sawyer, S. (2010) 'Visual storytelling: A beneficial but challenging method for health research with young people', *Qualitative Health Research*, 20(12): 1677–1688.

Driessnack, M. (2006) 'Draw-and-tell conversations with children about fear', *Qualitative Health Research*, 16: 1414–1435.

Due, C., Riggs, D. and Augoustinos, M. (2014) 'Research with children of migrant and refugee backgrounds: A review of child-centered research methods', *Child Indicators Research*, 7: 209–227.

Duncan, R., Drew, S., Hodgson, J. and Sawyer, S. (2009) 'Is my mum going to hear this? Methodological and ethical challenges in qualitative health research with young people', *Social Science and Medicine*, 69: 1691–1699.

Eder, D. and Fingerson, L. (2001) 'Interviewing children and adolescents', in J. Gubrium and J. Holstein (eds), *Handbook of Interview Research: Context and Method*. London: Sage. pp. 181–201.

Edwards, D. and Potter, J. (1992) *Discursive Psychology*. London: Sage.

Eggenberger, S. and Nelms, T. (2007) 'Family interviews as a method for family research', *Journal of Advanced Nursing*, 58(3): 282–292.

Einarsdottir, J. (2007) 'Research with children: Methodological and ethical challenges', *European Early Childhood Education Research Journal*, 15: 1752–1807.

Emmel, N., Hughes, K., Greenhalgh, J. and Sales, A. (2007) 'Accessing socially excluded people – trust and the gatekeeper in the researcher–participant relationship', *Sociological Research Online*, 12(2). Available at: http://www.socresonline.org.uk/12/2/emmel.html doi: 10.5153/sro.1512.

Etherington, K. (2001) 'Research with ex-clients: A celebration and extension of the therapeutic process', *British Journal of Guidance and Counselling*, 29(1): 5–19.

Evans, A., Elford, J. and Wiggins, D. (2008) 'Using the internet for qualitative research', in C. Willig and W. Stainton-Rogers (eds), *The SAGE Handbook of Qualitative Research in Psychology*. London: Sage. pp. 315–333.

Faulkner, A. (2004) *The Ethics of Survivor Research: Guidelines for the Ethical Conduct of Research Carried out by Mental Health Service Users and Survivors*. Bristol: Polity Press.

Fleitas, J. (1998) 'Spinning tales from the World Wide Web: Qualitative research in an electronic environment', *Qualitative Health Research*, 8(2): 283–292.

Flewitt, R. (2005) 'Conducting research with young children: Some ethical considerations', *Early Child Development and Care*, 175(6): 553–565.

Flewitt, R. (2014) 'Interviews', in A. Clark, R. Flewitt, M. Hammersley and M. Robb (eds), *Understanding Research with Children and Young People*. London: Sage. pp. 136–153.

Flynn, N. (2004) *Instant Messaging Rules: A Business Guide to Managing Policies, Security, and Legal Issues for Safe IM Communication*. Saranac Lake, NY: AMACOM.

Fontana, A. and Frey, J.H. (2003) 'The interview: From structured questions to negotiated text', in N. Denzin and Y. Lincoln (eds), *Collecting and Interpreting Qualitative Materials* (2nd edn). London: Sage. pp. 61–106.

Fontes, T. and O'Mahony, M. (2008) 'In-depth interviewing by Instant Messenger', *Social Research Update*, 53 [Online]. Available at: www.soc.surrey.ac.uk/sru (accessed 12 January 2016).

Francis, J., Johnston, M., Robertson, C., Glidewell, L., Entwistle, V., Eccles, M. and Grimshaw, J. (2010) 'What is adequate sample size? Operationalising data saturation for theory-based interview studies', *Psychology and Health*, 25(10): 1229–1245.

Fraser, S., Lewis, V., Ding, S., Kellett, M. and Robinson, C. (eds) (2004) *Doing Research with Children and Young People*. London: Sage.

Fraser, S., Flewitt, R. and Hammersley, M. (2014) 'What is research with children and young people?', in A. Clark, R. Flewitt, M. Hammersley and M. Robb (eds), *Understanding Research with Children and Young People*. London: Sage. pp. 34–50.

Free Dictionary (2016) Available at: http://www.thefreedictionary.com (accessed 9 January 2016).

Freeman, M. and Mathison, S. (2009) *Researching Children's Experiences*. New York: The Guildford Press.

Gallacher, L.-A. and Gallagher, M. (2008) 'Methodological immaturity in childhood research? Thinking through "participatory methods"', *Childhood*, 15(4): 499–516.

Gallagher, M. (2008) '"Power is not an evil": Rethinking power in participatory methods', *Children's Geographies*, 6(2): 137–150.

Garaway, G. (1996) 'The case-study model: An organizational strategy for cross-cultural evaluation', *Evaluation*, 2(2): 201–211.

Gaskell, G. (2000) 'Individual and group interviewing', in M. Bauer and G. Gaskell (eds), *Qualitative Researching with Text, Image and Sound*. London: Sage. pp. 38–56.

Geneva Declaration of the Rights of the Child (1924) UN Documents: Gathering a Body of Global Agreements. NGO Committee on Education of the Conference of NGOs from United Nations websites. Available at: http://www.un-documents.net/gdrc1924.htm (accessed 2 February 2016).

Giglio, M. (2012) 'Boston College's secret tapes could bring IRA exposure and retribution', *The Daily Beast*. Available at: http://www.thedailybeast.com/articles/2012/07/10/boston-college-s-secret-tapes-could-bring-ira-exposure-and-retribution.html (accessed 18 December 2015).

Giordano, J., O'Reilly, M., Taylor, H. and Dogra, N. (2007) 'Confidentiality and autonomy: The challenge(s) of offering research participants a choice of disclosing their identity', *Qualitative Health Research*, 17(2): 264–275.

Glaser, B. and Strauss, A. (1967) *The Discovery of Grounded Theory: Strategies for Qualitative Research*. New York: Aldine.

Government of Queensland (2015) *Child Protection Act*. Available at: https://www.legislation.qld.gov.au/legisltn/current/c/childprotecta99.pdf (accessed 8 December 2015).

Grant, J. and Luxford, Y. (2009) 'Video: A decolonising strategy for intercultural communication in child and family health within ethnographic research', *International Journal of Multiple Research Approaches*, 3: 218–232.

Green, J. and Thorogood, N. (2013) *Qualitative Methods for Health Research* (3rd edn). London: Sage.

Grover, S. (2004) 'Why won't they listen to us? On giving power and voice to children participating in social research', *Childhood*, 11 (1): 81–93.

Gubrium, J. and Holstein, J. (2008) 'The constructionist mosaic', in J. Holstein and J. Gubrium (eds), *Handbook of Constructionist Research*. New York: Guildford. pp. 3–12.

Guest, G., Bruce, A. and Johnson, L. (2006) 'How many interviews are enough? An experiment with data saturation and variability', *Field Methods*, 18(1): 59–82.

Guillemin, M. and Gillam, L. (2006) *Telling Moments: Everyday Ethics in Health Care*. Victoria, Australia: IP Communications.

Gunter, B. (2002) 'Online versus offline research: Implications for evaluating digital media', *Aslib Proceedings*, 54(4): 229–239.

Hamilton, R. and Bowers, B. (2006) 'Internet recruitment and e-mail interviews in qualitative studies', *Qualitative Health Research*, 16(6): 821–835.

Hamo, M., Blum-Kulka, S. and Hacohen, G. (2004) 'From observation to transcription and back: Theory, practice, and interpretation in the analysis of children's naturally occurring discourse', *Research on Language and Social Interaction*, 37(1): 71–92.

Harden, J., Scott, S., Backett-Milburn, K. and Jackson, S. (2000) '"Can't talk won't talk?" Methodological issues in researching children', *Sociological Research Online*, 5(2). Available at: http://www.socresonline.org.uk/5/2/harden.html (accessed 11 November 2015).

Harper, D. (2006) 'Discourse analysis', in M. Slade and S. Priebe (eds), *Choosing Methods in Mental Health Research: Mental Health Research from Theory to Practice*. Hove: Routledge. pp. 47–67.

Heath, H. and Cowley, S. (2004) 'Developing a grounded theory approach: A comparison of Glaser and Strauss', *International Journal of Nursing Studies*, 41(2): 141–150.

Heath, S., Charles, V., Crow, G. and Wiles, R. (2004) 'Informed consent, gatekeepers & go-betweens', paper presented at The Ethics and Social Relations of Research conference (Sixth International Conference on Social Science Methodology), Amsterdam.

Heath, S., Charles, V., Crow, G. and Wiles, R. (2007) 'Informed consent, gatekeepers and go-betweens: Negotiating consent in child and youth-oriented institutions', *British Educational Research Journal*, 33(3): 403–417.

Henderson, D. (2000) 'Play therapy', in C. Thompson and L. Rudolph (eds), *Counselling Children*. Belmont, CA: Wadsworth Brooks/Cole. pp. 373–399.

Heyl, B. (2001) 'Ethnographic interviewing', in P. Atkinson, A. Coffey, S. Delamont, J. Lofland and L. Lofland (eds), *Handbook of Ethnography*. London: Sage. pp. 369–383.

Hill, M. (1997) 'Participatory research with children', *Child and Family Social Work*, 2: 171–183.

Hiller, H. and DiLuzio, L. (2004) 'The interviewee and the research interview: Analysing a neglected dimension in research', *Canadian Review of Sociology*, 41: 1–26.

Hinchcliffe, V. and Gavin, H. (2009) 'Social and virtual networks: Evaluating synchronous online interviewing using instant messenger', *The Qualitative Report*, 14(2): 318–340.

Hinduja, S. and Patchin, J. (2008) 'Personal information of adolescents on the internet: A quantitative content analysis of MySpace', *Journal of Adolescence*, 31: 125–146.

Hollway, W. and Jefferson, T. (2008) 'The free association narrative interview method', in L. Given (ed.), *The SAGE Encyclopaedia of Qualitative Research Methods*. Sevenoaks, CA: Sage. pp. 296–315.

Holt, A. (2010) 'Using telephones for narrative interviewing: A research note', *Qualitative Research*, 10: 113–121.

Holt, L. (2004) 'The "voices" children: De-centring empowering research relations', *Children's Geographies*, 2(1): 13–27.

Horsman, C. (2008) 'The particular needs of children and adolescents – not just little adults', *The Foundation Years*, 5: 75–78.

Horstman, M., Aldiss, S., Richardson, A. and Gibson, F. (2008) 'Methodological issues when using the draw and write technique with children aged 6–12 years', *Qualitative Health Research*, 18(7): 1001–1011.

Hubbard, G., Backett-Milburn, K. and Kemmer, D. (2001) 'Working with emotion: Issues for the researcher in fieldwork and teamwork', *International Journal of Social Research Methodology*, 4(2): 119–137.

Hunt, N. and McHale, S. (2007) 'A practical guide to the e-mail interview', *Qualitative Health Research*, 17: 1415–1421.

Hussein, M., Hirst, S., Salyers, V. and Osuji, J. (2014) 'Using grounded theory as a method of inquiry: Advantages and disadvantages', *The Qualitative Report*, 19: 1–15.

Hutchby, I. (2005) '"Active listening": Formulation and the elicitation of feelings – talk in child counselling', *Research on Language and Social Interaction*, 38(3): 303–329.

Hutchby, I. and Wooffitt, R. (2008) *Conversation Analysis* (2nd edn). Cambridge: Polity Press.

Instone, S. (2002) 'Developmental strategies for interviewing children', *Journal of Paediatric Health Care,* 16: 304–305.

Irwin, L. and Johnson, J. (2005) 'Interviewing young children: Explicating our practices and dilemmas', *Qualitative Health Research*, 15: 821–831.

Ison, N. (2009) 'Having their say: Email interviews for research data collection with people who have verbal communication impairment', *International Journal of Social Research Methodology*, 12(2): 161–172.

Ivey, A. and Ivey, M. (2003) *Intentional Interviewing and Counselling: Facilitating Client Development in a Multicultural Society* (5th edn). Pacific Grove, CA: Thomson Brooks/Cole.

James, A., Jenks, C. and Prout, A. (1998) *Theorizing Children*. Cambridge, UK: Polity.

James, N. and Bushner, H. (2006) 'Credibility, authenticity, and voice: Dilemmas in online interviewing', *Qualitative Interviewing*, 6(2): 403–420.

Joffe, H. and Yardley, L. (2004) 'Content and thematic analysis', in D. Marks and L. Yardley (eds), *Research Methods for Clinical and Health Psychology*. London: Sage. pp. 56–68.

Johnson, A. (2002) 'So ...?: Pragmatic implications of so-prefaced questions in formal police interviews', in J. Cotterrill (ed.), *Language in the Legal Process*. Basingstoke: Palgrave MacMillan. pp. 91–111.

Johnson, B. and Macleod-Clark, J. (2003) 'Collecting sensitive data: The impact on researchers', *Qualitative Health Research*, 13(3): 421–434.

Jowett, A., Peel, E. and Shaw, R. (2011) 'Online interviewing in psychology: Reflections on the process', *Qualitative Research in Psychology*, 8: 354–369.

Keating, D. (1979) 'Adolescent thinking', in J. Adelson (ed.), *Handbook of Adolescent Psychology*. New York: Wiley. pp. 211–246.

Kellett, M. (2005) *Children as Active Researchers: A New Research Paradigm for the 21st Century?* UK: ESRC.

Kelly, A. (2009) 'In defence of anonymity: Rejoining the criticism', *British Educational Research Journal*, 35(3): 431–445.

King, N. (2004) 'Using templates in the thematic analysis of text', in C. Cassell and G. Symon (eds), *Essential Guide to Qualitative Methods in Organisational Research*. London: Sage. pp. 256–270.

King, N. (2012) 'Doing template analysis', in G. Symon and C. Cassell (eds), *Qualitative Organizational Research*. London: Sage. pp. 426–450.

Kinmond, K. (2012) 'Coming up with a research question', in C. Sullivan, S. Gibson and S. Riley (eds), *Doing your Qualitative Psychology Project*. London: Sage. pp. 23–36.

Kirk, S. (2007) 'Methodological and ethical issues in conducting qualitative research with children and young people: A literature review', *International Journal of Nursing Studies*, 44: 1250–1260.

Kiyimba, N. and O'Reilly, M. (in press; a) 'An exploration of the possibility for secondary traumatic stress amongst transcriptionists: A grounded theory approach', *Qualitative Research in Psychology*.

Kiyimba, N. and O'Reilly, M. (in press; b) 'The risk of secondary traumatic stress in the qualitative transcription process: A research note', *Qualitative Research*.

Komulainen, S. (2007) 'The ambiguity of the child's "voice" in social research', *Childhood*, 14(1): 11–28.

Koo, M. and Skinner, H. (2005) 'Challenges of internet recruitment: A case study with disappointing results', *Journal of Medical Internet Research*, 7(1): e6.

Kortesl{uoma, R., Hentinen, M. and Nikkonen, M. (2003) 'Conducting a qualitative child interview: Methodological considerations', *Journal of Advanced Nursing*, 42: 434–441.

Kvale, S. (2008) *Doing Interviews*. London: Sage.

Kvale, S. and Brinkman, S. (2009) *Interviewing: Learning the Craft of Qualitative Research Interviewing* (2nd edn). London: Sage.

Lamb, M., Hershkowitz, I., Orbach, Y. and Esplin, P. (2008) *Tell Me What Happened: Structured Investigative Interviews of Child Victims and Witnesses*. West Sussex: John Wiley and Sons.

Lansdown, G. (2000) 'Implementing children's rights and health', *Archives of Disease in Childhood*, 83(4): 286–288.

Lenhart, A., Madden, M. and Hitlin, P. (2005) *Teens and Technology: Youth are Leading the Transition to a Fully Wired and Mobile Nation*. Washington DC: Pew Internet and American Life Project.

Lester, J. and O'Reilly, M. (2016) 'The history and landscape of DA and CA', in M. O'Reilly and J.N. Lester (eds), *The Palgrave Handbook of Adult Mental Health: Discourse and Conversation Studies*. Basingstoke: Palgrave.

Levy, R. and Thompson, P. (2013) 'Creating "buddy partnerships" with 5- and 11- year old boys: A methodological approach to conducting participatory research with young children', *Journal of Early Childhood Research*, DOI: 10.1177/1476718X13490297.

Lewis, A. (1992) 'Group child interviews as a research tool', *British Educational Research Journal*, 18(4): 413–421.

Lewis, A. and Porter, J. (2004) 'Interviewing children and young people with learning disabilities: Guidelines for researchers and multi-professional practice', *British Journal of Learning Disabilities*, 32: 191–197.

Liebling, A. (1999) 'Doing research in prison: Breaking the silence?', *Theoretical Criminology*, 3(2): 147–173.

Liegghio, M., Nelson, G. and Evans, S. (2010) 'Partnering with children diagnosed with mental health issues: Contributions of a sociology of childhood perspective of participatory action research', *American Journal of Psychology*, 46: 84–99.

MacDonald, K. (2008) 'Dealing with chaos and complexity: The reality of interviewing children and families in their own homes', *Journal of Clinical Nursing*, 17(23): 3123–3130.

Mahon, A., Glendinning, C., Clarke, K. and Craig, G. (1996) 'Researching children: Methods and ethics', *Children and Society*, 10: 145–154.

Mander, R. (1992) 'Seeking approval for research access: The gatekeeper's role in facilitating a study of the care of the relinquishing mother', *Journal of Advanced Nursing*, 17: 1460–1464.

Mann, C. and Stewart, F. (2000) *Internet Communication and Qualitative Research: A Handbook for Researching Online*. London: Sage.

Marshall, M. (1996) 'Sampling for qualitative research', *Family Practice*, 13(6): 522–525.

Mauthner, M. (1997) 'Methodological aspects of collecting data from children: Lessons from three research projects', *Children and Society*, 11: 16–28.

McGuinness, S. (2008) 'Research ethics committees: The role of ethics in a regulatory authority', *Journal of Medical Ethics*, 34: 695–700.

McPherson, A. (2010) 'Involving children: Why it matters', in S. Redsell and A. Hastings (eds), *Listening to Children and Young People in Healthcare Consultations*. Oxon: Radcliffe Publishing Ltd. pp. 15–30.

Meho, L. (2006) 'E-mail interviewing in qualitative research: A methodological discussion', *Journal of the American Society for Information Science and Technology*, 5(10): 1284–1295.

Miller, T. and Boulton, M. (2007) 'Changing constructions of informed consent: Qualitative research and complex social worlds', *Social Science and Medicine*, 65: 2199–2211.

Morrow, V. and Richards, M. (1996) 'The ethics of social research with children: An overview', *Children & Society*, 10(2): 90–105.

Morse, J.M. (2007) 'Ethics in action: Ethical principles for doing qualitative health research', *Qualitative Health Research*, 17(8): 1003–1005.

Morse, J. and Field, P. (1995) *Qualitative Methods for Health Professionals* (2nd edn). California: Sage.

Munford, R. and Sanders, J. (2004) 'Recruiting diverse groups of young people to research: Agency and empowerment in the consent process', *Qualitative Social Work*, 3(4): 469–482.

National Voices (2015) *My Life, My Support, My Choice: Children and Young People Call for Coordinated Care and Support on their Terms*. Available at: http://www.nationalvoices.org.uk/my-life-my-support-my-choice (accessed 16 October 2015).

Niewenhuys, O. (2001) 'By the sweat of their brow? Street children, NGOs and children's rights in Addis Abab', *Africa*, 71(4): 539–557.

NSPCC (2015) *The Child Protection System across the UK*. Available at: https://www.nspcc.org.uk/preventing-abuse/child-protection-system/ (accessed 9 December 2015).

Ochs, E. (1979) 'Transcription as theory', in E. Ochs and B. Schiefflin (eds), *Developmental Pragmatics*. New York: Academic Press. pp. 43–72.

Onwuegbuzie, A. and Leech, N. (2007) 'Sampling designs in qualitative research: Making the sampling process more public', *The Qualitative Report*, 12(2): 238–254.

Opdenakker, R. (2006) 'Advantages and disadvantages of four interview techniques in qualitative research', *Forum Qualitative Sozialforschung/Forum: Qualitative Social Research*, 7(4). [Online] Available at: www.qualitative-research.net/index.php/fqs/rt/printerfriendly/175/391 (accessed 17 November 2015).

O'Reilly, M. (2005) 'Active noising: The use of noises in talk, the case of onomatopoeia, abstract sounds and the functions they serve in therapy', *TEXT*, 25(6): 745–761.

O'Reilly, M. and Kiyimba, N. (2015) *Advanced Qualitative Research: A Guide to Contemporary Theoretical Debates*. London: Sage.

O'Reilly, M. and Parker, N. (2013) '"Unsatisfactory Saturation": A critical exploration of the notion of saturated sample sizes in qualitative research', *Qualitative Research*, 13(2): 190–197.

O'Reilly, M. and Parker, N. (2014a) *Doing Mental Health Research with Children and Adolescents: A Guide to Qualitative Methods*. London: Sage.

O'Reilly, M. and Parker, N. (2014b) '"She needs a smack in the gob": Negotiating what is appropriate talk in front of children in family therapy', *Journal of Family Therapy*, 36(3): 287–307.

O'Reilly, M., Parker, N. and Hutchby, I. (2011) 'Ongoing processes of managing consent: The empirical ethics of using video-recording in clinical practice and research', *Clinical Ethics*, 6: 179–185.

O'Reilly, M., Karim, K., Taylor, H. and Dogra, N. (2012) 'Parent and child views on anonymity: "I've got nothing to hide"', *International Journal of Social Research Methodology*, 15(3): 211–224.

O'Reilly, M., Ronzoni, P. and Dogra, N. (2013a) *Research with Children: Theory and Practice*. London: Sage.

O'Reilly, M., Vostanis, P., Taylor, H., Day, C., Street, C. and Wolpert, M. (2013b) 'Service user perspectives of multi-agency working: A qualitative study with parents and children with educational and mental health difficulties', *Child and Adolescent Mental Health*, 18(4): 202–209.

O'Reilly, M., Karim, K. and Lester, J. (2014) 'Separating "emotion" from "the science": Exploring the perceived value of information for parents and families of children with ASD', *Clinical Child Psychology and Psychiatry*, DOI: 10.1177/1359104514530735.

Pantell, R., Stewart, T., Dias, J., Wells, P. and Ross, W. (1982) 'Physician communication with children and parents', *Pediatrics*, 70(3): 396–402.

Parker, N. and O'Reilly, M. (2012) '"Gossiping" as a social action in family therapy: The pseudo-absence and pseudo-presence of children', *Discourse Studies*, 14(4): 1–19.

Parker, N. and O'Reilly, M. (2013) '"We are alone in the house": A case study addressing researcher safety and risk', *Qualitative Research in Psychology*, 10(4): 341–354.

Paterson, B., Gregory, D. and Thorne, S. (1999) 'A protocol for researcher safety', *Qualitative Health Research*, 9(2): 259–269.

Patton, M. (1990) *Qualitative Evaluation and Research Methods* (2nd edn). California: Sage.

Paul, M. (2007) 'Rights', *Archives of Disease in Childhood*, 92: 720–725.

Paulus, T., Lester, J.N. and Dempster, P. (2013) *Digital Tools for Qualitative Research*. London: Sage.

Piaget, J. (1950) *The Psychology of Intelligence*. London: Routledge and Kegan Paul.

Piercy, H. and Hargate, M. (2004) 'Social research on the under-16s: A consideration of the issues from a UK perspective', *Journal of Child Health Care*, 8(4): 253–263.

Potter, J. (1996) *Representing Reality: Discourse, Rhetoric, and Social Construction*. London: Sage.

Potter, J. (1997) 'Discourse analysis as a way of analysing naturally occurring talk', in D. Silverman (ed.), *Qualitative Research: Theory, Method and Practice*. London: Sage. pp. 144–160.

Potter, J. (2002) 'Two kinds of natural', *Discourse Studies*, 4(4): 539–542.

Potter, J. and Hepburn, A. (2005) 'Qualitative interviews in psychology: Problems and possibilities', *Qualitative Research in Psychology*, 2: 1–27.

Potter, J., and Wetherell, M. (1987) *Discourse and Social Psychology*. London: Sage.

Powell, C. (2011) *Safeguarding and Child Protection for Nurses, Midwives and Health Visitors: A Practical Guide*. Maidenhead: Open University Press.

Punch, S. (2002) 'Interviewing strategies with young people: The "secret box", stimulus material and task-based activities', *Children and Society*, 16: 45–56.

Punch, S. (2007) '"I felt they were ganging up on me": Interviewing siblings at home', *Children's Geographies*, 5(3): 219–234.

Rice, M., Bunker, K., Kang, D., Howell, C. and Weaver, M. (2007) 'Accessing and recruiting children for research in schools', *Western Journal of Nursing Research*, 29(4): 501–514.

Richmond, H. (2002) 'Learners' lives: A narrative analysis', *The Qualitative Report*, 7(3). Available at: www.nova.edu/ssss/QR/QR7-3/richmond.html (accessed 7 August 2015).

Riessman, C.K. (2008) *Narrative Methods for the Human Sciences*. Thousand Oaks, CA: Sage.

Robb, M. (2014) 'Disseminating research: Shaping the conversation', in A. Clark, R. Flewitt, M. Hammersley and M. Robb (eds), *Understanding Research with Children and Young People*. London: Sage. pp. 237–249.

Roberts, F. and Robinson, J. (2004) 'Interobserver agreement on first-stage conversation analytic transcription', *Health Communication Research*, 30(3): 376–410.

Roszkowski, M. and Bean, A. (1990) 'Believe it or not! Longer questionnaires have lower response rates', *Journal of Business and Psychology*, 4(4): 495–509.

Roulston, K. (2010) *Reflective Interviewing: A Guide to Theory and Practice*. London: Sage.

Rycroft-Malone, J., Harvey, G., Seers, K., Kitson, A., McCormack, B. and Titchen, A. (2004) 'An exploration of the factors that influence the implementation of evidence into practice', *Issues in Clinical Nursing*, 13: 913–924.

Sacks, H., Schegloff, E. and Jefferson, G. (1974) 'A simplest systematic for the organization of turn-taking for conversation', *Language*, 50: 696–735.

Sampson, H. (2004) 'Navigating the waves: The usefulness of a pilot in qualitative research', *Qualitative Research*, 4(3): 383–402.

Schegloff, E. (1987) 'Analyzing single episodes of interaction: An exercise in conversation analysis', *Social Psychology Quarterly*, 50(2): 101–114.

Schön, D.A. (1983) *The Reflective Practitioner: How Professionals Think in Action*. London: Temple Smith.

Shaw, C., Brady, L.-M. and Davey, C. (2011) *Guidelines for Research with Children and Young People*. London: NCB Research Centre.

Shaw, S. and Barrett, G. (2006) 'Research governance: Regulating risk and reducing harm?', *Journal of the Royal Society of Medicine*, 99: 14–19.

Shopes, L. (2013) 'Oral history', in N.K. Denzin and Y.S. Lincoln (eds), *Collecting and Interpreting Qualitative Materials*. Thousand Oaks, CA: Sage. pp. 119–150.

Shuy, R. (2001) 'In-person versus telephone interviewing', in J. Gubrium and J.A. Holstein (eds), *Handbook of Interview Research: Context and Method*. London: Sage. pp. 537–556.

Silverman, D. (2013) *Doing Qualitative Research* (4th edn). London: Sage.

Sinclair, J. and Coulthard, M. (1975) *Towards an Analysis of Discourse*. Oxford: Oxford University Press.

Sinclair, J. and Coulthard, M. (1992) 'Towards an analysis of discourse', in M. Coulthard (ed.), *Advances in Spoken Discourse Analysis*. London: Routledge. pp. 1–34.

Smith, J. (2004) 'Reflecting on the development of interpretative phenomenological analysis and its contribution to qualitative research in psychology', *Qualitative Research in Psychology*, 1(1): 39–54.

Smith, J., Flowers, P. and Larkin, M. (2009) *Interpretative Phenomenological Analysis: Theory, Method and Research*. London: Sage.

Smith, P.K., Cowie, H. and Blades, M. (2015) *Understanding Children's Development*. Chichester: John Wiley and Sons.

Social Research Association (2005) *Staying Safe: A Code of Practice for the Safety of Social Researchers*. Available at: www.the-sra.org.uk (accessed 18 October 2015).

Söderback, M., Coyne, I. and Harder, M. (2011) 'The importance of including both a child perspective and the child's perspective within health care settings to provide truly child-centred care', *Journal of Child Health Care*, 15(2): 99–106.

Sokolowski, R. (2000) *Introduction to Phenomenology.* New York: Cambridge University Press.

Solberg, A. (2014) 'Reflections on interviewing children living in difficult circumstances: Courage, caution and co-production', *International Journal of Social Research Methodology*, 17(3): 233–248.

Sparrman, A. (2005) 'Video recording as interaction: Participant observation of children's everyday life', *Qualitative Research in Psychology*, 2: 241–255.

Spradley, J. (1980) *Participant Observation.* New York: Holt, Rinehart and Winston.

Stafford, A., Laybourn, A., Hill, M. and Walker, M. (2003) '"Having a say": Children and young people talk about consultation', *Children and Society*, 17: 361–373.

Starks, H. and Trinidad, S.B. (2007) 'Choose your method: A comparison of phenomenology, discourse analysis, and grounded theory', *Qualitative Health Research*, 17(10): 1372–1380.

Sturges, J. and Hanrahan, K. (2004) 'Comparing telephone and face-to-face qualitative interviewing: A research note', *Qualitative Research*, 4(1): 107–118.

Tausig, J. and Freeman, E. (1988) 'The next best thing to being there: Conducting the clinical research interview by telephone', *American Journal of Orthopsychiatry*, 58(3): 418–427.

te Riele, K. and Brooks, R. (2013) *Negotiating Ethical Challenges in Youth Research.* London: Routledge.

Teijlingen (van), E., Rennie, A.M., Hundley, V. and Graham, W. (2001) 'The importance of conducting and reporting pilot studies: The example of the Scottish births survey', *Journal of Advanced Nursing*, 34(3): 289–295.

Temple, B. and Young, A. (2004) 'Qualitative research and translation dilemmas', *Qualitative Research*, 4(2): 161–178.

Thomas, A. and Chess, S. (1977) *Temperament and Development.* New York: Brunner/Mazel.

Thomas, N. and O'Kane, C. (1998) 'The ethics of participatory research with children', *Children and Society*, 12: 336–348.

Thorne, S. (2000) 'Data analysis in qualitative research', *Evidence Based Nursing*, 3(3): 68–70.

Tishler, C. (2011) 'Pediatric drug-trial recruitment: Enticement without coercion', *Pediatrics*, 127(5): 949–954.

Trivedi, P. and Wykes, T. (2002) 'From passive subjects to equal partners: Qualitative review of user involvement in research', *British Journal of Psychiatry*, 181: 468–472.

Tuckett, A. (2004) 'Part 1: Qualitative research sampling – the very real complexities', *Nurse Researcher*, 12(1): 47–61.

UNICEF (n.d) *Child-centred Development: The Basis for Sustainable Human Development.* New York: UNICEF. Available at: http://www.unicef.org/dprk/ccd.pdf (accessed 25 November 2015).

UNICEF (2015) *The United Nations Convention on the Rights of the Child (1989).* Available at: http://www.unicef.org.uk/UNICEFs-Work/UN-Convention/ (accessed 4 January 2016).

United Nations Convention on the Rights of the Child (UN) (1989) *Conventions on the Rights of the Child*. London: UNICEF. Available at: http://www.unicef.org.uk/Documents/Publicationpdfs/UNCRC_PRESS200910web.pdf (accessed 7 December 2015).

Uphold, C. and Strickland, O. (1993) 'Issues related to the unit of analysis in family nursing research', in G. Wegner and R. Alexander (eds), *Readings in Family Nursing*. Philadelphia: JB Lippincott. pp. 151–161.

Vaughan, J. (1990) 'Foreword', in R.T. Clift, W.R. Houston and M.C. Pugach (eds), *Encouraging Reflective Practice in Education: An Analysis of Issues and Programs*. New York: Teachers College Press.

Waller, T. and Bitou, A. (2011) 'Research *with* children: Three challenges for participatory research in early childhood', *European Early Childhood Education Research Journal*, 19(1): 5–20.

Westby, C. (1990) 'Ethnographic interviewing: Asking the right questions to the right people in the right ways', *Communication Disorders Quarterly*, 13(1): 101–111.

White, A., Bushin, N., Caperna-Mendez, F. and Laoire, C. (2010) 'Using visual methodologies to explore contemporary Irish childhood', *Qualitative Research*, 10: 143–158.

White, P. (2009) *Developing Research Questions: A Guide for Social Scientists*. Basingstoke, Hampshire: Palgrave MacMillan.

Wilkes, L., Cummings, J. and Haigh, C. (2014) 'Transcriptionist saturation: Knowing too much about sensitive health and social data', *Journal of Advanced Nursing*, DOI: 10.111/jan.12510.

Willig, C. (2008) *Introducing Qualitative Research in Psychology* (2nd edn). Milton Keynes: Open University Press.

Willmott, A. (2010) 'Involving children: How to do it', in S. Redsell and A. Hastings (eds), *Listening to Children and Young People in Healthcare Consultations*. Oxon: Radcliffe Publishing Ltd. pp. 45–55.

Wilson, C. and Powell, M. (2001) *A Guide To Interviewing Children: Essential Skills for Counsellors, Police, Lawyers and Social Workers*. Sydney: Allen and Unwin.

Wimpenny, P. and Gass, J. (2000) 'Interviewing in phenomenology and grounded theory: Is there a difference?', *Methodological Issues in Nursing Research*, 31(6): 1485–1492.

Woodhead, M. and Faulkner, D. (2000) 'Subjects, objects or participants? Dilemmas of psychological research with children', in P. Christensen and A. James (eds), *Research with Children: Perspectives and Practices*. London: Falmer Press. pp. 9–35.

Wooffitt, R. (2005) *Conversation Analysis and Discourse Analysis: A Comparative and Critical Introduction*. London: Sage.

Wright, K. (2005) 'Researching internet-based populations: Advantages and disadvantages of online survey research, online questionnaire authoring software packages, and web survey services', *Journal of Computer-Mediated Communication*, 10(3): article 11. Available at: http//jcmc.indiana.edu/vol10/issue3/wright.html (accessed 18 December 2014).

Yuille, J., Hunter, R., Joffe, R. and Zaparnuik, J. (1993) 'Interviewing children in sexual abuse cases', in G. Goodman and B. Bottoms (eds), *Child Victims, Child Witnesses; Understanding and Improving Testimony*. New York: Guilford. pp. 95–115.

Zezima, K. (2011) *College Fights Subpoena of Interviews tied to IRA*. Available at: http://www.nytimes.com/2011/06/10/us/10irish.html (accessed 4 August 2015).

INDEX